# GERMANY since 1918

# GERMANY since 1918

## David Childs
Reader in Politics,
University of Nottingham

**Batsford Academic and Educational Ltd**

First published 1971
© David Childs, 1970
Second Edition 1980

ISBN 0 7134 3673 5 (hardback)
       0 7134 3674 3 (paperback)

Printed and bound by
Billing & Son Ltd, Guildford and Worcester
for the publishers
Batsford Academic and Educational Ltd
4 Fitzhardinge Street, London W1H 0AH

# Contents

# Acknowledgment

I want to express my thanks to Professor Michael Balfour, CBE, of the University of East Anglia, for giving me, in the form of his detailed comments on the manuscript for this book, some of the benefits of his long interest in Germany. Obviously, any errors, omissions or shortcomings which remain, are entirely the author's responsibility.

KEY
•••• Frontier between DDR and BRD.
■■■■ Effective German frontier since 1945.
▬▬▬ Eastern German frontiers on 31 December 1937.
▨▨▨ Territory to Poland.
▦▦▦ Territory to U.S.S.R.

# 1  The Making of Weimar

Most travel brochures which include Weimar show the famous Goethe-Schiller statue in the town's main square, establishing it as an historical town closely connected with Germany's greatest cultural ambassadors. Also in the centre is the theatre in which the deputies of the first assembly of the German Republic met in 1919. To get to Weimar today presents the Western visitor with certain difficulties for it is in the German Democratic Republic, East Germany as we know it. It is plausible to suggest that Weimar and East Germany are cut off from the West because of the failure of the first German 'Weimar' Republic. Not far from Weimar is another monument to Germany's past, another symbol of that republic's failure, symbol of the regime which followed and which made the division of the nation more likely—Buchenwald concentration camp. There thousands of Germans and thousands more foreigners suffered and died. In all 56,000 died there, more people than the population of Weimar today or in 1932 when the majority of the town's people voted for the regime which was to set up that evil place, for the Nazis and the Nationalists.

The frock-coated deputies who assembled in Weimar in 1919 had been called there because of its associations with Germany's humanistic traditions, which they preferred to Berlin's militaristic and monarchical past. Despite the glowing democratic sentiments expressed by many of the deputies dark shadows already hung over the Republic.

Disaster threatened the German Empire (founded at Versailles in 1871 after the defeat of France) when in 1917 the mighty weight of the virile United States of America was thrown in behind the Anglo-French alliance. If Britain and France were by that time tired of the war which the European powers had unleashed upon themselves in the summer of 1914, Germany was even more so. By 1918 agricultural production was 40-60 per cent below prewar levels. The official food rations of 1917-18 were well below average prewar levels of consumption. Germans were allowed only about 20 per cent of their prewar consumption of meat, 13 per cent of eggs, 21 per cent of butter, 41 per cent of vegetable fats and about 47 per cent of flour. The official ration could rarely be honoured. Food and other prices had risen dramatically and Germans were working longer hours to meet those higher prices. More than 60 per cent of large and medium-sized factories in the Berlin armaments industry, which worked nine hours a day before the war, worked 10-12 hours a day in 1917. In more than half the factories the workers had to work regularly on Sundays as well. More than a third of those employed in industry were women as compared with about 20 per cent before the war. At the front victory and defeat alike resulted in very heavy casualties. Germany lost nearly two million dead and over double that number wounded in the fighting. In these circumstances it is not surprising that Germans should go on strike, some in anger, others in desperation.

The Russian revolutions of 1917 helped to focus discontent on a level higher than concern for mere material things, important though they were. This revolutionary upsurge in Russia also gave some Germans an example just as it frightened others.

In November 1917 there were demonstrations in Berlin, particularly in the working-class areas, demanding peace. In the same month peace demonstrations took place in certain other German towns as well. Again in November, and at the beginning of December, strikes broke out in a number of important factories. In Berlin, for instance, 2,600 workers at the Daimler Motor Works struck. In January 1918 over 400,000 workers downed tools in Berlin's metal industry. Their demands were political as well as economic. They took up the slogan of Lenin for a peace without annexations or indemnities, and demanded a democratic regime based on universal suffrage. The strike leadership coopted six leaders, three from the Social Democratic Party, and three from the Independent Social Democratic Party. The Independent Social Democrats were the minority movement of the Social Democratic Party who had been expelled from the party for opposing the world war. Some of them were pacifists, others revolutionaries. They were really only united on the question of their opposition to the war, and then not on the tactics to be pursued, and by their adherance to that ill-defined principle 'Socialism'. Friedrich Ebert, leader of the Majority Social Democrats who supported the war and one of the six coopted leaders, later commented that he joined the strike leadership in order to get the strikers back to work as soon as possible. The strike lasted only a few days but before it ended over a million workers in various parts of Germany had come out and violence erupted, several workers being killed or wounded. Germany was at this time officially under 'state of siege' which meant wide powers for the military and regimentation for the workers; consequently, military courts dealt with thousands jailing them or sending them off to the front. Other strikes followed.

Despite Germany's critical strategic position, due to American intervention, the worsening situation of Germany's Austrian ally and the clamour of many German workers for peace, the Reich's military leaders, Ludendorff and Hindenburg, showed themselves in no mood for negotiations. How they would deal with defeated nations was revealed by the peace of Brest-Litovsk between Germany and Bolshevik Russia agreed in March 1918. This required that large areas of the former Czarist Empire be either incorporated into the Reich or maintained as German puppet states. In the same month a new German offensive was launched on the Western Front which gained some initial success. However, it soon became clear that military victory for Germany was impossible and that with every day complete military collapse drew nearer: Germany lacked the human and material reserves to sustain prolonged military effort and the American troops were pouring into France. In the hope of impressing the Allies and improving their negotiating position, the German military leadership advised the establishment of the broadest possible coalition government in Berlin.

In October Prince Max of Baden took over from Count Georg von Hertling as Chancellor of the German Reich. Prince Max was doubtful about the wisdom of bringing in the Social Democrats for he knew a political price would have to be paid. This price was the introduction of universal adult suffrage and secret ballot in all German Länder or regions (something mighty Prussia did not yet have), the abolition of censorship and acceptance of President Wilson's 14 Points Declaration. The Prince had also rejected the idea of an armistice and only agreed when told by Hindenburg that the armed forces could not hold out even a day longer.

Two Social Democrats entered the new government, Philipp Scheidemann as Minister without Portfolio, and Gustav Bauer as *Staatssekretär* for Labour. These were not very exalted posts for members of a party which in fact had been the largest party in the Reichstag since 1912! The new government included the Centre Party, the second largest in the Reichstag, and the Left Liberals as well as the Social Democrats who entered a German government for the first time. On 5 October the new government approved in principle the change to a parliamentary system in which the Chancellor or Prime Minister would be responsible to the Reichstag rather than to the Monarch, and in which war and peace were the responsibility of the Reichstag as elected parliament of the German people.

The Reichstag then went into recess until 22 October while the necessary legislation was being drafted. The Reichstag passed the bills on 26 October but then adjourned until 9 November. Considering the crisis Germany was facing this was remarkable. The slowness of parliamentary developments and the infrequency of that body's deliberations during this period was a sign that Germany's leaders had not yet decided to end the war. On 17 October Ludendorff was still voicing illusions about Germany's military future at a meeting of the Cabinet. Scheidemann sounded a more realistic note by pointing out, ' We have no meat. We cannot provide potatoes . . .!' In its telegrams to President Wilson of America negotiating an armistice the German government still prevaricated. As they did so the situation got worse. Wilson hinted strongly that Emperor Wilhelm would have to go and Ludendorff too. The general went on 26 October, the Emperor attempted to hold on. But the developing situation in Germany made it impossible for him to stay.

On Wilson's demand, the Germans had agreed to stop submarine warfare. Now the admirals of the fleet, whose ships had been inactive for some time, decided on their own initiative, without consulting the government, to put to sea and engage the British fleet. In all probability they would have been destroyed and the rank-and-file sailors, who had endured bad conditions for some years, were not prepared to sacrifice themselves in any last-minute, futile, grand gesture. They mutinied and hoisted the red flag. They declared that they would defend Germany against any attack by the British fleet but they would not undertake offensive operations. Had they not taken this action the war might have dragged on with far worse consequences for Germany. They were German patriots who risked being shot as traitorous mutineers. The mutiny started on 30 October. Already, in August of 1917 there had been a mutiny in the fleet. On that occasion two of the leaders, Albin Köbis and Max Reichpietsch, had been court-martialled and shot, many others suffered imprisonment. On this occasion too it looked for a time as though the officers would re-establish their authority for briefly, with the help of marines, they managed to restore ' order '. But as the mutiny was being put down in Wilhemshaven it was breaking out in Kiel (3 November). There it spread to troops stationed in the area and to the citizens of the town. Within days it had spread throughout the coastal towns of North Germany. By the 7-8 November it had spread inland to all major centres of the Reich. In its outward aspects it was similar to what had happened in Russia after February 1917—councils of workers and servicemen were being set up and were either taking over control of the towns or were exercising control jointly with the existing authorities. On 7 November the first royal house fell in Bavaria where a democratic republic was proclaimed. Kurt Eisner became the Prime Minister of a coalition government made up of Independent Social Democrats and Majority Social Democrats.

The leaders of the Majority Social Democrats were under increasing pressure from their rank-and-file to pursue a more militant policy. They feared losing support to the Independent Social Democrats or, worse still, to the Spartacus League, the forerunner of the German Communist Party. They had to demand from Prince Max the abdication of Wilhelm, warning that if this demand were not met they would be forced by their own members to leave the government. Friedrich Ebert further warned the Prince, according to the latter's memoirs, that if the abdication were not announced, there would be a social revolution, ' which I hate like sin '. Both the Majority Social Democratic leaders and the Prince hoped to save the monarchy by securing Wilhelm's departure. This he still refused to do. The Social Democrats therefore left the government and, by the time Wilhelm had agreed to go, on 9 November, the cause of the monarchy was lost in Germany. On that day Karl Liebknecht, one of the Spartacus leaders and Reichstag member, just released from prison where he had been held for opposing the war, led a demonstration to the Berliner Schloss. In front of the building he proclaimed a German Socialist Republic. Fearing the consequences of opposing such a proclamation, Philipp Scheidemann made his own proclamation of a ' free German Republic ' on the same day. For this, for which he had no authority but his own political instinct, Scheidemann was criticised by Ebert. But there was no going back. The next day, as Kaiser Wilhelm ii, last of the Hohenzollern monarchs, German Emperor for 30 years, fled to Holland, a mass meeting of the Berlin workers' and soldiers' councils formally elected six People's Commissioners to form a Council to rule Germany. The new Council of People's Commissioners consisted of three Majority Social Democrats, Ebert, Scheidemann and Otto Landsberg, and three Independent Social Democrats, Hugo Haase, Wilhelm Dittmann and Emil Barth. Friedrich Ebert was elected chairman.

Meanwhile, in the forest of Compiègne, Germans and Frenchmen were meeting to arrange an armistice. Marshal Foch of France was the Allies' representative and handed the Allies' conditions to the German commission. The chief German delegate was Matthias Erzberger, a Centre Party member of the Prince Max government, who had been prevailed upon by Hindenburg to go to Compiègne. On 11 November the Germans signed the armistice agreement.

Foolishly, the Allies did not require any high-ranking German officer to sign the agreement, though a major-general and a naval captain did sign. Consequently, after the war German militarists were to claim that it was not the work of the German armed forces, who had been ' stabbed in the back ' by the politicians.

The coalition government led by Ebert was soon faced with difficult decisions. Its members were men who had suddenly had power thrust upon them. They were used to waging great struggles to get small reforms. Now power was in their hands. What to do with it? Ebert felt that order was to be maintained at all cost. If it were not, and Germany were plunged into anarchy, the people, and particularly the working people (as always), would be the sufferers. He also felt that if the government degenerated into a small, revolutionary junta, it would be forced to take ever more repressive steps to maintain itself (as was happening with the Bolsheviks in Russia). Furthermore, he feared that if a German government appeared incapable of maintaining order the Allies would occupy the whole country. To achieve his primary objective he did two things.

Firstly, as General Wilhelm Groener later testified, Ebert secured the support of the Army High Command for his government. ' We allied ourselves to one another to fight against the revolution, to fight against Bolshevism. . . . The purpose of this alliance, that we concluded on the night of 10 November was the total putting down of revolution, the re-establishment of ordered government power, the support of such government power by an armed force, and the soonest possible summoning of a national assembly. That was the aim.' They further agreed to the sending of ten divisions of troops to Berlin to carry out the ' disarmament of Berlin, the clearing of Berlin of Spartacists, etc '. Ebert's second aim, as mentioned above by Groener, was the summoning of a National Assembly. On this point there were differences of opinion in the government. The more Left-inclined Independents agreed in principle but thought the Council should get on with the job of transforming the power structure immediately and thus prevent the re-emergence of those capitalist-imperialist forces which were responsible for Germany's present plight. The Spartacists desired immediate action, including the establishment of a dictatorship based on the workers' and soldiers' councils—which they wrongly believed Russia had. They felt betrayed by men like Friedrich Ebert, the professional politicians who, by working-class standards, had long since secured for themselves a good life based on a career in the Socialist movement. Had not such men been the ones who had supported the imperialist war? Was it not a fact that while such men urged caution the reactionary forces were regrouping? Taking up what had been the slogan of Lenin *before* he got power, *Die Rote Fahne,* the organ of the Spartacists, demanded all power to the workers' and soldiers' councils.

On 20 December the first all-German congress of these councils rejected by 344 votes to 98 the demand for a government based on the councils and agreed that on 19 January elections should take place for a national assembly. As these votes suggest, the congress was totally dominated by Ebert's men. The Spartacist leaders Karl Liebknecht and Rosa Luxemburg were unable to secure election to the congress. The congress passed two other significant resolutions which were not to be realised. One of these was a call for the socialisation of all ' ripe ' industries, especially coal mining. The other was for the establishment of a People's Militia, a traditional Social Democratic demand, with elected leaders (rather than officers) and responsible to the People's Commissioners. This resolution was an embarrassment to Ebert in view of his alliance with Hindenburg and Groener.

A week before the congress met the promised divisions of loyal troops had arrived in the suburbs of Berlin and General Groener was getting impatient with the slowness of the operations against ' unauthorized military groups ' (i.e. Left-wing groups). One of the most important of these was the People's Marine Division which, although now tending to the Left, had been recognised by the People's Commissioners to the extent that they had provided its members with pay. This pay was cut off and in order to ' negotiate ' with him the marines seized Otto Wels, Social Democrat Berlin City Commandant. Under pressure from General Groener, Ebert agreed to troops being used against them. This attack failed and Spartacus demonstrations followed in Berlin, where the offices of the organ of the Ebert party were taken over, and in other German towns. Fighting broke out in various places. On 29 December the Independents decided to leave Ebert's Council of People's Commissioners and their places were taken by Majority Social Democrats.

At the end of December 1918 the Spartacus Leagues decided to break their (by then) very precarious ties with the Independent Social Democrats and set themselves up as the German Communist Party. Against the advice of their two most important leaders Liebknecht and Luxemburg, they decided not to contest the elections to the national assembly. In this way they showed their disdain for this body and strengthened the suspicions of the Social Democrats and others that their aim was purely armed insurrection. On 6 January the representatives of the new Communist Party, Karl

Liebknecht and Wilhelm Pieck, agreed with representatives of the Berlin Independent Social Democrats, the People's Marines and the revolutionary shop stewards, to an armed struggle for the conquest of power. Strikes and the occupation of buildings in Berlin followed. Weapons were distributed but the attempted coup was badly led and ill-coordinated; the result was that the pro-government troops turned the action into a blood bath. The fighting ended on 12 January with the storming by government troops of the Berlin police headquarters. Many of the rebels were shot out of hand. Three days later Liebknecht and Luxemburg, who against their better judgement had supported the rising in print, were hunted down, beaten and shot.

The murder of Luxemburg and Liebknecht (for it was later recognised as murder by the authorities) helped to perpetuate the bitterness which existed between Communist and Social Democrat. This was to be of great importance in the last years of the Weimar Republic. Had Luxemburg and Liebknecht lived they might have led the Communist Party out of the cul-de-sac of mere oppositionism and dependence on Moscow. Rosa Luxemburg had already denounced Leninism long before the Russian Revolution, though she greatly admired the courage and sincerity of Lenin, and by 1918 was disturbed by events in Russia. Had she survived she very probably would have seen through Stalinism.

The armed struggle of the Left in Berlin was not yet at an end. Early in March renewed fighting broke out in the capital during a general strike called by the revolutionary shop stewards to achieve socialisation of the factories and the dissolution of the Free Corps.* Gustav Noske, a Social Democrat who had been put in charge of the Republic's armed forces by Ebert in December, once again acted as the state's ' bloodhound ', as he himself put it. Government troops went into action killing anyone who was found armed. Roughly 1,200 died on both sides in the fighting. Skirmishing went on in other parts of the Reich too but by the end of May the government/Right-wing troops were in command.

In Bavaria where a Left coalition had been functioning under Kurt Eisner, an Independent Social Democrat, trouble started when Eisner was assassinated on 21 February 1919. Eisner was in fact on his way to the regional parliament to announce his resignation as his party had been severely defeated in elections held the month before. Eisner had been killed by a Rightist, but angered by it, one

* These were armed units of volunteeers, including many Right-wing, former officers. They were officially supposed to protect the frontiers and keep ' order '.

of his supporters shot the leader of the Majority Social Democrats in the parliament. Violence now swept through Bavaria. A revolutionary council was set up and a general strike called. In April the council prevented the parliament from meeting and then declared a republic based on workers' councils citing the Russian Soviets as its model. The official government of Bavaria led by a Majority Social Democrat was not prepared to capitulate and government troops moved in to settle the issue. This they did with great brutality, shooting anyone whom they suspected. A group of 21 members of a Catholic organisation who were holding a meeting were shot down as suspected revolutionaries. They were not the only ones. After the carnage the legal government was allowed to return to Munich.

In January 1919 Ebert had been able to keep his promise to hold elections throughout the Reich for a national assembly. The Majority Social Democrats gained 11.5 million votes or 37.9 per cent and 165 seats. To the Left the Independents received 2.3 million votes or 7.6 per cent and 22 seats. The Centre Party's share was 5.9 million votes or 19.7 per cent and 90 seats. The Democratic Party (left Liberals) won 5.6 million votes (18.5 per cent) and 75 seats. On the right, the German Nationalists got just over 3 million votes (10.3 per cent) and 42 seats. Also on the right the German People's Party attracted 1.3 million votes (4.4 per cent) and 22 seats. Minor groups received another 1.6 per cent of the vote and seven seats. Participation in the election had been high, 82.7 per cent of the electorate having voted. Voting was under a new franchise. Women had been granted the vote which they and male Germans now had the right to exercise from the age of 20 (previously it had been from 25 for men). The Social Democrats could claim that in spite of everything their advance was continuing. As a united party they had gained 34.8 per cent of the poll at the last elections of 1912. In 1919 the two Social Democratic Parties had received 45.5 per cent of the vote. It looked as though the parliamentary, gradualist tactic was paying off, for the years before the war had been years of almost uninterrupted advance. That advance appeared to be continuing. Right-wing groups seemed to be on their way out, for their share of the vote had dropped from 36.6 per cent in 1912 to 16.3 per cent in 1919.

From the election results it was obvious that the first elected government of the Weimar Republic would have to be a coalition government. Meeting at Weimar the national assembly elected Ebert President of the Republic by a decisive majority over his Nationalist opponent. Ebert then appointed a government of seven Social Democrats, three Centre Party members, three Democrats and one

B

non-party, Foreign Minister Count von Brockdorff-Rantzau. The Independent Social Democrats had refused to take part in the government.

Apart from the precarious state of law and order the new government faced the problem of negotiations with the Allies and the maintenance of the unity of the Reich.

When Allied peace terms became known in Germany in May 1919 there was great disappointment and equally great anger. The Germans claimed they had expected a peace based on President Wilson's 14 Points and that the terms were not consistent with them. They had neglected to remember that Wilson had had no authority to speak for Britain, France or Belgium, and that these states had carried the main effort of the war against Germany. And, of course the terms were, to a considerable extent, based on Wilson's 14 Points. Ebert spoke of the delivering up of the German workers to wage slavery for foreign capitalism. The parliamentary group of the Majority Social Democrats rejected the terms as unacceptable. Scheidemann, as head of the government, and most of his cabinet resigned as a gesture against the terms. He was replaced on 22 June by another Majority Social Democrat, Gustav Bauer, who formed a government of Social Democrats, Centre and Bavarian People's Party. Chancellor Bauer declared that the new government would be prepared to sign if the articles requiring Germany's sole responsibility for the war, and the articles requiring Germany to hand over its citizens wanted by the Allies as war criminals were deleted. The majority of the national assembly voted for this compromise. The Allies refused these concessions; they had earlier granted other concessions, because the Germans, against the terms of the treaty, had just scuttled their fleet at Scapa Flow. Further, captured flags due for handing back to the French had been burned. The Allies warned the Germans of the consequences of any additional delay. In view of this situation the national assembly agreed to give the government a mandate to sign. The Nationalists, German People's Party, part of the Centre and part of the Democratic Party voted against. The Independent Social Democrats had advised voting for the treaty from the start. Their view was that although it was ' a forced peace of the worst kind ', they had got to think of the consequences of not signing: continued internment for German prisoners of war, the occupation of Germany's raw materials' areas, the stepping up of the blockade, unemployment, starvation, death and terrible cataclysm—then Germany would still have to sign. This commonsense view of the Independents was in marked contrast to the daydreaming of the Nationalists, and many of the officers.

And in view of what later happened in Germany it should be stressed that Ebert and Noske only used their influence in favour of signing when they had heard from General Groener that the military situation was hopeless. In fact he begged them to stay at their posts. Hindenburg, who also clearly understood the situation, sought to evade the responsibility by resigning. The two unfortunate German ministers who signed the Treaty of Versailles were Hermann Müller, a Social Democrat and Foreign Minister, and Dr Johannes Bell.

The main aims of the Treaty of Versailles appear to have been to reduce Germany from the status of a world power to being merely a European power; to rob Germany of its territorial conquests; to destroy Germany as a military power, and to make Germany pay for the devastation Imperial troops had inflicted on other nations. All German colonies were allotted to Allied states as League of Nations' trust territories. The Imperial fleet was also required to be handed over to the Allies but, as we have seen, it was scuttled before this transfer could be effected. The articles of the Treaty dealing with territory stipulated the return of Alsace-Lorraine to France; the creation of an independent Polish state with a ' a free and secure access to the sea '; the restoration of Belgium, Romania and Serbia, and the creation of a Czechoslovak state; the carrying through of plebiscites to determine the frontiers with Denmark and Poland; the cession of the Eupen and Malmédy districts to Belgium and the transfer of the Saar to French control under a League of Nations' Commission for 15 years; the prohibition of any future union of Germany and Austria. The Treaty reduced the mighty German military machine to an army of 100,000 and a navy of 15,000. It laid down the type and number of ships, forbade submarines, tanks, planes and offensive weapons. Article 231 stated: ' the Allied Governments affirm and Germany accepts the responsibility of Germany and her allies for causing all the loss and damage ', which the Allies and their subjects had suffered ' as a consequence of the war imposed upon them by the aggression of Germany and her allies '. Finally, to enforce the treaty, Allied armies were to occupy bridgeheads along the Rhine for 15 years and the Rhineland was to be permanently demilitarised.

The Constitution of the Weimar Republic, drafted by Hugo Preuss, was accepted on 31 July 1919. It established a federal system with a Reichsrat or house of states and a Reichstag or directly elected house. This was similar to the earlier Imperial Constitution. The President was to be directly elected. There was also provision for a *Reichswirtschaftsrat* or Reich Economic Council, which was no more than lip-service to the idea of economic democracy. The

Council played virtually no role in the affairs of the Republic. The Reichsrat was not in the powerful position of the old upper house, but it could delay legislation until overruled by a two-thirds majority of the Reichstag. The latter was the main constitutional organ. Elected for four years it controlled legislation and normally the government. The President did not appear to be in too strong a position on paper, though in practice his position turned out to be very strong. The fact that he was directly elected gave him prestige, and under Article 48 of the Constitution he could employ the armed forces for the restoration of order. In cases of emergency he could suspend most of the constitutional liberties. The same Article empowered the President to rule by emergency decrees. The decrees had to be counter-signed by the Chancellor or responsible Minister, and the Reichstag had to be informed of them and retained the power of rescinding them. As we shall see, these presidential powers were to be of vital importance later on.

The signing of the Versailles Treaty had incensed many Right-wing officers still more against the Republic. With little else to do with their time, groups of plotters were springing up all over Germany. In March 1920 one such group carried out a coup in Berlin. The originator of this particular plot was not an officer but a civil servant, an agricultural specialist, Wolfgang Kapp. The military figures connected with it were Generals von Lüttwitz and Ludendorff. The coup was actually executed by Ehrhardt's Marine Brigade, a Free Corps organisation. These troops had no difficulty in occupying key buildings in the capital, including the Chancellor's office. Luckily the President and the Government had fled to Dresden from where they successfully called for a general strike. Kapp and his followers were virtually powerless. Most of the army and the police at first remained neutral but slowly turned towards the Ebert regime for fear of worse to come, namely civil war or a more Left-wing regime.

A terrible sequel to the Kapp Putsch was the crushing of the remnants of the so-called 'Red Ruhr Army' which grew out of resistance to the Putsch in the Ruhr.

Thousands of workers had armed themselves and taken over large areas of the Ruhr. In certain instances they had shown they were more than a match for armed police, Free Corps and even Reichswehr units. After the collapse of the Putsch they were reluctant to surrender their weapons so soon after the loyalty of the official armed forces had proved to be so doubtful. They demanded guarantees against further militarist coups and introduction of the social changes which the Social Democratic leaders had promised endlessly before and after 1918. On 24 March an agreement was reached between representatives of the government and a very wide spectrum of political opinion including the Centre Party, the Democratic Party, the trade unions, Majority and Independent Social Democrats; representatives of local authorities and two Communists though did not sign for their party. Under the agreement, which became known as the Bielefeld Agreement, the workers agreed to hand over their weapons and return to work. The government side promised to disarm and punish those who had taken part in the Putsch; to disband all anti-republican organisations; to purge the administration of counter-revolutionary elements; to carry through ' as quickly as possible ' co-determination in economic organisations and administrative reform on a democratic basis; ' Immediate ' socialisation of ' ripe ' industries, especially coal and potash; formation of a local militias from the loyal republican circles of the population; extension of social welfare legislation; financial help from the state for the dependants of killed or wounded; no discrimination against those workers who had taken part in the struggle or against members of the police or Reichswehr; provided the agreement was loyally kept Reichswehr units would not move into the Ruhr industrial area.

This agreement remained a dead letter in virtually every respect. On 26 March the Weimar coalition was reshuffled with Hermann Müller as Chancellor and the participation his Majority Social Democrats, the Centre Party and the Democrats, but nothing was done to realise the promises given to the Ruhr workers. Most of them handed over their weapons and returned to work, some did not. Reichswehr and Free Corps units were sent into the area and even into towns in the demilitarised zone, thus breaking the Versailles Treaty (quite apart from any consideration of the Bielefeld Agreement). They brutally went about their business, killing both prisoners and wounded, including women. Had Ebert and his colleagues used the opportunity they had immediately after the collapse of the Kapp Putsch they would probably have secured once and for all a democratic, social republic enjoying the support of the majority of the people. As it was, by showing every tolerance to Right-wing plotters but none to workers who had defended the Republic, they alienated countless thousands of politically conscious workers from the Weimar Republic. The Left of the Independent Social Democrats joined the Communist Party and at the elections which followed the defeat of Kapp the Majority Social Democrats lost to the Left. They did not find much thanks from the right for their actions.

# 2  Weimar from Crisis to Stability

The elections of 6 June 1920 produced a swing away from the centre parties to the extremes—a result of the heat generated by the Kapp Putsch and discontent with the government. The Social Democrats remained the largest party but lost heavily to the Independent Social Democrats and even to the Communists, the latter being ably represented by two deputies Dr Paul Levi and Clara Zetkin. The Social Democrats felt that continued participation in government with bourgeois parties pursuing measures which were unpopular with many of their supporters would result in further erosion of their base. They therefore left the government and in 1922 were re-united with the Independent Social Democrats. Although they, more than any other party, became associated in the public mind with ' the Weimar System ', they did not provide a Chancellor again until Hermann Müller took over for a second time in June 1928 remaining in office till March 1930. After November 1923 the Social Democrats were no longer represented in a Reich government though, as we shall see, they were important in regional government and their man, Friedrich Ebert, was President of the Republic until his death in 1925.

The Centre Party politician Constantin Fehrenbach now took over the government. His party had joined with the Social Democrats in coalition in February 1919 and were participants in all 17 governments to May 1932 (and even after that if one includes expelled Centre Party politicians who remained in office). Thus they, even more than the Social Democrats, could be called the classic party of Weimar.

That during this period they usually had 60-odd seats out of a Reichstag of between 403 (in 1919) and 608 (in July 1932) seats indicates not only their weakness but also the weaknesses of the parliamentary system in Weimar Germany. The partners in the 17 coalition governments were usually united on very little, often carrying on contradictory policies in various ministries, and it is not surprising that by the end of 1932 the governments of the Weimar Republic had existed on average only eight months. In such circumstances interest groups and the permanent ' servants ' of the state, the bureaucracy and the military, exercised far more influence than was their due.

## SECRET REARMAMENT AND THE UNLIKELY ALLIANCE

The *Wehrgesetz* or Defence Law of 1921 set out the constitutional position of the armed forces in the Weimar Republic. This law paid lip-service to the Versailles Treaty, the democratic traditions of Social Democracy and the developments during the German revolution. The stipulations of the Treaty of Versailles regarding the maximum strength of the forces, their officers and organisation were duly recorded, the President was named as commander-in-chief and even the ghosts of the soldiers' councils crept in. There was an elected *Heerskammer* (Army Chamber) made up of officers, N C Os and other ranks with advisory functions. There were also *Vertrauensräte* in all units mainly concerned with the personal grievances of the ordinary soldiers. The position of the Defence Minister was not very clearly defined. He could issue orders but not commands. Servicemen were not allowed to engage in political activities and even membership of non-political clubs could be banned for reasons of military discipline. Many Social Democrats believed this would prevent soldiers being active in Right-wing parties and organisations. On the whole, however, officers clamped down on Left-wing activity in the barracks and turned a blind eye to or supported, Rightist activities. Although even on paper far from perfect, the *Wehrgesetz* shows the limited value of constitutional devices when democratic consciousness is lacking.

Remarkable in view of the precarious tenure of office enjoyed by his colleagues was the ability of Dr Otto Gessler, a member of the Democratic Party, to retain his position as Minister of Defence which he held from 1920 to 1928. It then passed into the hands of General Wilhelm Groener until June 1932 and from then, until Hitler became Chancellor in January 1933, the post was occupied by General Kurt von Schleicher. Even after that another general, Werner von Blomberg, was Defence Minister until the post was abolished in 1938. This is some indication of the resilience of the old military caste, for Gessler held office with the approval of the Reichswehr even though the generals did not always agree with everything he said or did.

Chief of the army from March 1920 to October 1926 was General Hans von Seeckt, very much an old-fashioned aristocratic officer. He was a monarchist. Of the Weimar Constitution he wrote, ' it's basic principles (are) contrary to my political thinking '. Seeckt's military policy, and that of his fellow officers, was secret rearmament while officially keeping to the limitations imposed by the Versailles Treaty. The armed forces were not allowed an air arm, so a shadow air force was built up by expanding, through subsidies, civilian flying clubs where officers trained, training pilots abroad, testing machines abroad and developing a strong civil aviation industry. Likewise the navy tested submarines and other equipment beyond the frontiers of the Reich, notably in Holland and Spain. Further, the Reichswehr maintained a large proportion of N C Os, the backbone of any army, who made rapid expansion after 1933 possible. There were also various military clubs, societies and organisations to foster the military spirit, pass on military knowledge or engage in paramilitary sports activities.

More astonishing than any of these activities was Seeckt's policy of secret military cooperation with Soviet Russia. What could possibly induce military cooperation between old-fashioned German militarists and Russian, in some cases Russian Jewish, Bolsheviks? Firstly, Seeckt was personally pro-Russian, though strongly 'anti-Marxist'. Secondly, both nations were losers of World War I. They felt they had been badly treated by the Anglo-Saxon-French alliance. Thirdly, industrial Germany had much to offer agrarian Russia. Fourthly, some German officers admired the 'strong' government of Bolshevik Russia. Finally, both were hostile to Poland. Poland's existence, so declared Seeckt, 'is intolerable, incompatible with the survival of Germany. It must disappear, and it will disappear through its own internal weakness and through Russia—with our assistance'. As for the Bolsheviks, they regarded one bourgeois capitalist regime much as another and bought where they could.

This cooperation involved the construction of aircraft factories, by Junkers, tanks, artillery, munitions and poison gas factories, the products of which were then used in training by Soviet and German troops. The Germans gave a wide assortment of specialist training to Soviet personnel including staff training to Soviet officers who went to Germany for the purpose. The German Navy too was involved in such cooperation, though much less so due to its suspicion of Soviet Russia and other opportunities.

Russo-German military joint ventures continued until Hitler gained power and would not have been possible without the interest of major industrial concerns as well as the military. What about the politicians? What was their attitude to it? Certainly until 1926, when it was attacked by the Social Democrats, most members of the Reichstag were unaware of it. Certainly most of them would have opposed it had they known. The Centre Party Chancellor

Wirth (Chancellor October 1921 to November 1922) knew and approved of it, favouring an Eastern orientation to German policy. He negotiated the Rapallo Treaty which heralded Russo-German *rapprochement* in 1922. His successor Cuno, who lasted until August 1923, opposed such cooperation but was unable to stop it. Stresemann was more sympathetic. The other Chancellors, if they knew about it, were unable to prevent it.

## THE RUHR OCCUPATION AND HITLER'S PUTSCH

Throughout 1921-22 tension continued in Germany. There were rumours of coups and political assassinations (including that of Matthias Erzberger, one of the signatories to the Armistice Agreement, and Walther Rathenau, Jewish Foreign Minister, both were murdered by Rightists). The trials of Germans before German courts for alleged war crimes—mainly the ill-treatment of prisoners of war and the sinking of a hospital ship—further stirred up the nationalists. Worse was to come. The fate of Upper Silesia was still in the balance. By a considerable majority the inhabitants voted in March 1921 to remain in Germany. Polish volunteers, encouraged by the Polish government, anticipated the decision of the Allies to partition Upper Silesia by staging a coup in the area. The French occupying forces did nothing, but the Poles were opposed by German Freikorps who successfully held the Poles. But the Reich government was forced to follow a verbally more conciliatory policy than the Freikorps, which once again increased the wrath of the nationalists. Eventually Upper Silesia was partitioned as a result of a recommendation by a League of Nations' committee drawn from Belgium, Brazil, China and Spain. Their decision was a disappointment to the Germans.

Hatred rather than disappointment was the response of the Germans to the Franco-Belgian occupation of the Ruhr which started in January 1923. Officially it was said that the French sought to ensure punctual delivery of reparations. The move, which was not supported by Britain, was declared an illegal violation of Versailles by the German government under Chancellor Cuno. The Reich government forbade German industry to export coal to France or Belgium, and ordered government officials and other public employees to ignore the instructions of the occupying forces. Many German officials obeyed their government, German workers went on strike. The French military authorities, no doubt remembering bitter situations when the boot was on the other foot, responded with vigour. They jailed hundreds, expelled hundreds more and killed 13 Krupps workers when they fired on strikers.

Faced with so many political difficulties, not to mention economic ones (discussed below), it would not have been surprising if the German governmental system had collapsed. Hitler thought it might —with a gentle push from Bavaria. His amateurish revolt was probably inspired by Mussolini who was busy toppling the Italian parliamentary system after his famous 1922 march on Rome.

Adolf Hitler was born in 1889, the son of a minor Austrian Custom's Official. Like Churchill and some others destined for fame he was not so good at his school subjects, though he made his mark in history classes. He left the *Gymnasium* without graduating with the intention of becoming an artist but he failed to get into the Vienna Academy of Fine Arts and apparently gave up this ambition. For several years he lived on a modest paternal inheritance and from money he earned doing odd jobs. He pursued his interest in architecture at this time.

It was in Vienna, a very politically aware city, that he came to full political consciousness. His views were not unusual for one from his background. As a petty bourgeois he despised the workers. As a German-Austrian he had little time for the lesser breeds of the Empire—Poles, Hungarians, Czechs, and Slovaks. He was conventionally anti-semitic when he arrived in Vienna from the city of Linz. The capital was at that time ruled by a Lord Mayor with strong anti-Jewish tendencies and Hitler was no doubt influenced by this atmosphere. He was probably angered too by finding Jews who were better educated or materially better off than himself. He became a pan-German nationalist in the years before the First World War as he contrasted the dynamism of Germany with the decay of the Hapsburg Empire. At the outbreak of the war he volunteered for service in a Bavarian rather than an Austrian regiment and was twice awarded the Iron Cross. He rose to the rank of corporal.

After Bavaria's brief experiment as a Marxist republic at the end of the war, Munich became a hotbed of Rightist agitation. Hitler attracted the attention of his officers for his Right-wing views and oratorical abilities. They, in fear of Marxism and seeking platforms for their own ideas, assigned him to investigate the activities of a group calling itself the German Workers' Party. He joined this movement, which had been set up by a nationalist locksmith Anton Drexler, and left the army. By the time the party changed its name to the National Socialist German Workers' Party (NSDAP) on 1 April 1920 he was already among its leaders. The NSDAP adopted a programme, taken over from the earlier party, including: the uniting of all Germans in a greater Germany; such a Germany to have a strong central government; abolition of unearned incomes; nationalisation of trusts: abolition of land rents and land speculation; maintenance of a sound middle class; municipalisation of department stores and their lease at cheap rates to small traders; death for traitors and profiteers and, so important after 1933, ban on Jews from holding public office and loss of citizenship, and renunciation of the Versailles Treaty.

In the summer of 1921 Hitler succeeded in fighting Drexler for the party leadership and from then on was the party's Führer, a position which it seems the founders of the movement had not regarded as part and parcel of National Socialism. About this time Hitler got his first financial backers—two wealthy ladies. One of these was Frau Helene Bechstein, wife of the famous piano maker, the other was Frau Gertrud von Seidlitz, who had a considerable holding in some Finnish paper mills. Hermann Göring, famous for his exploits as a fighter pilot, also contributed to Hitler's and the party's upkeep. He had been lucky enough to marry into affluence. Hitler himself did not marry, he was married to the movement and gradually built up an image as an austere, devoted leader. He was a non-drinker, non-smoker and vegetarian. It was in these early years that some of the later internationally-known Nazis joined the movement. Men like Rudolf Hess, son of a German merchant in Egypt and wartime flyer, Max Amann, Hitler's wartime sergeant, and Alfred Rosenberg, the Estonian-German graduate of Moscow University.

Another important, in many respects decisive, figure in the Nazi movement claimed earlier membership than Hitler—a fact probably held against him by his Führer; this was Ernst Röhm. He had served Kaiser and Fatherland as a captain in the army and built up the Nazi movement's military wing, the S A. Early in 1923 Röhm engineered an alliance of a number of militant Right-wing groups including many former officers and N C Os, something Hitler, as a former corporal, could not have succeeded in doing. This brought Hitler on to the same platform as General Ludendorff who was always ready to ' have a go ' if he thought he could advance the Right-wing cause.

On 26 September 1923 Gustav Stresemann, who had become Chancellor in August, announced, no doubt to the surprise of those who remembered him as a hardline nationalist during the war, the end of resistance to the French in the Ruhr. He had taken the precaution of getting President Ebert to declare a state of emergency under Article 48 of the Constitution, tantamount to turning the country over to the army under General Seeckt. Seeckt saw his task as maintaining the unity of the Reich and of ' law and order '. How-

ever, he had greater ambitions too. He planned to take over as
Chancellor and actually drew up a ' government programme ' along
authoritarian lines. Germany might well have got a military regime
at that time had not some Right-wing officers, and later Hitler,
jumped the gun. Led by former Major Ernst Buckrucker Right-wing
rebels attempted to seize Berlin. Seeckt put down this rebellion. He
continued to be pressed by his own officers to take over and in
the end it appears to have been a combination of lack of unity on
the Right, Hitler's impetuosity and Seeckt's indecisiveness, which
saved Germany from military dictatorship in 1923.

Bavaria, which since the fall of the Kaiser had been operating
almost as an independent state, was run by an extremely reactionary
clique headed by Dr Gustav Ritter von Kahr. After a personal
attack on General Seeckt in the *Völkischer Beobachter*, the Nazi
newspaper, he ordered its prohibition. The Reichswehr commander
General Lossow refused to execute the order and was backed by
von Kahr. The situation gradually deteriorated and open secession
broke out with officers taking a new oath to Bavaria replacing the
one they had taken to the Reich. Hitler hoped to exploit this
situation and tried to force the hand of von Kahr, Lossow and
police chief Col. Hans von Seisser. He hoped to get them to launch
a complete takeover in Munich leading to a march on Berlin. Using
the S A he arrested them as they attended a businessmen's meeting
in a Munich beer hall. At first reluctant to cooperate with him, they
agreed when threatened with a revolver and when they heard that
Ludendorff was behind the Nazi leader. Hitler now made a fatal
mistake of leaving them in the custody of his subordinates. The three
Bavarians slipped away and being enraged by their treatment they
ordered troops and police to deal with the Nazis. The putsch of
8-9 November ended in bloodshed with 16 S A and three police killed
and many others wounded.

There was bloodshed in other parts of Germany that autumn. In
Hamburg the Communists revolted from 23 to 26 October. Ernst
Thälmann was in charge and it was hoped that the rising would
spread throughout the country. In fact it was put down without too
much difficulty. In Saxony and Thuringia Left-Socialist and Communist coalition governments had been established. Seeckt acted
with much more decisiveness than he had shown in dealing with
Bavaria. These governments were perfectly legal though the
Communist partners foolishly called for the setting up of the
dictatorship of the proletariat throughout Germany. Workers'
militias were formed. Seeckt ordered the Reichswehr in, disbanded
the armed workers' organisations and arrested the governments.

This action led to the break-up of the coalition government in Berlin
due to the withdrawal of the Social Democrats. Stresemann fell on
30 November and was replaced by the Centre Party politician Marx
who ruled with the help of an enabling act until February of the
next year. Stresemann was included in the government as Foreign
Minister, a post he occupied until his death in 1929. General Seeckt
gradually relinquished control of things after the crushing of the
revolts. Why he did so is not clear though he may have felt by so
doing he could legally get power by becoming next President. As
it turned out his fellow officer Hindenburg was elected to that
position after the death of Ebert in 1925. In the autumn of 1926
the politicians felt the position of the Republic had been so stabilised
that they could dismiss Seeckt, officially for introducing a member
of the old royal family in uniform to a regimental exercise, without
any fear of a military coup. They were over-optimistic. The officers
had merely changed their loyalty from Seeckt to Hindenburg and
he was to lead them and the country into Hitler's lap.

## FROM INFLATION TO STABILISATION

Germany's political troubles of the early 1920s were made much
worse by economic problems (in turn to a considerable degree
caused by political difficulties). The peace terms, the Kapp putsch,
the troubles in Upper Silesia, the coups and rumours of coups,
created loss of confidence in the currency and inflation followed. The
reparations crisis and the French occupation of the Ruhr led to a
catastrophic fall in the value of the mark. Domestic prices became
fixed according to the mark's relation to the dollar. In July 1914 this
had been 4.2 marks to the dollar by July 1919 it was 14 marks. In
July 1922 493.2 marks were exchanged for one dollar and a year
later 353,412.0. Runaway depression was now fully under way and
by December 1923 4,200,000 million marks were needed to purchase
one dollar! The situation was so out of hand that shops closed at
midday with one set of prices and reopened in the afternoon with
another higher set. Those on fixed incomes or with property invested
at fixed money values, in government bonds for example, lost everything as did holders of savings bank deposits. This fairly large group
of normally conservative people equated their personal misfortune
with the Weimar system and were more than ever prepared to listen
to the representatives of the old order. But some other people were
doing well out of the collapse of the monetary system. Businessmen
flourished as their physical assets increased in value daily and even
hourly. On the other hand, their debts declined. Obviously, as new
loans were advanced those granting them tried to take account of

further depreciation of the currency when fixing the rate of interest, but they were never quite successful. The result was that there was a boom in investment activity as new plant and equipment were being acquired virtually without cost. Great fortunes were made. In this connection the name of Hugo Stinnes is well known. He inherited a coal-mining and shipping firm. After the war the inflation enabled him to expand and diversify his holdings until he became one of the most powerful men in Germany. He used his economic power to gain political influence which he exercised as one of the leaders of Gustav Stresemann's German People's Party, the party which was in government from May 1923 to May 1932, and through his ownership of the newspaper *Deutsche Allgemeine Zeitung*. Stinnes died in April 1924.

Apart from internal measures, such as a radical credit freeze imposed in April 1924, financial stabilisation was brought about by the Dawes Plan, drawn up on American initiative. Named after General Charles C. Dawes, the chairman of the committee which worked it out, the plan was recommended as offering a temporary solution to Germany's reparations difficulties. The Americans hoped, for their part, that the plan would help them to find some outlet for their own excessive gold reserves and markets for their industrial production. Under the plan the Germans were offered an immediate loan of 800 million gold marks, and, though the final reparations total remained unsettled, annual payments of reparations of a size within the Reich's capacity to pay were fixed. In return the Germans had to accept that their railways and the Reichsbank were removed from German control, and the Reparations Commission, under an American financier, Parker Gilbert, exercised a degree of supervision over the Republic's financial arrangements. The Plan, and certain political initiatives abroad by Stresemann, heralded a period of economic recovery and expansion rivalling any other in previous German history. Germany, which for a number of years had been both politically and economically a sleeping giant, now returned to the international scene. One index of this economic return was the expansion of exports. In 1929, despite the loss of Reich territory and of all her colonies, exports were up on the 1913 level by 34 per cent. Germany's share of world production rose from 8 per cent in 1923 to 12 per cent in 1928, and of world trade from 8.1 per cent in 1925 to 9.5 per cent in 1929. Between the years 1923 and 1928 total industrial production was doubled thus overtaking the highest pre-war level. The following figures of production help to illustrate that development:

| Year | hardcoal in mill. tons | brown coal in mill. tons | raw steel in mill. tons | electricity in mill. kWh. |
|---|---|---|---|---|
| 1913 | 190.1 | 87.2 | 20.8 | — |
| 1923 | 62.3 | 118.8 | 6.3 | — |
| 1926 | 145.3 | 139.2 | 12.3 | 21,218 |
| 1929 | 163.4 | 174.5 | 16.1 | 30,660 |

The development of German industry during this period was due to German willingness to learn from American experience of the rationalisation of industry, and to the inflow of foreign investments. Seventy per cent of the latter came from American banks. In 1925 I. G. Farben, the huge firm dominating the chemical and dyestuff industries, was set up. And in 1926 Albert Vögler formed the giant steel trust Vereinigte Stahlwerke A.G. In the electrical industry Siemens had a virtual monopoly.

Naturally, in these conditions of economic expansion the industrial workers were able to improve their position. But not as much as one might have expected. It was only in 1928 that real wages reached the prewar level. And there remained a pool of unemployed though nothing like what was to come.

### Unemployment in Germany, 1926-29   (in millions)

| Year | | number |
|---|---|---|
| 1926 | January | 2.2 |
| | July | 2.0 |
| 1927 | January | 2.2 |
| | July | 0.9 |
| 1928 | January | 1.7 |
| | July | 1.0 |
| 1929 | January | 2.8 |
| | July | 1.2 |

Many workers improved their housing conditions during these years. This was due to a considerable extent to their own efforts and those of their representatives in, above all, the Länder or regional governments. In the years 1920-30 the workers' building cooperatives alone built some 100,000 homes. Of greater importance was the Prussian housing law of 1918 which empowered local authorities to enact planning measures, provide open spaces, and erect small dwellings and buildings of public utility: it directed further that all districts with more than 10,000 inhabitants to issue police ordinances concerning housing hygiene. The larger towns were required to open offices for the allocation of dwellings and for the control of housing hygiene. The Act of 1918 had been passed because the introduction of universal suffrage had made Prussia a

Social Democratic stronghold. Similar measures were introduced in other areas subject to Social Democratic influence. The Reich, again under Social Democratic influence, subsidised house building and controlled rents.

### STRESEMANN'S FOREIGN POLICY

As mentioned above, Stresemann's foreign policy helped to produce the international confidence in Germany which produced the conditions for economy recovery. Like the nationalists he wanted to end the encirclement of Germany, German military weakness and foreign occupation. Unlike them he was prepared to seek the friendship of Britain and France to achieve this and prepared for a reasonable compromise settlement on reparations. When that had been brought about, and only then, could the problems of revision of the eastern frontier be approached with any likelihood of success. The Locarno Pacts of October 1925 by which Britain, France, Italy and Germany all guaranteed the Franco-German and Belgian-German frontiers were the first part of his aims and were followed, after some delay, by Germany's entry into the League of Nations with a permanent seat upon the Council. This was in September 1926. Another part of the Locarno agreement was the reduction in the number, and cost to the Germans, of the occupation forces in the Rhineland and the British withdrawal from Cologne on 30 January 1926. Finally, at the beginning of the following year the Inter-Allied Commission of control of German armaments was dissolved. Stresemann's policy of conciliation and gentle revision ran into temporary difficulties later in that year after Poincaré, who had been largely responsible for the Ruhr occupation, replaced the more ' dove '-like Herriot as French Prime Minister. By early 1928 Stresemann was complaining that the Allies were not granting further concessions of the kind his policy of fulfilment deserved. On 30 October he sent an urgent request for a new and final settlement of the reparations question. The Allies agreed and appointed an expert committee to investigate the issue. On 7 June 1929 it produced the Young Plan. Weeks later Stresemann accepted this and got the immediate evacuation of the Rhineland by the British and Belgians, and the promise of French evacuation by the end of June 1930 ' if physically possible '. He did not live to see this or the subsequent failure of his policy due to economic and political changes in Germany. Gustav Stresemann died on 2 October 1929.

### THE FAILURE OF DEMOCRACY IN EUROPE

The German education system with its emphasis on obedience and authority had long been the target of Social Democrat and liberal critics of the old order. Once that order collapsed they hoped to be able to do something to alter the education system as well. Apart from any general improvement in standards the reformers sought the breaking-down of the old religious barriers which kept Catholic children separated from Protestant children; the development of a democratic consciousness among teachers which would be passed on to their pupils and, thirdly, the ending of the virtual monopoly by the middle classes of secondary-grammar and higher education. Despite brave efforts the reformers failed to achieve these aims.

As far as standards were concerned, in these areas where the reformers were in charge—Prussia, Hamburg, Saxony, Thuringia—standards did rise. Even in these areas less progress was made in overcoming religious differences though some secular schools were set up in a few areas, notably Hamburg and Berlin. In south-western Germany interdenominational schools were established. The majority of schools though remained denominational, so-called *Bekenntnisschulen*. Disagreement over the maintenance of these denominational schools was one of the main differences between the Social Democrats and the Catholic Centre Party which not only prevented the formulation of national educational policy but interfered with their cooperation on other issues. Particularly among secondary-school teachers the old monarchical-conservative ideas persisted and they ignored appeals from above for the teaching of loyalty to the Republic's democratic ideals. History textbooks remained nationalist orientated. In the reform-controlled Länder some efforts were made to make secondary education available to children from working class, peasant or poorer homes. In 1925 the *Aufbauschulen* were set up in certain parts of Germany to provide an alternative secondary education for gifted pupils who had completed their elementary school courses, but had, for one reason or another, failed to obtain entrance to a secondary school. Nevertheless, the lack of an adequate scholarship system still prevented most gifted non-middle-class children from getting secondary education. In 1931, the working-class population made up over 50 per cent of the total population, but only about seven per cent of secondary-school pupils were from this social class.

In 1918 Germany was much better endowed than Britain with universities. Greater respect for learning was a possible reason for this. Continuing religious rivalries, the existence of so many independent states in nineteenth-century Germany, and the importance of a legal training in public administration and industry, a training only obtained at a university, were other decisive factors. A number of

c

technical universities were established in the latter part of the nineteenth century, to help Germany develop its technology. Unlike
Britain there was a tradition of dependence on the state and senior
members of the academic staff had the status of civil servants.
Professors were appointed by the state and apart from any attitude
of conformity this might have engendered, in Prussia at any rate,
Social Democrats were excluded from professorships under a law
of 1899. In the few years at their disposal the Weimar reformers
could do little to alter this situation. If the great majority of
professors were not members of the N S D A P before 1933 they were
nationalist inclined.

The situation among the students was not very much different.
Again, the great majority were not consciously Nazi-inclined, rather
vaguely nationalist though not very political. However, a considerable minority of them were members of the traditionalist fraternities.
Most of these had their origins in the struggle against the French,
Napoleonic invaders when they had liberal as well as nationalist
ideas. But gradually, later on in the nineteenth century, they became
reactionary. Membership came to be regarded as a passport to a
top job. Moreover membership did not lapse on graduation, former
students became much respected *Alte Herren* taking part in cere-
monies and get-togethers with each succeeding generation of students.
In this way each generation of student members was brought under
the influence of the survivors of past generations with all their ideas,
prejudices and opportunities for patronage.

Over the Weimar years there were a number of incidents at
German universities which seemed to be harbingers of what was to
come in 1933. There was the case of E. J. Gumbel, an ex-serviceman
turned pacifist who lectured on mathematical statistics at Heidelberg
University. He was hounded from 1923 onwards by Right-wing
students backed up by teachers. In 1930, by which time he was an
' extraordinary professor ', he had his ' licence to teach ' cancelled
by the Ministry of Education in Baden. This was after protests by
Right-wing students over remarks he made about the war while
addressing a meeting of socialist students. Prof. Theodor Lessing of
Hanover Technical University published an attack on Paul von
Hindenburg when the latter was running for President in 1925. He
was then hounded for the rest of the years of the Republic. At the
start of the campaign his lectures were broken into, mobs stood
outside the building and jeered at him, others surrounded him and
his family, jostled him and desisted only when he agreed to cease
lecturing for a term. In 1930 Günther Dehn was elected by the
theological faculty of Heidelberg to a full professorship. A violent

campaign was started by nationalist students accusing him of having called the soldiers of the World War 'murderers' and, although an enquiry by the Church authorities proved the falsity of the charge, the appointment was withdrawn under student pressure. There were many examples of Right-wing professors giving encouragement to their cause and denouncing the Republic in their lectures without suffering any inconvenience.

In a few years the two universities of Berlin, the universities of Heidelberg, Halle, Munich, Cologne, Marburg, Greifswald, Kiel, Königsberg, Hamburg, Hanover and Brunswick all suffered from political disturbances. Towards the end of the Republic the universities were radicalised in the way the German people as a whole were being radicalised. The result of the *Astawahlen*, the non-party organisation of the general student body at each university, available for 14 out of 33 universities, or university-level institutions, in 1933, indicated the Nazis commanding majorities in all 14.

## CULTURAL FERMENT AND POLITICAL COMMITMENT

The Weimar period stands out as an era of intellectual ferment, of rich diversity in motivation and idiom in the arts, of revolutionary content and experimentation in form. This ferment affected all branches of the arts. Here we can only mention some of the significant names, and erect a few sign-posts in literature, the cinema and architecture.

On the Left, the period opened with Heinrich Mann's lampoon of the Germany of the Kaisers, *Der Untertan*, which earned him the hatred of the traditionalists for the rest of his life. Erich Maria Remarque echoed and encouraged the pacifist wave sweeping Europe with *Im Westen Nichts Neues*, a book made famous by Hollywood as *All Quiet On The Western Front*. Arnold Zweig's *Sergeant Grischa* exposed the inhumanity of war on the Eastern Front. In their satirical magazine *Die Weltbühne*, Carl von Ossietzky and Kurt Tucholsky used their considerable talents against militarism, revanchism and authoritarianism. The one later died in a concentration camp, the other despaired and committed suicide in lonely exile. Thomas Mann renounced his earlier nationalism, and recognised the new enemy, laying bare the psychological character of Fascism in his allegorical tale of *Mario und der Zauberer*. In 1931, Erich Kästner, in *Fabian*, narrated the troubles, temptations, and final destruction, of the lower middle class young man in the Berlin of mass unemployment, political gangsterism and avant-garde sex. And Hans Fallada asked, as so many were asking, 'What Now Little Man?', in his novel of the same name. Bertolt Brecht

Ludwig Renn, Anna Seghers, Arnold Zweig, and some other writers, felt the answer was to be found in Communism.

On the right, the poet Stefan George, consciously non-political, published a collection of poems in 1921, entitled, *Das neue Reich.* In one of these poems he prophesied that out of the new youth would emerge the new leader. He would set up the new Reich. Deliberately political, Moeller van den Bruck, attacked Versailles, the November Revolution, Social Democracy, Liberalism, Democracy and Communism. His *Das Dritte Reich* was at least one of the most influential books of the period. Oswald Spengler fought the same foes, adding a new one, the coloured races. To prevent *The Decline of the West* a strong, new, military Reich was necessary. Spengler, together with Ernst Jünger and a host of now forgotten popular writers, stressed the heroics of war, and even went so far as to claim that it was natural, inevitable and invigorating. The book which later became the literary Bible of National Socialism, Hans Grimm's *Volk ohne Raum* (*A People Without Space*), whose proletarian hero comes to accept the nationalist credo after learning to hate the British in South Africa, was also written in this period.

Much of German film production between 1918 and 1933 was concerned, like much of production elsewhere, with escapist themes —comedies, adventures in far-off places, detective stories, fantasies and musicals. As the censorship had been abolished in 1918, both the educational and commercial sides of sex could be, and were, fully exploited. But more serious themes were dealt with too, and politics strayed into the cinema.

Serious film directors were preoccupied with the same problems as serious writers. Unlike the writers, they had the problem of financing their projects. The U F A organisation possessed a dominant position both in the production and distribution of films. From 1927 this company was in the hands of Alfred Hugenberg, a reactionary banker, nationalist and later ally of Hitler. Though he did not exploit his position to the full he had no enthusiasm for critical and controversial themes.

One of the directors who did manage to handle controversial themes was G. W. Pabst, an Austrian. His pacifist-inclined *Westfront 1918* gave the public a frank look at the horror of war. In his *Kameradschaft* (*Comradeship*), made in 1931, he preached international solidarity with a story about German miners going to the aid of French colleagues, trapped in a mine on the other side of the frontier. Another film made by Pabst in 1931 was his rendering of *Dreigroschenoper* by Bertolt Brecht. All three films still attract film enthusiasts. Two other critical films which have stood the test of time are Leontine Sagan's *Mädchen in Uniform*, exposing the effects of Prussianism in a girls' boarding school, and Richard Oswald's *Captain of Köpenick*, an amusing attack on militarism based on a true story.

The Blue Angel, the best-known film of the Weimar era was, unlike the five mentioned above, a U F A production. Directed by another Austrian, Joseph von Sternberg, it tells the story of the decline and fall of a secondary school professor through his infatuation with, and subsequent marriage to, a night-club singer. Emil Jannings, who became infamous for his parts in Nazi films, played the teacher, Marlene Dietrich, who emigrated to America, the singer. This cautionary tale of sex and sadism has been interpreted by students of the German film as symbolic of the destruction of the Weimar system.

More nationalist in tone were the historical and war films directed by Gustav Ucicky and Luis Trenker.

'A hotbed of cultural Bolshevism' was the description given by Hitler to the Weimar Republic's most famous experiment in architecture and design. Founded in 1919 by Walter Gropius, the Bauhaus was conceived as a school which would unite the arts, technology and industry to promote the quality of life. It united the architects Gropius, Ludwig Mies van der Rohe and Marcel Breuer, with painters such as Paul Klee, Wassily Kandinsky and Lyonel Feininger, and others besides. The school greatly influenced the design of furniture, pottery and posters, as well as painting and architecture. Its basic idea was to discard conventional ornamental styles for functional ones of steel, glass and concrete. The new designs were meant to give people a greater insight into reality, and make life easier—especially for women. In Germany their architectural ideas were realised in the complex of Bauhaus buildings at Dessau, the communal theatre at Jena, and the trade union school at Bernau near Berlin.

Politically on the Left, the Bauhaus school had its ideas rejected just as much by Stalin as by Hitler, and by many with money to build in Britain and America. In the postwar era, however, Bauhaus-influenced styles gradually became the accepted convention in the West and, after the death of Stalin, in the East too.

### HITLER IN THE WILDERNESS

On 1 April 1924 Adolf Hitler faced the judges in a Munich court to hear them pronounce sentence on him for attempting to alter the German constitution by force—the result of his revolutionary escapade of the previous November. He could have got life imprisonment; in fact he was sentenced to five years. Less than nine months later on 20 December he was released from Landsberg fortress. His light sentence was no doubt partly due to the presence of General Erich Ludendorff with him in the dock—the general was acquitted—and to the nationalist sympathies of the judges. Ludendorff, as one of Germany's most famous military men, ensured the presence of journalists from all over Germany and Europe. Hitler used the opportunity presented to get some free publicity. In so many words he told the old ruling classes. ' I want to march with you, not against you '. He actually said : ' I believe that the hour will come when the masses, who today stand in the street with our swastika banner, will unite with those who fired on them '. He was a revolutionary against the revolution (of 1918), a destroyer of Marxism and a friend of the Reichswehr for ' the hour will come when the Reichswehr will stand at our side, officers and men '. Considering he was only a half-educated former corporal, many representatives of the old order must have thought him an arrogant upstart, even a bit mad. But they had to admit he was a courageous fellow, willing to ' have a go ' for the old cause, and that his heart was in the right place. And, after all, good old Ludendorff thought him worthy of support. This view of the likely effect of his trial is shown to be plausible when we learn that during his period of internment he received a good many well-to-do visitors at Landsberg. They saw to it that his detention was not uncomfortable.

Hitler did not merely spend his time in Landsberg fortress entertaining wellwishers from high society. He turned his attention to literary activities. He wrote what was to be his autobiography and political testament rolled into one, *Mein Kampf* or *My Struggle*. In its preface he wrote that he realised that men ' are won over less by the written than by the spoken word ' but ' Nevertheless, for a doctrine to be disseminated uniformly and coherently, its basic elements must be set down for all time '. We need not say too much about this rambling, two-part, volume written in a style which is a mixture of contemporary popular journalism and south German dialect. The central point of the book is the struggle against the Jews who are at the back of every difficulty Germany had recently experienced. The Jew is ' a parasite on other peoples ' who has to lie to convince other people that ' he is not a people but a " religious community ", though of a special sort '. In order to infiltrate into a society, he uses a thousand different guises and methods, from debased culture and weakening a nation through intermarriage, to posing as an intellectual benefactor of mankind or a popular political leader. Doctrines such as equality and democracy help the Jew by allowing full freedom to exploit the gullibility of his fellows. Most of all he controls the nation's life through his control of economic affairs especially through the stock exchange. The labour movement becomes ' a pure movement entirely of manual workers under Jewish leadership, apparently aiming to improve the situation of the worker, but in truth planning the enslavement and with it the destruction of all non-Jewish peoples '. Marxism is the doctrine of that movement. Also, ' the Jew by means of the trade union, which could be a blessing for the nation, shatters the foundations of the national economy '.

This then was how the Jews were operating against Germany's interests within the country itself. What about in the international arena? There Germany faced ' chauvinistic France ' struggling to turn Germany into ' a hotch-potch of little states '. This is what France fought for in 1914, ' though at the same time in reality it sold its people as mercenaries to the international world Jew '. Britain had fought to annihilate Germany as a colonial and commercial rival but Britain needed Germany as a check to the power of France. As for Russia, it was ruled by ' the scum of humanity ' and ' in Russian Bolshevism we must see the attempt undertaken by the Jews in the twentieth century to achieve world domination '. What Germany needed was an alliance with Britain and Italy. With such an alliance Germany could ' break off the soil ' the colonial and commercial policy of the prewar period and shift to the soil policy of the future. If we speak of soil in Europe today, we can primarily have in mind only Russia and her vassal border states '. In order to justify his aggressive foreign policy Hitler evoked ' Fate ' and the ' Court of History '. He was applying the theory of the survival of the fittest to international affairs.

In order for Germany to realise its foreign policy aims it needed a strong internal order, a centralised state, freed from Jews and Marxists and their ideas, practising ' racial hygiene ' based on a people trained in will-power and determination.

Hitler was not expecting to win converts with *Mein Kampf* and said this frankly in his preface. This was just as well, for in the years immediately after it was written the Nazi movement did not appear to be getting very far. Membership was rising, but only slowly: 27,000 in 1925; 49,000 in 1926; 72,000 in 1927 and 108,000 in 1928. In these years the Nazi leader had to be largely content with slowly building up his organisation and strengthening his own position within that organisation. He established himself as sole leader to whose decisions all members of the movement were subordinate. He created the s s (*Schutzstaffel* or protective squad) as a special bodyguard bound by an oath of loyalty to his person. That was in April 1925. In 1926 he obtained the support of the crippled, yet intellectually very able, Dr Paul Joseph Goebbels, who had first been attracted to National Socialism by Gregor Strasser's 'Left-wing' version of the Nazi gospel. In that year he deserted the North German Nazi leader Strasser for Hitler who was none too pleased with Strasser's 'socialism'. Despite these successes within the movement Adolf Hitler was not making much impact on the masses outside it.

The elections of 20 May 1928 seemed to augur well for German democracy. Those stalwart supporters of Weimar the Social Democrats increased their vote significantly and their parliamentary strength went up accordingly from 131 to 153. On their left the Communists increased their representation from 45 to 54. The Centre more or less held its position but lost eight seats, being reduced to 61. Stresemann's moderate nationalist German People's Party also lost slightly dropping from 51 to 45 seats. The Bavarian People's Party lost two seats returning 17 members to the Reichstag. The Nationalists, later to be Hitler's allies, faced a slump of support and fell in seats from 111 to 78. As for the Nazis, their strength was reduced from 14 to 12. In May 1924 they had won 32 seats. Their prospects looked bleak yet within two years they were to change dramatically.

# 3    Weimar Crisis and Collapse

After the elections of May 1928 President Hindenburg called upon Social Democrat Hermann Müller to form a government. This he only managed to do with great difficulties about a month later. Müller's coalition partners were the Centre Party, the (Conservative Catholic) Bavarian People's Party, the Democratic Party and the German People's Party.

Müller's 'Grand Coalition' was soon faced with a crisis which gave the enemies of democracy in Germany useful ammunition. The outgoing Government and the Reichstag had approved in principle the building of a naval cruiser. This decision had been fought by the parties of the Left at the elections. What now? The Müller cabinet reaffirmed the earlier decision to build the ship. The Social Democratic parliamentary group criticised their ministers for not openly attacking the plan but agreed to continued Social Democratic participation in the government. Agitation, mainly from the Communists, continued over the issue and on 17 November a remarkable scene took place in the Reichstag. The Social Democrats, including the ministers who had agreed it in the Cabinet voted against the decision to construct the ship. As it turned out, the Social Democrats and the Communists were outvoted on the issue by 202 to 257 in favour. To many in Germany the incident seemed to prove the futility of the parliamentary system. Apart from this it probably led to the weakening of the Social Democratic Party due to internal dissension and loss of grass roots support.

Changes were also taking place in other parties which facilitated the Nazi seizure of power in 1933. After their electoral set-back the Nationalists engaged in post-mortem feuding. The result was that their chairman resigned and was replaced by Alfred Hugenberg on 20 October. As we shall see, this was to be of decisive importance in 1933. The Centre Party changed its leadership about the same time. A party congress elected Professor Monsignor Ludwig Kaas as successor to Wilhelm Marx who had resigned. This represented a shift to the right at a time when Centre-Social Democratic cooperation was of the greatest importance for the maintenance of the Republic.

During the summer of 1928 the sixth congress of the Communist International, Comintern, met in Moscow and announced a new line which was of the greatest importance for Germany. It forbade member parties from engaging in collaboration with parties belonging to the Second (Social Democratic and Labour) International. The German Communists from then on treated the Social Democrats as their main enemies, dubbing them ' Social Fascists '. At the 12th party congress of the K P D in June 1929 the Communist leader Ernst Thälmann accused the Social Democrats of trying to establish a fascist dictatorship. The Communists started using up their energies fighting the Social Democrats and in futile attempts to set up their own trade union organisation to rival that under Social Democratic .influence. They later recognised, when it was too late, the falseness of these efforts.

The Communists' thesis was wrong and had been thought up in Moscow. It was not the product of a German critique of the Weimar Republic, yet the Social Democrats had a case to answer. They were demanding loyalty to a state which was headed by a militarist Hindenburg. They were in coalition with some profoundly clerical and reactionary politicians in the Bavarian People's Party and the Right of the Centre Party. The state machine was manned by monarchist bureaucrats and ' defended ' by monarchist officers who were plotting to destroy its democratic provisions. Further, in the Weimar Republic the industrialists, as in the case of the Rhenish-Westphalian iron industry lock-out of November 1928, could openly defy government decisions on labour disputes. And did not governments in which Social Democrats participate exercise financial stringency when dealing with the unemployed but not when handing out millions upon millions of marks to the enemies of Weimar, the Junkers, to maintain their tottering estates? Finally, the forces of ' law and order ', including those controlled by Social Democrats. seemed, in nine cases out of ten, to hit out harder when dealing with Left-wing radicals than when dealing with those on the right. Only a matter of weeks before the 12th Communist congress 31 people had been killed and hundreds more wounded when police, under Berlin's Social Democratic police chief, Karl Zörgiebel, opened fire on a banned Communist May Day demonstration. The Communists had attempted to resist the police and used firearms.

OPPOSITION TO THE YOUNG PLAN

The 12th Communist Party congress attacked the Young Plan and declared the intention of the party to fight it. More important than

Communist opposition to the Plan was that of the Nazis and Nationalists.

As we have seen, the acceptance of the Plan by Germany in 1929 resulted in the withdrawal of Allied occupation forces, and re-established Germany's exclusive responsibility for its own finances and economy. However, it foresaw Germany continuing to make payments to the Allies until 1982! It is only to be expected that very many Germans resented this as, apart from the additional financial burdens it laid upon their shoulders, it was based on the assumption that it was the Germans who were mainly responsible for the horrors of the 1914-18 war. Most ordinary Germans were inclined to think that it was the ' upper ten thousand ' in Germany and in the Allied countries who between them shared responsibility for the outbreak of hostilities and that crimes were then committed on both sides. Hugenberg hoped to cash in on the resentment of reparations and of the branding of the Germans as criminals. He launched a referendum campaign demanding that the German people be given the opportunity to vote on the issues related to the Versailles agreement and subsequent agreements which followed from it, including the issue of further reparations. His allies in the campaign were Franz Seldte, leader of the paramilitary nationalist Stahlhelm organisation, of which Hindenburg was the most prominent honorary member, and Nazi leader Hitler. In order for a referendum to be held under the Constitution the organisers had to collect the signatures of 10 per cent of the electorate. This they managed to do, most of the signatories residing East of the Elbe. The next step was for the demands of Hugenberg-Hitler to be presented to the Reichstag in the form of a so-called ' freedom law '. This was defeated causing a split in the Nationalist Party. The actual referendum then followed and was heavily defeated only 5.8 million Germans voting in favour as against the 21 million necessary for it to have become law.

Though the referendum vote represented a decisive defeat for the Rightist alliance the campaign leading up to it represented an important step forward for the Nazi movement. Firstly, it helped to establish the Nazis' respectability by associating them in the middle-class mind with respectable Conservative politicians. The alliance with Hugenberg brought Hitler into closer contact with wealthy industrialists. Already since 1923, according to his own testimony, Fritz Thyssen, head of the steel trust, *Vereinigte Stahlwerke,* had been supporting the Nazis. In 1929 Emil Kirdorf, a top man in the Ruhr coal industry, gave assistance to the Nazis. Hitler's destruction of Strasser's Left-wing Nazi organisation about this time and new association with Hugenberg paved the way for others to do the same. The Hugenberg contact further meant that the Nazis had greatly benefited from the Nationalist leader's publicity empire. He owned newspapers, an agency, cinemas and Germany's most important film company, U F A, which produced a weekly newsreel.

When the world economic crisis broke out after the Wall Street crash in autumn 1929 the Nazis were therefore in a position to exploit it. The crisis had severe repercussions in Germany because of the nature of German industry and credit. Roughly one-third of German production was exported by the late twenties. Which meant that when other nations started to cut their imports from Germany, German workers lost their jobs. From 1929 to 1933 German exports fell by almost two-thirds. During the years of boom and prosperity German industrial expansion had been financed to a considerable degree by foreign, very often American, loans. About one half of the credits were short term. Obviously, at the first sign of trouble the foreign investors pulled out their funds. These troubles were in the first place economic ones connected with the world economic situation. By September 1930 there were fears about Germany's political future which caused a massive repatriation of short-term credits. This helps to explain why Germany suffered more from the crisis than other highly industrialised nations, except the United States.

International Industrial Production 1928-31
*1929 output equals 100*

| Year (monthly average) | Germany | USA | UK | France | Sweden |
|---|---|---|---|---|---|
| 1928 | 98.6 | 94.1 | 94.3 | 91.4 | 81.5 |
| 1929 | 100.0 | 100.0 | 100.0 | 100.0 | 100.0 |
| 1930 | 82.4 | 80.7 | 100.7 | 100.7 | 97.1 |
| 1931 | 69.1 | 68.6 | 83.5 | 89.3 | 85.3 |

NAZISM: A MASS MOVEMENT

In March 1930 the Grand Coalition fell apart. Disagreement broke out over the financing of unemployment relief. In December 1929 there were 1.5 million workers on relief and during the next month unemployment grew by nearly another million. The unemployment insurance fund was in deficit and it was considered necessary either to cut down relief payments or increase contributions. The Social Democrats were against the former and the German People's Party, which was closely connected to industry, opposed the latter course. As no compromise was found, Hermann Müller resigned. He died the following year.

Heinrich Brüning of the Centre Party took over from Müller forming a right-of-centre government including many of the old faces from the bourgeois parties of the Grand Coalition. Elections followed in September at which there was what amounted to a landslide to the National Socialists. In 1928 they had only won 810,000 votes and 12 seats. They now received 6.4 million votes and 107 seats becoming second only to the Social Democrats in the Reichstag. The latter won 8.6 million votes and 143 seats, a loss of half a million votes and ten seats. The Communists picked up 4.6 million votes or 1.3 million more than last time. Their strongholds being East Berlin, East Düsseldorf and Merseburg where they emerged as the strongest party. They also did well in Potsdam, Chemnitz, Hamburg, West Düsseldorf and Leipzig. With 77 seats, as against 54 in the outgoing Reichstag, they overtook the Centre Party as third largest parliamentary group. The Centre though increased its representation from 61 to 68 seats, based on an increased vote, together with the other Catholic party the Bavarian People's Party, of half a million giving them nearly 5.2 million votes. The Bavarian People's Party got 19 seats, two more than in 1928. The really big losers of the election were the Nationalists and the German People's Party. The former lost two million votes, leaving them just under 2.5 million, the latter one million, retaining 1.6 million. They were awarded 44 seats (78 in 1928) and 30 seats (45 in 1928) respectively. The small parties attracted over six million votes, some winning, some losing votes. They gained 89 seats.

As the gain in the Communist votes and the loss of votes by the Nationalists and the People's Party indicate, the Nazis did not cash in on the disatisfaction of the unemployed proletarians. Rather they were able to attract the temporary loyalty of disappointed Right-wing voters. They got their biggest increase in Schleswig-Holstein, East Prussia and Pommerania, in Breslau and Hanover South. In other words, they did well in agricultural districts, especially Protestant ones, rather than industrial areas. They further won over the non-political elements, for another characteristic of this election was the increase in turn out. In 1928 75.6 per cent had voted, in 1930 82 per cent did so. Finally, the Nazis, like the Communists, were attractive to the young, the new voters.

Brüning continued as Chancellor but without a majority in the Reichstag. He was able to do so only because he was backed by Hindenburg and was able to use emergency decrees under Article 48 of the Constitution, and then inducing enough groups in the Reichstag to vote against their repeal. His answer to the crisis was basically one of deflation. He cut down wages, salaries and prices in an effort to restore confidence in the German financial and industrial system. His efforts met with no significant, immediate success. By the end of 1931 there were some 4.5 million out of work and many others on short-time working.

The Nazis continued their rapid advance. This was made possible by the continuing crisis and by their ever closer ties with the monied circles of the old 'National Camp'. On the 11 and 12 October 1931 they took part in a rally of the Right at Bad Harzburg in Braunschweig. Called on the initiative of Hugenberg, it became known as the Harzburg Front. It consisted of the Nazis, the Nationalists of Hugenberg, the Stahlhelm and other militarist organisations, even the small Economic Party and the German People's Party were represented. Former admirals and generals abounded as did representatives of the old aristocratic families. Of even greater significance, industry was well represented. The gathering called for the resignation of Chancellor Brüning. Hitler further consolidated his links with industry at meetings he had on 9 December in Berlin with Fritz Thyssen and Albert Vögler, another leading industrialist, and on 27 January 1932 at a meeting of the Düsseldorf Industrial Club. In his Düsseldorf address he won the applause of the businessmen for his denunciation of Democracy and Communism and his praise for authoritarianism, the 'white race' and economic imperialism. With such speeches he could be sure of increasing funds from the industrialists. Already in 1931 Kirdorf had secured for the Nazis a levy of 50 pfennig on every ton of coal sold by the German Coal Trust.

It is remarkable that Hitler's nationalist and business friends did not see through him about this time, did not realise that although they thought they were using him and could tame him, he was determined to use them. They had enough evidence of his arrogant and dangerous ambitions in what he said. They also found him a tough customer in any negotiations for joint action. Once again he exposed himself early in 1932 when he decided to stand against Hindenburg for the Presidency. This was surely a very undiplomatic move? Like the Munich putsch of 1923 it was a move which could have cost Hitler his career. Perhaps more surprisingly, in view of the fact Hindenburg was in the race, Hugenberg's Nationalists also presented a candidate. Theodor Duesterberg, the deputy head of the Stahlhelm. Thälmann, the Communist, was the only other candidate. Hindenburg accepted the nomination of a nonparty committee mainly composed of members of the parties he despised, the Social Democrats and the Centre Party and the other moderate groups. Some nationalist groups also supported him. The

84-year-old field marshal needed two attempts to pull off his
re-election. On 13 March he won 18.65 million votes to Hitler's
11.4 million. Thälmann attracted 5 million and Duesterberg about
half that number. The old man was just 0.4 per cent short of a
majority and therefore a second ballot was necessary. Duesterberg
decided not to try again and asked his supporters to vote for the
field marshal while Hugenberg opted for neutrality between the
remaining Right-wing candidates. Hitler found a useful ally in
Frederick William, the former Crown Prince. Once again however
he lost to Hindenburg by 13.4 million to the field marshal's
19.4 million. Thälmann got just under 4 million. As Goebbels' diary
shows, the Nazis were very disappointed with the result even
though these two ballots marked a considerable rise in their vote
over 1930. One aspect of the ballots worth mentioning is that
women, who predominated, voted more heavily for Hindenburg
than for any other candidate.

THE BARON'S GOVERNMENT

Having elected him, the moderates hoped Hindenburg would help
them strengthen the Republic. For a brief moment it looked as
though their hope would become reality. Just before the regional
elections in Prussia, the President issued a decree dissolving the S A
and S S. But two days later he was calling for action against Left-
wing paramilitary bodies. The President could not get the agreement of the government to ban non-Nazi paramilitary organisations
and consequently only the S A and the S S were dissolved. This
angered the army leaders who saw the S A as a useful addition to
Germany's small Reichswehr. Through General Kurt von Schleicher
and the President's son, Oskar, they turned Hindenburg against
Brüning. Relations between the two were in any case not good.
Brüning had not complied with the President's demand for a cabinet
reshuffle to the Right. The breaking point between Chancellor and
President came over the government's proposals to cut subsidies to
the Junkers' estates and buy up bankrupt ones for smallholders.
Hindenburg regarded this as ' agrarian Bolshevism '. Under pressure
from President and Reichswehr Brüning resigned.

The appointment of Franz von Papen as Chancellor in May 1932
represented another nail in the coffin of the Weimar Republic.
Papen, a wartime cavalry major and a Catholic noble allied to
industry by marriage, owed his opportunity largely to Schleicher's
influence with the President. Schleicher took over the Defence
Ministry in this ' Barons' Cabinet ' as it became known, or ' gentle-
men's Government ' as Papen called it. It would have done justice to

the Kaiser for it was made up of aristocratic officers of the reserve with one exception, the exception being the Minister of Economics who was in reality the representative of heavy industry. Most of the ministers had Nationalist connections though formally they were non-party. Papen himself had been nominally a member of the Centre Party but resigned from that party when it criticised his decision to form such a government. Another important fact to note about this government is that five of its eight members went on to serve in Hitler's government of 1933, one remaining a minister until 1945 and some of the others retaining posts in Hitler's Germany.

The government of Franz von Papen was in an even more hopeless position in the Reichstag than that of Brüning had been. Even had they had a firm alliance of Nazis, Nationalists, German People's Party and Economic Party, which they did not, they would not have had a majority. The alternatives were a change of government or fresh elections, the government and the Nazis wanted elections. In order to improve relations with the Nazis further, Papen decided to lift the ban on the S A and S S, an action which could only lead to a new outbreak of disorders throughout the Reich.* Another move which made Papen very popular on the Right was the ejection of the Social Democratic-Centre coalition government in Prussia where he made himself Reich Commissar by presidential decree. By this action, he gained control of three-fifths of Germany. Recent elections in Prussia had led to large Social Democratic losses and the coalition was carrying on as a caretaker regime. This furnished Papen and Hindenburg with their excuse.

Three weeks before the election the Papen regime got a boost from the decisions of the Lausanne Conference on reparations. The Young Plan was replaced by a new agreement which scaled down reparations once again and only obliged the Germans to pay when their economic position enabled them to do so. In fact they made no further payments. By 1933 Hitler came to power and he unilaterally abrogated earlier agreements.

As expected, the elections of July 1932 resulted in a great victory for the Nazis. They more than doubled their parliamentary strength returning 230 Reichstag members. This was a greater number of seats than any other party had ever succeeded in winning in the Weimar Republic, or, for that matter, in the Reichstag of the Kaisers. However, as a percentage of the votes the Nazi victory was still behind that of the Social Democrats in 1919 (excluding the Left Socialists) and in actual votes it was behind the number cast for

---

* Within one month 99 people died and 1125 were wounded in street skirmishes.

both Social Democratic groups in that year. Moreover the result indicated other, more important, weaknesses of the National Socialists. Compared with the presidential election their advance seemed to be slowing down. And it was being gained very largely, as in 1930, by winning over voters from other Right-wing parties and new voters or those who normally did not bother. Despite their good result the Nazis, even with the other Right-wing groups, were without a majority. Finally, in view of what was to happen later, it should be mentioned that only 37.2 per cent of the votes went to the Nazis, though, admittedly, some of their worst ideas were held by many on the Right.

Of the other big groups in German politics the Social Democrats lost another ten seats, winning 133 seats and 7.9 million votes (against 13.7 million for the Nazis); the two Catholic parties increased their seats to 97, attracting 5.7 million; the Communists also got more seats and votes—89 and 5.2 million; the Nationalists and the German People's Party lost heavily—the former returned 39 members, a loss of 5, the latter only 7, a loss of 23. These parties received roughly 5 million votes.

From the point of view of parliamentary government the elections had made the situation worse than ever. Negotiations followed between Papen, Hitler and Hindenburg. The Centre Party politicians were included as well. These negotiations came to nothing because Hitler was not prepared to be number two to von Papen—who could blame him? What the Reichstag thought of von Papen was shown in September when a Communist censure motion was passed with all groups except the Nationalists voting for it. Seldom had the Reichstag been so unanimous. Papen had attempted to prevent the Reichstag from voting on this and another motion repealing his emergency decree. But Hermann Göring, newly elected as its president, refused to accept Papen's decree, signed by Hindenburg, dissolving the so recently elected parliament. By dissolving the Reichstag again von Papen was gaining months during which he could carry on as Chancellor ruling by emergency decrees signed by the ailing President.

The most important aspect of the elections of 6 November was the loss by the Nazis of over two million votes and 34 seats. The Nationalists improved their position by 15 seats giving them 54. The German People's Party improved its representation too from 7 to 11. These results give us the clue to what had happened: the old Right-wing parties were winning back their middle-class followers. These waverers had been put off the Nazis by Hitler's sectarian ambitions. Göring's treatment of Papen no doubt contributed to this

D

result. Another factor was the sudden lurch to the Left by the Nazis just before the elections. They had supported a Communist-led strike of Berlin transport workers, an unofficial strike at that. The strike continued until after the elections. The anti-working-class, bourgeois, supporters of stability and ' law and order ' were dismayed at the sight of Reds and Brownshirts picketing together. Nazi losses were also attributable to a decline in turnout from 84 per cent to 80.6 per cent. Further evidence that the high watermark of the Nazi tide had passed was provided in local elections a few days later and even in student union elections. Perhaps this lulled the non-Nazis into complacency.

On the Left the election results seemed to prove that militancy paid off. The Communists again improved their position gaining just under 6 million votes and 100 seats. The Catholics suffered slight losses probably due to the decline in turnout. Social Democratic representation was reduced to 121 for 7.3 million votes. The Communists were no doubt the beneficiaries here.

Once again the elections solved nothing. Once again there was no workable coalition in sight. Hindenburg interviewed the leaders of the Centre and Right-wing groups. Kaas for the Centre Party declared his readiness to take part in a government which included the Nazis. Hitler once again refused to participate in a government which he did not lead. General Kurt von Schleicher, still officially Defence Minister, now attempted to bring together the Left-wing of the Nazi party, the Centre, the trade unions, but not the Social Democratic Party, and the armed forces in a ' strong ' government which would introduce a more authoritarian system of government. Schleicher was not very successful in his endeavours, but he persuaded the President to let von Papen go and appoint himself as Chancellor. At the beginning of December the General took over announcing a Cabinet which looked very much like the old one. Military dictatorship appeared imminent. Unlike Papen, however, General Schleicher was realist enough to comprehend that a few officers and aristocrats could not rule a great industrial nation for very long. So he continued in his efforts to win trade-union support as well as attempting to detach the Left of the Nazi party from Hitler. He even tried to bring in the Social Democratic Party. But Otto Wels, who had taken over the leadership after the death of Hermann Müller, was not prepared to form an alliance with Schleicher even when the General offered to ban the Nazi movement. Considering Germany's experience with military men both before and after 1918 this was understandable; knowing what we now know, we can regret it.

Franz von Papen, angry at the way he had been replaced by General von Schleicher, and with plenty of time on his hands, started to intrigue against his erstwhile friend and minister. Although Papen no longer held any official position he still had his powerful friends including the President. The powerful men of industry also wanted a solution and preferably one without the trade unions and the Social Democratic Party. Schleicher's failure to produce a government with any likelihood of success played into Papen's hands. Another factor which helped to break Schleicher was the outcome of the regional election in Lippe, an area with a population of only about 100,000. This was a *Land* in which the socio-economic structure was favourable to the Nazis. They increased their score at the expense of the Nationalists. This helped to convince many influential figures that the Nazis were a necessary part of any government (even though the Social Democrats and the other moderate parties improved their positions in the Lippe election). Papen and Hugenberg reactivated the Harzburg Front. The Cologne banker Kurt von Schröder acted as marriage broker for this alliance. Schleicher also had other enemies in the shape of the East Prussian estate owners who feared his plans for redistributing land to small-holders. They helped to turn the President against him. In the end, however, it seems it was Franz von Papen who persuaded Hindenburg that Hitler was more modest than he seemed and that he and Papen should be given the chance to form a government of ' National Concentration '.

# 4　Hitler's *Gleichschaltung* and Gambles

It is impossible to pinpoint the moment when Hitler's dictatorship was firmly and irrevocably established. When one considers his position on being appointed Chancellor on 30 January 1933 one can forgive observers at that time for thinking his regime was not likely to last. First of all, his party, the N S D A P, even with its Nationalist allies did not command a majority in the Reichstag. In the Cabinet there were only three Nazis as against nine other members with the apparently key post of Minister of Defence and Vice-Chancellor in non-Nazi hands. The latter post was held by Franz von Papen. Moreover, though Hitler was Chancellor, he was overshadowed in respect and influence by President Hindenburg and Hindenburg was in a position to dismiss him. And the armed forces, which stood on the Right politically, were loyal to Hindenburg rather than to Hitler. The police forces too were generally not, as they were to shortly become, totally subservient to Nazi wishes. The German press was very largely regional rather than national in circulation and in any case the Nazis ran only 2.5 per cent of all German newspapers. The parties which opposed Nazism also appeared to be in a strong position at the beginning of 1933. They were well organised and, especially the Social Democrats, possessed a large number of loyal, indoctrinated members. The Social Democrats dominated the powerful, though formally independent, trade unions, unions which had been largely responsible for bringing down one would-be dictator, Kapp, in 1919. Finally, there was the Catholic Church, that authoritarian body which controlled the hearts and minds of about one-third of the population, which was wealthy and had world-wide connections and which had, like the Social Democrats, successfully resisted the attacks of the Kaiser's state in the nineteenth century.

Apart from these factors outside the Nazi party setting limits to its power there were three limiting factors within the movement. The leaders were men with no experience of government and little experience of anything else. The majority of the members were fairly new to the movement which already appeared to be past its zenith. Nor were the Nazis completely united over their goals. Some stressed their social revolutionary mission while others, including Hitler, proclaimed their nationalist and anti-semitic aims.

Hitler clearly recognised this situation and set about to change it dramatically, both by exploiting available opportunities and by creating opportunities. It is impossible to say whether the Reichstag fire falls into the category of an opportunity exploited or one created. On the night of 27 February 1933 the Debating Chamber of the Reichstag was set on fire with explosive consequences for Germany. Up till 1962 the great majority of historians had assumed that this was the work of the Nazis who wanted a pretext to eliminate their Left-wing opponents and who needed a crisis to panic the electorate into voting for them. Hitler claimed the fire had been started by Communists to signal the outbreak of a Left-wing rising throughout Germany. For months the Nazis tried to pin the crime on a group of Communists including Ernst Torgler, chairman of the Communist parliamentary group, and Georgi Dimitroff, a Bulgarian and Communist International official. Also in the dock was Marinus van der Lubbe, a young Dutchman who had been a member of the Dutch Communist Party but was associated in 1933 with a Dutch Left-wing splinter group. Van der Lubbe admitted the crime from the start, steadfastly maintaining that he was the sole culprit. He claimed he had started the fire as a political protest against the Nazis and the capitalist system. The others, despite the torture of five months in chains, denied any responsibility and were eventually acquitted after a well organised international protest action against their trial. Van der Lubbe was convicted and subsequently beheaded on very doubtful legal grounds.

A re-examination of the evidence by Fritz Tobias led him to the conclusion that although the Communists were undoubtedly not involved in the crime neither were the Nazis. The fire was the work of Marinus van der Lubbe alone. However, neither Herr Tobias nor Mr A. J. P. Taylor, who supported this view, were adequately able to explain away some prominent Nazi witnesses, such as Hermann Rauschning and General Halder, who later testified that Hermann Göring, at the time of the fire President of the Reichstag and Prussian Minister of Interior, had boasted he was responsible for the fire.

Whatever the origins of the Reichstag fire it was exploited by Hitler with diabolical brilliance. As the Nazis and their allies did not have a majority in the Reichstag, elections had been set for 5 March. With Göring as head of the Prussian police the Nazi S A could increasingly control the streets in large areas of the country and harass their opponents. On 22 February Göring enrolled large numbers of S A, S S and Stahlhelm members as auxiliary police. The next day the police raided Karl Liebknecht House, headquarters of the Communist Party. Officially they were seeking evidence of a plot. They found no evidence though no doubt the raid yielded material which later helped them to suppress the K P D. As the Reichstag burned four days later Hitler got Hindenburg to issue an emergency decree which he could do under Article 48 of the Constitution. This decreed 'for the Protection of People and State' set aside normal civil liberties:

> Restrictions on personal liberty, on the right of free expression of opinion, including freedom of the press; on the rights of assembly and association; and violations of the privacy of postal, telegraphic and telephonic communications; and warrants for house searchers, orders for confiscations as well as restrictions on property, are also permissible beyond the legal limits otherwise prescribed.

The same decree gave the central authorities the right to exercise the powers of the organs of regional and local government and introduced the death penalty for a wide range of offences. With one stroke the Weimar Constitution was virtually destroyed. Immediately the arrest was ordered of all Communist members of the Reichstag together with other leading Communists and certain other anti-Nazis. During the night of 28 February over 10,000 arrests were made in various parts of Germany. Communist leader Ernst Thälmann was hunted down and taken on 3 March. He later met his death in a concentration camp.

### THE ENABLING ACT AND GLEICHSCHALTUNG

The results of the elections held on 5 March were not as decisive as Hitler had wished. The Nazis got 44 per cent of the seats, their allies 7 per cent. The Social Democratic vote held firm while the Communists did not do at all badly in the situation. The Centre Party actually made slight gains. The main effect of the Nazi propaganda campaign which played on fear of civil war and Red revolution was to drive Conservatives, Nationalists and traditionalists into the Nazi Camp.

When the new Reichstag assembled in the Kroll Opera House on 24 March it was confronted with an Enabling bill giving the government unlimited power for four years. A two-thirds majority was required before this bill could become law. The Social Democrats led by Otto Wels refused to have anything to do with it. Of the 94 Social Democrats who voted against the measure 24 were later murdered. Twenty-six Social Democrats had been prevented from attending as had the 81 Communists who had been elected. They were either under arrest or in hiding. The major responsibility for the passage of the bill with the necessary majority must be held to fall upon the Centre and the Bavarian People's parties, whose combined votes of 92, if cast against the measure, instead of for it as they were, would have increased the minority to 186, or 11 more than was required to prevent a constitutional amendment from becoming law. The Catholic deputies had allowed themselves to be persuaded by Hitler's promises of freedom for the churches. They were influenced too by the pleas of their former party colleague Franz von Papen who was a member of the government asking for supreme power. Finally, apart from Nazi threats, they were influenced by the fact that Hindenburg was still President. They believed he could restrain the government. It is interesting to speculate what might have happened had the Catholic parties not surrendered. Many influential people on the Right, including the President, some in the civil service, some industrialists and officers might have thought again about supporting Hitler. On the Left the Social Democrats and the trade unions, who both later tried to pursue a conciliatory policy towards the Nazis, might have showed more fight.

Having armed themselves with dictatorial powers the Nazis issued further decrees to consolidate their position. On 2 May the trade unions were dissolved; on 18 May the cooperative societies were taken over; on 27 June, the Nationalist leader Hugenberg was removed from his place in the Cabinet; on 7 July, the Social Democrats were deprived of their seats in the Reichstag; and on 14 July, all political parties except the Nazis were outlawed. The democratic institutions of Weimar went the same way as its parties and popular bodies. The Reich Governor Law of 31 March established Reich supervision over the States or Länder. On 30 January 1934 State law was replaced by delegated Reich law. The parliaments of the Länder were dissolved without provision for re-election, and the Länder ministers were henceforth appointed by the appropriate Reich ministers, to whom they were responsible. The Upper House or Reichsrat was dissolved in February 1934. The Reichstag continued to exist as a single-party, rubber-stamping body. It was mockingly described as the most highly paid choral society in Germany: its members received their salaries for singing the first stanzas of the National and Nazi anthems once or twice a year when they were called upon to applaud Hitler's various outpourings and edicts. In November 1933 the non-Nazi members were ousted by a one-party general 'election'. By February 1934 the total *Gleich-*

*schaltung* or 'coordination' of all German parliamentary institutions had been achieved.

Dr Goebbels, who on 13 March 1933 had been appointed Minister of Popular Enlightenment and Propaganda, was also very active in the first months after the Nazi take-over. Under a decree issued in June other ministries had to turn over some of their responsibilities to Goebbel's new ministry. The Ministry of Interior gave up the supervision of radio, films, press, theatre; the protection of works of art and memorials, and the regulation of state celebrations and holidays; the Foreign Ministry handed over its propaganda activities abroad. Even material for tourists came under Goebbel's control. As mentioned above, in 1933 the Nazis were not strongly represented in the press. They sought to remedy this situation by banning the 'Marxist' press, by forced sales of newspapers and control of news agencies and personnel. The *Schriftleitergesetz* issued on 4 October laid down that the office of editor was an official position, which could not be held by a person without German citizenship, or who had been deprived of his rights as a citizen, who was a Jew, or who was married to one. In their work editors were placed under various restrictions. The law, especially those parts of it concerned with the functions of the editor, destroyed any possibility of editorial independence. It made it impossible for German journalists to express a personal view of politics. The law gave Dr Goebbels an instrument for the achievement of a complete uniformity of the press: censorship was not necessary because the editor became a *de facto* censor.

The fate of the film industry was the same as that of the press. The film companies were taken over one by one including the largest of them, the U F A, which had belonged to the Nationalist leader Hugenberg. In less than five years the film department of the Goebbels' ministry gained a monopoly position in film production. It goes without saying that the showing of foreign films was strictly controlled. Finally, all journalists, film directors, broadcasters, actors and others at work in the mass media were required to belong to the appropriate Nazi-dominated professional organisation. The results of this on the information and entertainment media we shall examine later.

In Hitler's moves to consolidate his regime the attitude of the armed forces was of the greatest importance. In the person of General von Blomberg, who had been appointed Defence Minister, Hitler found an enthusiastic supporter. Many of the other senior officers were less enthusiastic. Among the junior officers enthusiasm was much more widespread. Hitler lost no time in attempting to win over the senior officers. On 3 February he confided his military and political ideas to the German military leadership. These included the destruction of Marxism and democracy, military equality for Germany, the reintroduction of conscription, and the conquest of living space in the East and its ruthless Germanisation. Of more immediate importance to the officers was the assurance that there would be no moves to bring them under S A or Party control. Hitler was able to give the forces more tangible assurances in June of the following year.

## THE 'NIGHT OF LONG KNIVES'

Unlike many of his rank-and-file Hitler had never taken the socialist slogans of his movement seriously and had already fallen out with some of his lieutenants, notably the Strasser brothers, because they had. In the summer of 1933 some of his S A men were getting restless and calling for a 'second revolution' to deal with the capitalists, Junkers and reactionaries. At the head of these discontented elements was Ernst Röhm, commander of the S A and Hitler's closest friend in the Nazi movement. In May 1934 Hitler is believed to have negotiated with the military leaders on the cruiser *Deutschland* an agreement which involved their support for him as head of state on the death of Hindenburg in return for the emasculation of the S A. Hitler also intrigued with Göring and Himmler, who saw Röhm as a stumbling block to their own power ambitions, against the S A chief. Meanwhile Papen, angry about the suppression of a speech he had made at Marburg University, inveighed against Hitler to his old friend Hindenburg. When on 21 June Hitler visited the President, he was met by General von Blomberg who warned him that Hindenburg had threatened to declare martial law and turn over power to the armed forces, if Hitler did not reduce tension by dealing with his party radicals. Hitler now acted. He put Göring and Himmler, head of the secret state police or Gestapo, in charge of eliminating 'disloyal' S A leaders in Berlin, while he personally dealt with matters in Bavaria where S A leaders were conferring.

Hitler later admitted that some 77 people had been shot down in that 'night of long knives' on 30 June 1934. After the war the figure of more than 1,000 was given. The victims included not only S A leaders such as Röhm, but also such prominent non-Nazis as General and Frau von Schleicher, General Kurt von Bredow and Erich Klausener, leader of Catholic Action.

Although the 'night of long knives' horrified many people both inside and outside Germany, it misled others into believing that the worst of the Nazi revolution was over, and that Germany would now settle down to a normal existence again. Many of those who harboured such illusions were shocked the following month by the attempt of the Austrian Nazis, with arms and encouragement from Berlin, to seize power. The coup failed. However, Dr Dollfuss, the Austrian Chancellor, was murdered and the episode created bad feeling between Hitler and Mussolini, who regarded himself as ally and protector of Austria, one of the very few friends Hitler had abroad.

In August 1934 the final consolidation of Hitler's position was achieved. Hindenburg died and Hitler took over the powers of head of state and commander in chief of the armed forces. The title of President was abolished and Hitler styled himself Führer (Leader) and Reich Chancellor. All officers and men of the armed forces were required to swear an oath of allegiance to Hitler personally rather than to the German state or people. This oath was to prove important later on when officers were to claim that they could not support action to remove the Führer because of it.

Hitler's new office was formally ratified by a plebiscite of the German people. One interesting aspect of the ' campaign '—no opposition was permitted—leading up to the vote which is of minor historical importance, was the use of what was claimed to be the political testament of Hindenburg. It praised the Nazis for leading the German nation to ' internal unity '. The testament, which was given the blessing of the President's son, Oskar, is generally believed to have been forged.

ECONOMIC RECOVERY

One of the reasons Hitler had not been prepared to push his Austrian ambitions too far in 1934 was Germany's lack of military preparedness. This was as much a question of economics as of military capabilities. Hitler was also concerned about economic affairs because of the problem of unemployment. Whatever he thought of his promises of ' work and bread ' he realised that the continuation of widespread unemployment represented a source of potential instability to the regime. His economic plans therefore aimed at two major objectives—creating jobs and making Germany economically independent as a means of strengthening the Reich's military capacity. Within a few years of taking power the Nazis were able, as the table below shows, to claim success in combating unemployment. Indeed, they were more successful than were the governments of Britain and the U S A and other countries. How were they able to achieve this result?

Employment and Unemployment in Germany
1932-38   (*in millions*)

| Year | | Employed | Unemployed |
| --- | --- | --- | --- |
| January | 1932 | 12.73 | 5.5 |
| January | 1933 | 11.5 | 6.0 |
| September | 1933 | 14.5 | 3.7 |
| September | 1934 | 16.1 | 2.3 |
| September | 1935 | 17.0 | 1.8 |
| September | 1936 | 18.3 | 1.1 |
| September | 1937 | 19.7 | 0.5 |
| September | 1938 | 20.8 | 0.2 |

In the spring of 1933 Hitler issued a proclamation promising a Four-Year Plan ' to rescue the German people, to safeguard German food supplies, and to rescue the German worker through a powerful attack on unemployment '. The measures subsequently introduced were not the product of a specific Nazi ideology of economics. They were rather the type of scheme adopted, though with much less vigour, in many countries in the 1930s nowadays summed up in the term ' Keynsianism '. They were in part based on the ' war socialism ' introduced in Germany during the First World War. Further, they were based on measures already undertaken by previous governments.

The Papen government of 1932 had offered tax incentives to businesses to increase the number of their employees. In addition Papen drew up a programme for expenditure on housing, house repairs, land improvement and capital expenditure by the railways and the Post Office. This was followed under the von Schleicher government by the appointment in December 1932 of a Commissioner for the Creation of Employment, who issued, just two days before the Nazis took over, a programme of expenditure on roads, housing, public utilities and inland water transport. Also in existence before 1933 was the voluntary labour service which by the end of 1932 was 250,000 strong. Its funds were provided partly out of the Reich budget, but primarily from the resources of the Unemployment Insurance Fund. The members of the service were mainly engaged in land improvement schemes. They received food and lodging but no pay. Another scheme worth mentioning was the compulsory reduction of interest on agricultural mortgages. This was introduced in September 1932. Obviously, the effects of these schemes would take time to make themselves felt. When they did so the Nazis were in power and enjoyed the political advantage they conferred. Nevertheless, we should not underestimate the importance of measures initiated by the Nazis, or rather, by Dr Schacht. These were more thorough than those brought in by previous governments, and unorthodox by most people's standards at the time.

Hitler's Four-Year Plan for the abolition of unemployment was given effect by the Law for the Reduction of Unemployment of 2 June 1933. It meant a great extension of public works; tax remissions and subsidies for profits reinvested in industry and agriculture; tax abatements for the employment of female domestic servants (thus reducing the number of women competing with men for industrial or agricultural employment); marriage bonuses for each newly married couple providing the wife did not continue to work outside the home. A separate law, also introduced in June 1933, inaugurated an ambitious scheme for the construction of 7000 km (4,375 miles) of motorways, the famous *Autobahnen*. The general transport tax was raised to help finance this project but taxes on new cars had been abolished in April 1933 to boost the automobile industry. The labour service was greatly expanded and in the early years of Nazi rule was an important factor in reducing the number of unemployed. In January 1933 there were some 180,000 persons engaged in labour service or on some other kind of relief works. By June of the same year the number had risen to over half a million and by June 1934 it was some 800,000. The figure was later reduced as industrial expansion got under way. In March 1935 military conscription was reintroduced, which further helped to mop up the unemployed. It has been estimated that by the time full employment was reached in 1938 about one and a half million men were either doing military service or labour service, and another one to two million were occupied in the service of the Nazi party, the police, and the management of the state-controlled economy.

Another part of the measures introduced in 1933 was designed to foster new industries which would increase the country's defence capacity. Tax exemption was granted for a number of years to enterprises engaged in developing new processes provided these were considered to be of the national importance. Under the Second Four-Year Plan announced in September 1936, which was under Hermann Göring's control, much greater emphasis was placed on German economic independence. In order to develop the materials and processes to make this possible the state offered long term contracts with guaranteed profits to firms and went into industry itself. The most important case of the latter was the Hermann Göring Works for the extraction and utilisation of low-grade ore. By controlling imports and subsidies new raw materials such as staple fibre, magnesium and aluminium alloys, plastics, artificial rubber

(Buna) and industrial oils from coal were developed. Production of traditional raw materials and agricultural products was given new emphasis. Despite the successes, some of which are benefiting Germany today, the Third Reich was not able to make itself economically independent—as it was to learn to its cost in the war.

All these projects had to be paid for and it was the ordinary people who paid most with lower wages and higher prices. In 1928, a ' normal ' year, wage and salary earners received 62 per cent of the national income. Under the Nazis their share fell year by year until in 1938 it was only 57 per cent. It is true that by that time there was work for all and virtual security of employment. In addition, working-class housing projects had continued to expand as under the Weimar regime and the Nazis developed cheap sports facilities and cheap holidays. Six million persons are said to have taken part on such holiday excursions in 1936. But the worker no longer had any freedom to take industrial action, to elect his own representatives or leave his employment without permission.

### HITLER AND THE CHURCHES

The Nazis were a *Weltanschauungspartei*, a party having a total world outlook which they thought everyone else should accept. They also intended keeping power indefinitely. It was therefore intolerable, from their point of view, that there were any institutions not completely subservient to them and not completely imbued with their outlook. Having achieved the annihilation of organised political opposition and having brought about the control of the organs of government, the armed forces and the information media, they sought to bring those other two alternative sources of ideas and information under their control, the churches and the educational institutions.

In many respects the Catholic Church appeared a greater potential threat to Nazism than the other churches because of its own authoritarian views, the loyalty of many of its followers to Catholicism before all else and its international prestige and ties. The Catholic Church, however, no less than the other organisations which faced the Nazis in 1933, suffered from not knowing its own mind. As we have seen, a considerable number of Catholic clergy had at least some sympathy for Nazism. They were impressed by its old-fashioned moral tone and by its strong line against Communists, Social Democrats, Jews, Masons, Liberals and Anarchists. Its ideas of political and social institutions were similar to the Catholic idea of the corporate state and in Italy, where a party with which the

62                          HITLER'S *Gleichschaltung* AND GAMBLES

Nazis claimed affinity was in power, relations between Church and State were excellent. And although they had their doubts about the Nazis they feared, particularly after the March elections, that to be too outspoken might lead to a split in the church and tough sanctions against it by the state. At the last contested elections in March 1933 the bishops issued a statement urging the faithful to vote for candidates whose proven character and proven attitudes gave evidence of their concern for the rights of the church. The fact that the bishops had not explicitly mentioned the Catholic parties was exploited by Catholic Nazis. As we have seen, after the elections Hitler promised the Centre and Bavarian People's parties to guarantee the rights of the church in return for their voting for the Enabling Act. The Catholic bishops for their part withdrew their earlier prohibitions concerning Nazism. Catholics were told to be loyal to the state, to carry out their civic duties and to avoid anything subversive. Catholic lay bodies started to declare their loyalty to the new regime. On Hitler's birthday on 20 April 1933 the leader of the Centre Party Monsignor Kaas sent the Nazi leader a telegram of congratulations giving an assurance of ' unflinching cooperation '. This further accelerated the movement of Catholics towards Nazism. The Fulda bishops' conference of 30 May – 1 June issued a pastoral letter which promised loyalty to the new regime though it voiced certain misgivings over the position and treatment of the church. Despite these Catholic moves towards a reconciliation with the Nazis, attacks on Catholic organisations continued. On 28 June a wave of arrests took place in Bavaria. These arrests brought about the dissolution of the Bavarian People's Party on 4 July. The Centre Party was dissolved a day later.

In view of these events it is remarkable how easy the Nazis found negotiations which led to the Concordat signed at the Vatican on 20 July by Papen, for the Reich, and Cardinal Pacelli, later Pope Pius XII, for the Church. Superficially the agreement offered the church much. It accorded it full freedom of profession and public practice of the Catholic religion and the right of the church to manage its own affairs, ' within the limits of laws applicable to all '. It also gave priests certain privileges and continued state subsidies to the church. Most important from the church's viewpoint, Articles 19-25 protected the Catholic educational system. Article 23 even guaranteed the maintenance of existing Catholic schools and the establishment of new ones. The church made concessions on Catholic organisations and on the question of the control of military chaplains. Though the Vatican later commented that the agreement did not imply acceptance of Nazi ideology or methods it undoubtedly gave great international prestige to the Nazi regime at a time when Hitler had few friends outside Germany. It should be remembered that the Vatican and the Weimar Republic had failed to reach agreement on a concordat. Despite the concordat the Catholic Church soon found it had much to complain about in Nazi Germany. Its organisations were harassed, its publications suppressed and thousands of priests were arrested on various pretexts. In 1937 Pope Pius XI decided to protest about the situation in an encyclical, *Mit brennender Sorge*, in which he pointed out that Christianity could not be imprisoned within the frontiers of a single people, within the pedigree of one single race. Nevertheless, most Catholic bishops continued their cooperation with the Nazi authorities and five days after *Mit brennender Sorge* it was balanced by another encyclical which strongly condemned Communism.

The Protestant clergy were probably more enthusiastic about the 'Government of National Concentration' formed by Nazis and Nationalists than were their Catholic colleagues. It had the backing of Hindenburg, a pious Protestant, and the majority of its members were loyal Protestants. But the Protestant clergy were Monarchist, Nationalist and Conservative rather than Nazi and it was not long before many started to have misgivings about the new regime. Few of them objected to the setting up of a Reich Church which replaced the existing loose association of regional churches, but argument broke out about who was to be its head. Hitler favoured Army Chaplain Ludwig Müller and by propaganda and intimidation succeeded in getting him elected as Reich Bishop. Opposition soon started notably from the 'Confessional Church' led by Pastor Martin Niemöller, a World War I U-Boat officer who had originally backed the 'National Government'. The Confessional Church rejected the authority of the Reich Bishop and the right of the state to interfere in matters of religious faith. Niemöller was later arrested after an outspoken sermon at his church in Dahlem, Berlin. On acquittal, in March 1938, of a charge of an underhand attack against the state, he was immediately taken into 'protective custody' and spent the rest of Nazi years in concentration camps. In the period 1937-39 hundreds of Confessional pastors were arrested and those who were not lost the state subsidies which formed a large part of their incomes. Most Protestant pastors did not choose Niemöller's road to Calvary, they swore a personal allegiance to the Führer. They were following the traditional policy of their church of acting as a state-supporting organisation. On the other hand, they prevented the Nazis setting up a Nazi-style pagan church.

## EDUCATION AND CULTURES IN THE THIRD REICH

In order to make the educational system subservient to their aims the National Socialists had to centralise it and expel the 'politically unreliable' elements. Full centralisation was achieved in April 1934 when a Reich Ministry of Education was given responsibility for all levels and forms of education from kindergarten to universities though certain Nazi educational establishments remained under NSDAP or SS control. The Nazis kept an eye on teachers through the National Socialist Teachers' League to which 98 per cent of all teachers, including university teachers, in 1942 belonged. All non-Nazi teachers' organisations were dissolved as were all non-Nazi youth and student bodies. Children and young people were under strong pressure to join the *Hitler Jugend* (for boys) or the *Bund Deutscher Mädel* (for girls). By 1938, when Catholic student associations were finally dissolved, the only body open to university students was the Nazi Students' Organisation.

In addition to camping and the usual type of Boy Scouting activities the *Hitler Jugend*, under an Act of December 1936, had the task of educating 'the entire German Youth' in the 'spirit of National Socialism'. Increasingly it put emphasis on the pre-military training of youth. Very many German school teachers were nationalist-inclined before 1933 and welcomed the 'National Revolution'. Probably the majority of their university colleagues shared their views but a higher proportion of them were purged. By May 1939 the Nazis claimed that 45 per cent of university teaching staff had been replaced by good Nazis.

In addition to centralising and purging the Nazi revolution affected German education in other ways. Nazi racial doctrines were compulsory subjects at all levels and religious teaching was gradually pushed out. In 1939 prayers were abolished in elementary schools. School discipline became stricter and corporal punishment, abolished under the Weimar Republic, was reintroduced. The whole education system was given a more vocational slant. Courses were also shortened to provide young people with more time for their compulsory military-political training. Women's education suffered in the Third Reich due to the official belief that a woman's place was in the home. Consequently there was greater stress on domestic science and nursing for girls to the detriment of their general education. Women found it more difficult to get into the universities and the professions. The impact of war losses forced some modification of this policy.

Despite the positive attitude of many students and university teachers to the Nazi takeover the N S D A P remained suspicious of the universities. It became more difficult than before 1933 to gain admission to higher education. Apart from academic qualifications, only those whose racial descent, physical fitness and record of service to the *Hitler Jugend* were satisfactory found places. These regulations and the greater opportunities available in the armed forces, industry and political organisations, reduced the number of university students by 1939, to less than half that of 1931-2.

In addition to the normal education system the Nazis set up a number of educational organisations of their own. These were supposed to train a specially selected élite for future political and military leadership. The *Napolas* were paramilitary boarding schools of which there were 23 in 1940 with about 5,000 pupils. Even more select were the Adolf Hitler Schools admission to which was open only to those who had, among other things, an unimpeachable family-tree going back to 1800.

What Nazi cultural policy was going to be was shown already on 10 May 1933 when a vast crowd watched the burning of ' decadent ' and ' hostile ' books in the square in front of Berlin's main University. Condemned were the works of such writers as Heinrich Heine, Thomas Mann, Stefan Zweig and very many others. In literature, painting, architecture, the cinema and the other creative fields artists had either to conform or get out. Jews of course did not have even this choice.

What were these new standards the Nazi sought to impose? If they were not of a directly propagandist nature they had to at least emphasise old Germanic ' folk ' traditions or simply suit the personal whims of Hitler. The piece of contemporary literature most favoured by Hitler was Hans Grimm's *Volk ohne Raum* (A People Without Space), the title of which conveys something of the contents. Painting had to be poster-style representational rather than, say, abstract, and was supposed to concern itself with Germanic or Nordic themes. Adolf Ziegler was one of the main protagonists of this kind of painting. In architecture Hitler preferred neo-classical style, a poor imitation of Greece and Rome rather than modern architecture based on contemporary needs and contemporary techniques and materials. Such neo-classical structures were designed by Albert Speer, later Minister of War Production, for the mass meetings and parades held at Nuremberg.

The Nazis realised the importance of the cinema. Dr Goebbels came to realise that people could not be serious all the time; consequently, especially after the outbreak of war, many escapist films were produced. The Nazi film-makers also proved themselves

E

extremely clever in using half-truths for propaganda purposes. An instance of this was the film by Hans Steinhoff called *Ohm Krüger* which was about the Anglo-South African War. The famous actor Emil Jannings played the title role of Krüger, the Boer leader. In the film the Nazis exploited the fact that General Kitchener set up the first concentration camps to intern civilian Dutch South Africans suspected of aiding Boer military formations. Churchill, who was a war correspondent in that war, was shown gloating over the plight of the inmates. As the writer found out when studying in Germany in the 1950s, Britain's 'invention' of the camps was firmly fixed in the minds of even those who were too young to have seen the film and seemed to them to at least greatly reduce German guilt. A film about the Irish struggle for independence, *Der Fuchs von Glenarvon*, the Fox of Glenarvon, and one about the *Titanic* are further examples of skilful exploitation of the half-truth. In addition the Nazis used the documentary technique with amazing results. Two of the best known of this type of film are Leni Riefenstahl's pictorial epic of the 1934 N S D A P congress and one on the 1936 Olympic Games. Both are still regarded as important by students of the film today. Nazi racial and imperialist policies were allocated their ration of celluloid. In 1940 Viktor Tourjanski produced *Feinde* (Enemies), in order to justify the German invasion of Poland. A little earlier Veit Harlan directed the notorious *Jud Süss* (Jew Süss) to fan the flames of anti-semitic feeling.

Music was more difficult to interpret in a strictly ideological way but the works of Jewish composers were banned.

Quite apart from those of Jewish ancestry, many members of Germany's cultural élite were not prepared to accept Nazi standards and went abroad. There they produced work which has proved more significant than most which appeared in Nazi Germany. There were the writers Thomas and Heinrich Mann, Bertolt Brecht, Anna Seghers, Ludwig Renn and Erich Maria Remarque. Then there were the specifically Jewish writers like Arnold and Stefan Zweig, Lion Feuchtwanger and Friedrich Wolf. These few will stand for the thousands of writers, artists, actors and directors who left Germany. They helped to enrich the countries which took them in. In Britain the high standard of Glyndebourne Opera was a product of the work of refugee musicians. In America Hollywood greatly benefited from refugees. The two giants of modern American architecture Walter Gropius and Ludwig Mies von der Rohe were refugees.

But Nazi Germany became poorer not only in the arts and architecture. Hundreds of university teachers—there were over 300 registered in Britain in 1944—left Germany. About 5,000 medical practitioners entered the U S A from Europe between 1933 and 1940. Many of them were Nazi victims. This number was as many as graduated in one year from all the medical schools in the United States. Worse still, from the point of view of the Nazi war economy, there were the scientists such as Albert Einstein and James Franck, whose theories helped to produce the atom bomb. Hundreds of others worked on various war projects in industry. Finally, many German refugee academics worked for American intelligence agencies as their contribution to the defeat of Nazism. There were the sociologists, Hans Speier, Leo Lowenthal and Max Horkheimer, political scientists such as John Herz and Otto Kirchheimer, philosophers like Herbert Marcuse, and many others.

### THE CONCENTRATION CAMP SYSTEM

Known anti-Nazis who did not manage or desire to go abroad were in danger of finding themselves in prison or, more likely, in a concentration camp for an indefinite period/The first Nazi concentration camp appears to have been set up by Himmler as head of Munich police in March 1933. It was in the grounds and stone huts of a former gunpowder factory near Dachau. It was said to be necessary because the normal prison system could not cope with the sudden influx of prisoners. Other camps were being set up around Berlin, particularly notorious was the one at Columbia-Haus, and in other parts of the country. At the end of July 1933 26,700 persons were in 'protective custody' (Schutzhaft). Conditions in the camps were primitive as they were either in disused or hastily-constructed premises. Those in charge—S A and S S before June 1934, S S after that date—were virtually free to do as they pleased with prisoners, except that is for a few who the regime wanted to be kept alive for possible future bargains or for propaganda reasons.

The head of the administration of all camps from 1934 to 1939 was Theodor Eicke, a former Imperial Army N C O and later I G-Farben employee in charge of factory security, who at the time of his appointment was undergoing psychiatric treatment. He imposed martial-law conditions as normal treatment for prisoners and not surprisingly many died under torture or from the back-breaking work or were 'shot while trying to escape'. For those who were not so dispatched isolation from the outside world, total insecurity and the thought that they could be detained for life were almost as fearful. By 1937 Eicke had reorganised the camps reducing them to four Dachau, Sachsenhausen, Buchenwald and Lichtenburg. Hardened criminals, vagabonds and homosexuals started to be sent to the camps and were often used as Kapos or trusties to oversee and inform on the political prisoners. About this time forced labour was developed in a more systematic form. In the spring of 1938 the s s firm Deutsche Erd-und Steinwerke GmbH (Dest) was founded to exploit quarries and establish brickworks.

It was the job of the secret police to hunt down those destined for 'protective custody'. A law of April 1933 set up the Gestapo (the German abbreviation for Secret State Police) which however only had jurisdiction in Prussia at that time. Ironically, its headquarters were in Prinz-Albrecht-Strasse in the former H Q of the Communist Party. In Bavaria Himmler was in charge of the political police. He gradually extended his writ until in April 1934 when he became Deputy Chief and Inspector of the Prussian Gestapo, he was *de facto* head of all secret police forces in Germany though in Prussia he was still nominally responsible to Göring. In June 1936 he was appointed Chief of the (now completely centralised) German Police as well as retaining his position as s s Führer. Reinhard Heydrich was his deputy. Heydrich was also head of the *Sicherheitsdienst* (Security Service) or s D. This was set up in 1931 as the intelligence service of the Nazi Party. The Gestapo operated through a network of offices throughout the Reich and a well developed system of informers. In the period October 1935—March 1936 over 1,000 persons per month were arrested by the Gestapo for alleged Left-wing activities alone.

PERSECUTION OF THE JEWS

Apart from the political opponents of the regime the Jews were the other main category of prisoners in the camps. The first general, organised attack on the Jews was in April 1933 when a boycott of Jewish businesses and professional people was instigated. It was accompanied by much violence. In the same month an Act was promulgated which excluded from the civil service those who had one or more Jewish grandparents. Due to the intervention of Hindenburg specific groups of 'non-Aryans' were excluded from the provisions of the Act. These were those who had held office since 1 August 1914, former front-line soldiers, and those whose sons or fathers had been killed in action. This hit academics too for they were regarded as civil servants in Germany. In the next months various professional organisations—of medical practitioners, dentists and lawyers—expelled their Jewish members or even non-Jews with Jewish spouses. A law of September 1933 prevented Jews from inheriting farms. During the next two years a series of laws and orders were introduced extending the purge of Jews to virtually every profession. When compulsory military service was reintroduced in 1935 Jews were excluded from its provisions. In September 1935 the notorious Nuremberg Laws, so called because they were made known at the Nazi party rally in that city, were announced. They were the Reich Citizenship Act and the Act for the Protection of German Blood and German Honour. The first law deprived Jews of their citizenship and revoked the earlier, more lenient attitude to Jewish ex-servicemen, their dependants and long-serving Jewish civil servants. All were now removed from the public service. The German Blood Act prohibited marriage and extra-marital relations between ' Jews and nationals of German or allied blood ' in order to ensure the ' survival of the German race '. It further prohibited a Jew from employing a female national of German or allied blood under 45 years of age in his household. An order dated 17 August 1938 forced male Jews to add the name ' Isràel ' and female Jews the name ' Sara ' to their non-Jewish first names. Jewish passports were marked with the letter ' J ' under an order of 5 October of that year.

A number of measures had been introduced during the years 1933-38 to exclude the Jews from the economic life of the country. These had not been entirely successful. The Nazis sought a pretext which would give them the opportunity to bring matters to a head. They got this chance when a German diplomat, von Rath, was assassinated by a 17-year-old Jew in Paris on 7 November 1938. The result was a ' spontaneous ' outbreak of violence which became known as the *Reichskristallnacht* (Reich Crystal Night). Over 7,000 Jewish shops were destroyed and synagogues burned throughout Germany. Jews were beaten up, about 90 of them killed and some 30,000 herded into concentration camps. Further measures for the ' Aryanisation ' of Jewish businesses followed and a large fine was levied on the Jewish community. Jews were also excluded from German schools and universities (this had been already largely achieved in practice), banned from places of public entertainment and cultural institutions and even had their driving licences invalidated. They were ordered to hand over their jewellery and were frequently forced to live together in ' communal Jewish houses '.

During these prewar years Jews were allowed, and sometimes even encouraged, to emigrate. It made it easier for the Nazis to take control of their businesses and clear them from responsible positions without measures which would get them a bad press abroad. However, too many German Jews abroad were witnesses against the Nazi regime. In September 1933 the Haavara Agreement was drawn up between the Zionist organisation and the Reich Ministry of

Economics. Would-be emigrants paid in funds to a Trust Company which then used the funds to finance German exports to Palestine. Half of the exports had, however, to be paid for by the Jews in foreign currency. Jews who so contributed were later reimbursed in Palestine by the Company. Some 170,000 Jews had emigrated under this scheme by November 1938. As one might expect, emigration was not very popular among Jews, particularly the older and better-off ones. After all, Palestine was not Europe and emigration, whether to Palestine or elsewhere, invariably meant a considerable financial sacrifice as the true value of properties were never fully realised. There was also the problem of one's profession. Apart from the language difficulty many emigrants found it difficult to start again in their old professions abroad.

Perhaps harder to bear than all the legal actions against the Jews was the cruel social ostracism. Jews found neighbours no longer greeted them on the streets, shops no longer wanted their trade, ' Aryan ' friends no longer called. Jewish children no longer had playmates and many Jewish partners in mixed marriages found that husbands or wives sought renewed respectability through divorce. There was the mental anguish and incomprehension of Jews whose families had lived in Germany for centuries, who were Germans to their very roots, who, in some cases, were even old-fashioned German nationalists themselves. Suddenly they were no longer wanted by the community they had admired so much.

### FOREIGN GAMBLES

Nazi foreign policy in the years before the outbreak of World War II represented a series of bold, even reckless, gambles. Hitler undertook these gambles, often against the advice of the military, because he had a primitive conception of politics and society, especially the politics and society of Britain and France (and of great importance later, of the U S S R and the U S A). It was a case of fools rush in where angels fear to tread. A more sophisticated view would have led to greater caution. His view of Britain was a mixture of admiration and contempt. He admired the British for having built up and maintained the greatest empire the world had ever seen, but he regarded the British ruling élite as effete and decadent, increasingly the pawns of Jewish wire-pullers in the City of London. For him Britain meant the bowler-hatted brigade, armed with umbrellas and elaborate titles and an outmoded view of chivalry. Perhaps Britain was somewhat to blame for Hitler's view for so many of the ' top people ' he met were of this variety, members of the Anglo-German Fellowship or The Link, two organisations sympathetic to Germany enjoying considerable support in Britain in the higher echelons. Even among those he met who were not connected with these organisations, many felt he represented a bulwark of 'law and order' at a time when European society was in danger of disintegrating. Many others did not like Hitler but they liked Stalin even less, and they wrongly supposed the alternatives were a strong Germany or Communism in Europe.

It must not be thought though, that the British politicians who had to deal with Hitler were merely ill-advised, gullible fools taken in by anti-Communist patter. Their attitudes of appeasement, like those of their French colleagues, reflected their very real desire to avoid another holocaust. They were impressed by the overwhelming suffering produced by the 1914-18 war. Unfortunately for the world Hitler was not. Unfortunately too for the world very few people could take in the fact that Hitler, the ruler of a great nation, could be totally indifferent to human suffering, his own people's as well as that of other nations. Again, it was difficult to believe that the men around Hitler—the admirals and generals, the industrialists and civil servants, the academics and scientists—would back a megalomaniac and allow themselves to be led to disaster by him. The British and French politicians had two further weaknesses *vis-à-vis* the Nazi leader. They, unlike him, had to seek re-election, and quite understandably the voters were more interested in fighting unemployment than fighting Hitler. Secondly, and this was more true of the British than the French, they felt that perhaps the victors had been hard on Germany in 1919 and that most of Hitler's claims were reasonable even if the man who was voicing them was not.

The claims themselves were never entirely clear. Hitler had always demanded the complete abrogation of the Versailles Treaty which meant restoration of Germany to her 1914 boundaries, the return of Germany's overseas colonies, and military equality for the Reich with the other major European powers. Clearly France would not be ready to surrender Alsace-Lorraine originally taken from her in 1870 after the Franco-Prussian War and regained in 1919. And Poland would not be prepared to relinquish *all* the territory gained at Germany's expense in 1919. But much of what Germany had lost was negotiable and many foreign politicians were sympathetic to the unification of Germany and Austria. An equally resolute, yet more reasonable, more peace-orientated German leader, might have gone a long way to achieving these aims without war.

Hitler's methods in other countries, as much as in his own, caused increasing suspicion. And was the end Versailles the height of Hitler's ambitions? How important were the statements made in

*Mein Kampf*, his book written in 1924, and in the Nazi party programme? These called for German 'living space' at the expense of Russia, and the uniting of all Germans living abroad, which implied a threat to many nations in Eastern Europe. Some Western politicians and experts thought Hitler, like most other politicians, would not be too concerned about not fulfilling pledges made years before he got power. Others took hope from the fact that these aims would lead him into eastern, and not western Europe. The latter were impressed by his anti-Communist posturing in the form of the Anti-Comitern Pact of 1936 signed by Germany, Italy and Japan, and the help he gave to General Franco in fighting 'Communism' in Spain. Hitler also misled the anti-Russian, anti-Communist Polish generals by signing a non-aggression pact with them in January 1934. He then moved rapidly in all directions, whether as the result of a carefully conceived plan or in response to the opportunities which presented themselves is in some doubt.

In 1935 he reintroduced conscription in defiance of Germany's obligations. In the same year he negotiated a naval agreement with Britain which greatly improved Germany's naval position. He won back the Saar in 1935 by League of Nations' plebiscite. In the following year his troops reoccupied the Rhineland which had been recognised as part of the Reich but was demilitarised. This made it more difficult for the French and British to help the Czechs and Poles later. Up to this point few politicians in Britain felt very hostile to this apparent assertion of German nation rights. In March 1938 Hitler seized Austria after a campaign of murder and blackmail, though afterwards he held a Nazi-style plebiscite to justify his actions. Once again there were many who were prepared to argue that this was a natural, logical, even historically inevitable development. Austria, without its empire, it was said, was neither economically nor politically viable. Before 1933 many German and Austrian democrats had wanted such a union and, as for the Austrian regime, as it was not very democratic or progressive, its passing would not be mourned.

The next item on the Nazi dictator's agenda was the destruction of Czechoslovakia. This he had talked about, together with the annexation of Austria, at a meeting of his top officers in November 1937. In Czechoslovakia he could use the German-speaking minority as a stick with which to beat the Prague government. Yet again he was able to mislead many reasonable people in Britain and France —as well as some who wanted to be misled—and lead them to believe he was merely interested in the rights of his compatriots outside the Reich. These 'Germans' had never been under German rule. Before 1919 they had been citizens of the Austro-Hungarian Empire. But after 1933 the majority of them increasingly looked to Germany for help and guidance. They supported the Sudeten German Party of Konrad Henlein. Many informed people in the West were coming to have their doubts about the wisdom of setting up Czechoslovakia after the world war. The trouble was the dominant Czechs—about 6.5 million of them—were a minority in their own state. With them were (roughly) 3.25 million Germans, 700,000 Hungarians, 400,000 Ruthenes, 70,000 Poles, and 3 million Slovaks. The latter, like the others, were restless. They wanted at least autonomy within a Czecho-Slovak state. The Czechoslovak state was more democratic, prosperous and progressive than the other states of central and eastern Europe. Yet the fact that it had not solved the problem of its nationalities made it easy prey for Hitler.

Less than three months after the Austrian Anschluss, Hitler sent a secret directive to the Wehrmacht announcing his ' unalterable ' decision to smash Czechoslovakia by military action in the near future. In Czechoslovakia Henlein's supporters stepped up their campaign of demonstrations and terror. In view of the deteriorating situation Britain sent a special envoy, Lord Runciman, to investigate German allegations of oppression in Czechoslovakia. Meanwhile the Führer ordered the German forces to be in a state of combat readiness by 1 October. At the annual Nazi rally in Nuremberg in September Hitler made an angry, threatening speech. There followed a two-day revolt of Henlein's organisation which was put down by the Czechs. War appeared imminent.

Neville Chamberlain, British Prime Minister, had for some time been thinking in terms of a solution based on the Czechs ceding the Sudetenland, the area where most of the German-speaking population lived. Three days after Hitler's Nuremberg speech he flew to Germany, at the time an unusual and indeed courageous step for a 69-year-old who had never flown before, to seek a solution. The crux of his conversation with Hitler was that the Sudeten area would go to Germany and that he would try to persuade British and French colleagues to accept this. The Führer went ahead with his military plans agreeing not to move until he had had a further talk with Chamberlain.

The British Prime Minister had no difficulty in convincing the French, even though they had a mutual assistance treaty with Czechoslovakia, or most of his political friends. Faced with this situation the Czechs were forced to capitulate. They had a treaty with the Russians. But the latter were only required to act if the French did so.

Chamberlain again went to Germany. This time meeting Hitler at Godesberg. The Nazi leader shocked the Prime Minister by raising his demands. In addition to getting the Sudetenland, he wanted the immediate military occupation of the area—to give the impression of a military victory. The whole operation had to be completed by 1 October. It was already 23 September! After much heart-searching the British statesman agreed to put Hitler's terms to his colleagues, the French and the Czechs. The Nazi assured him that he was making his ' last territorial demand ' in Europe. The Czechs refused to accept the German demands and mobilised. The French felt obliged to do the same. Britain mobilised the Home Fleet and the auxiliary Air Force. The Nazi dictator appeared to weaken. He sent a letter conciliatory in tone to Chamberlain on 27 September. Chamberlain grasped at this. He warned President Benes of Czechslovakia that even if Germany lost a world war, Czechoslovakia would still lose the Sudetenland. He proposed the Czechs should accept a limited German military occupation on 1 October of Egerland and Asch—outside the Czech frontier fortifications—and that a commission of Germans, Czechs and British, should quickly decide further areas to be handed over. To Hitler he proposed a conference to work out the details. Apparently it was Mussolini who got Hitler to agree to this. Hitler then issued invitations to Chamberlain, Mussolini, and the French Prime Minister, Edouard Daladier, to meet him at Munich on the following day. The Czechs were not invited.

The meeting at Munich was not a conference in any real sense, it was a gathering summoned to accept Hitler's demands. The leaders met on the afternoon of the 29 September. By 1 a.m. of the following day they signed the Munich Agreement. It provided for the German Army to begin moving into the Sudetenland on 1 October, and complete the occupation by 10 October. All areas considered to be more than 50 per cent German were to be cleared by the Czechs. They had to leave all installations, including military ones, in good order. They received no compensation.

Chamberlain returned home to a hero's welcome. A man of peace he feared war, especially the bombing of civilians, demonstrated so terribly for the first time in the Spanish Civil War which was then raging. Almost equally he feared the extension of Bolshevik influence in Europe. And, it must be admitted, Stalin's Russia was not a very attractive alternative to Hitler's Germany. He was fully aware of Britain's lack of military preparedness, less aware of Germany's military and economic weakness. Finally, he received little encouragement from the U S A whose help had been decisive in the 1914-18 war. He was ill-advised and a poor judge of men—should he not have thought that a man who treated an old man and leader of a great empire in the way Hitler treated him could not be trusted?

In March 1939 Chamberlain was to be completely disillusioned. The remainder of Czechoslovakia was incorporated into the Reich under threat of aerial bombardment. Slovakia masqueraded as an independent state but was *de facto* a German puppet. By May 1939 Hitler was telling his generals, ' Further successes can no longer be attained without the shedding of blood . . . Danzig is not the subject of the dispute at all. It is a question of expanding our living space in the East . . .' And ' There is no question of sparing Poland . . .'

Concerted Anglo-French action in 1933-36 would have resulted in the end of Hitler. His generals feared Anglo-French military moves over the reoccupation of the Rhineland, for instance, and urged Hitler to desist from implementing this policy. Later, an Anglo-French accord with Russia might have achieved the same result. In 1938 General Beck, Chief of the German General Staff of the Army, feared any move against Czechoslovakia would lead to joint British, French, Czech and Soviet action. He was preparing a coup against Hitler to meet such a situation.

Agreement with the U S S R was not to be. Many British, and to a lesser extent French, politicians were suspicious of Stalin. Many of them thought the Soviet armed forces of little military value. Stalin provided them with an additional argument when he purged his top officers as German spies in 1937. Yet in April 1939 there was a tiny glimmer of hope. Chamberlain, largely because of public pressure, agreed to negotiations with Moscow. On the British side these were at best half-hearted. In any case, Poland, Romania and the Baltic states voiced their objections to such an alliance with guarantees covering them. The negotiations dragged on ending in August with the bombshell of a non-aggression pact between Germany and Russia. The Soviets had been greatly disturbed by the Munich Agreement, which opened Hitler's way to the East and indicated Anglo-French preference for dealing with Hitler rather than them. They feared being caught in a war alone, without allies, a war on two fronts. Recently Japan had provoked a series of' armed clashes with the U S S R.

The published version of the Hitler-Stalin pact, valid for ten years, declared that neither party would engage in a warlike act against the other or join any third party in any such act. The additional secret protocols placed Finland, the Baltic states and Eastern Poland, ' in the event of a territorial and political transformation ' in the Soviet 'sphere of interest'. Bessarabia was also so placed. This gave Hitler the green light for action against Poland. He did not believe that without Russia, Britain and France would act to save Poland. But on 25 August Britain and Poland decided on a treaty of mutual assistance.

On 1 September German forces launched a full-scale attack on Poland the pretext being an attack on the German radio station at Gleiwitz, an 'attack' staged by the Nazis themselves. On the same day Britain and France warned Germany that unless 'all aggressive action against Poland' was suspended and German forces promptly withdrawn they would 'fulfil their obligations to Poland'. On Sunday 3 September with no response from Germany but growing unrest in Parliament, which had been recalled from holiday, Chamberlain repeated this intention giving the Germans until 11 a.m. to reply. Otherwise, 'a state of war will exist'. The German reply was the sinking of the British liner *Athenia* with the loss of 112 people on the same day.

# 5   Phoney War, Total War and Total Defeat

The author remembers as a small boy seeing pictures of the Polish armed forces in the London weekly *Picture Post* bearing the caption, 'Poland Is Ready'. In reality Poland was in no sense ready. When German forces went into action on 1 September the Poles lacked the necessary modern aircraft, tanks, anti-aircraft and anti-tank defences. Their communications and transport services were weak. German positions in East Prussia and in recently occupied Czechoslovakia gave the Wehrmacht a great strategic advantage. So that, although Poland had relatively large numbers of troops, its outlook was poor right from the start. By 8 September the Wermacht reached Warsaw. Any hope the Poles had of continuing open resistance ended on 17 September when Soviet forces crossed the frontier from the East.

In these circumstances it is perhaps surprising that remnants of the Polish forces were still resisting until well into October. Warsaw held out until 28 September when its garrison were forced to capitulate after repeated air attacks which had inflicted heavy civilian casualties and destroyed, among other things, the main waterworks.

Defeated Poland was then divided by Hitler and Stalin. The Soviets advanced to roughly along the Curzon Line (so called because it had been drawn up at the end of the 1914-18 war by the British Foreign Minister Lord Curzon). They could claim that they were only taking back by force what had been taken by force by the Poles in 1920. The area was mainly populated by Ukrainians and White Russians. They further claimed, with some justification, that the Poles had ill-treated these minority peoples. However, neither in 1920 nor in 1939 were the luckless peoples of these areas given any say in what was to happen to them. Germany and the Soviet Union came to a new agreement, officially called the German-Soviet Boundary and Friendship Treaty, concluded on 28 September. The secret part of the Treaty assigned Lithuania to the Soviet sphere of influence and, by way of exchange, gave the Germans the provinces of Lublin and Eastern Warsaw. The partners further agreed not to tolerate 'Polish agitation' in their respective territories. This agreement destroyed any hope that a rump Polish state would be permitted to exist.

In those early weeks of World War II Adolf Hitler was successful in other directions. His navy, which had been considered the weak arm of the German armed forces, scored some striking successes. On 17 September a German submarine sunk the British aircraft carrier *Courageous* off the coast of Ireland and on 14 October the Royal Navy battleship *Royal Oak* went to the bottom while at anchor at Scapa Flow after a daring U-boat attack. Hitler's wildest dreams seemed to be coming true. In the West where Anglo-French forces on one side, and German on the other, watched each other behind well-fortified positions the *Sitzkrieg* (sit-down or immobile war) contrasted greatly with the *Blitzkrieg* (lightning war) in Poland. The British called it the 'phoney war'. In this situation, and with Hitler announcing a 'peace offer' in the Reichstag on 6 October, the German people must have thought that Der Führer was once again delivering the goods and that there would be an early return to peace. In these circumstances, the bomb which exploded in the Munich Beer Cellar on 8 November just a few minutes after Hitler had finished making a speech to the old guard of the Nazi party, was without significance as a manifestation of opposition to the regime.

VICTORY IN THE WEST

Having knocked out Poland and got some kind of agreement with the USSR Hitler turned his attention to the West. He rightly concluded that, if left undefeated, Britain and France could only get stronger. He therefore aimed at a quick, yet decisive blow against France which would drive Britain from the mainland of Europe. Britain could then either be starved and bombed into submission or invaded. But before Hitler could turn his thoughts to France his attention was drawn to the situation in Scandinavia.

The Germans were heavily dependent on iron ore from Sweden for their war effort. For seven winter months of each year the ore from near Gellivare had to be hauled by rail to Narvik in Norway. From there it was shipped to Germany. Most of this journey was in Norwegian waters and Norway, like Sweden, was neutral. Winston Churchill, as Britain's First Sea Lord or Navy Minister, asked the British Cabinet to sanction the mining of Norwegian waters. This was rejected. But in December 1939 Britain saw a chance of intervention in Norway. This was due to the outbreak of hostilities between Finland and the Soviet Union.

The Soviets were concerned with building buffer zones between themselves and the Germans nothwithstanding the Hitler-Stalin Pact. They compelled Estonia, Latvia and Lithuania to sign treaties of 'Mutual Assistance' as a preliminary to taking them over. This gave the Soviet Navy what they considered to be useful bases in the Baltic. Immediately after the signing of the treaties Stalin put pressure on Finland to cede territory which he regarded as vital for Russia's defences. He was particularly concerned about an area where the frontier was only about 20 miles from Leningrad and the island naval base of Kronstadt, and about the lease of the Baltic port of Hangö as a naval base. When agreement was not reached the Russians attacked Finland. Most of the world sympathised with the Finns and were pleased about early Soviet reverses. The British and French intended to send an expeditionary force. This would have had to go through Norway with or without that country's acquiescence. Before such a force could be dispatched the Finns were defeated.

About one month after the Russo-Finnish Peace Treaty was signed, on 9 April German troops started their occupation of Norway and Denmark. This was not the result of Finnish defeat, for already in October 1939 Grand Admiral Raeder had been at work convincing Hitler of the importance of Norwegian ports for the German Navy both to defend German shipping and, offensively, to blockade the United Kingdom. Hitler was convinced that occupation was necessary after an incident in February involving the release of about 300 British seamen who were held aboard the German prison ship *Altmark*. The British destroyer *Cossack* intercepted the *Altmark* in Norwegian waters after it had been given clearance by the Norwegian naval authorities who apparently did not know this ship's mission. In Denmark the Germans found no opposition except for isolated shooting. In Norway things were different. Five German divisions were sent to occupy the main ports and the capital, Oslo. This was a potentially hazardous operation which could have led to disaster for the Germans. Everywhere the Germans met opposition. In the fjord leading to Oslo the guns of the Oskarsborg fortress sank the heavy cruiser *Blücher*, which had several important Nazi officials on board, and damaged the pocket battleship *Lützow*. Other German ships had been sunk or damaged when the invasion force had been challenged at the entrance to the fjord. This particular force was compelled to turn back. Nevertheless, the Germans quickly reduced the whole of Norway. They were able to do this by what became known as the classic Nazi military tactics. These were surprise, command of the air, parachute landings to take important military objectives (in this case Oslo's airport) and the use of internal subversion. In Norway the Germans had the help of Norwegian Nazis led by Vidkun Quisling, a former officer and former Defence Minister. They spread confusion and officers under their influence surrendered their units without a fight. This happened in Narvik. Poor British leadership also saved the day for the Germans.

Two days before the German attack on Norway and Denmark an Allied expeditionary force was due to sail for Norway. This force did not in fact sail as scheduled because of the news that the Germans were heading for Norway. By the time Allied troops were on their way the Germans already controlled much of the country including the vital ports and airfields. Nevertheless the British Navy went into action with some success. During the original German attack British ships and naval aircraft sank two German cruisers as well as smaller vessels. At Narvik, where the British lost two destroyers, they sank, in two engagements, ten better-armed German destroyers and a number of supply ships. In all the Germans lost, apart from these ten destroyers, three cruisers and the use of the badly damaged *Scharnhorst, Gneisenau* (both battle cruisers) and *Lützow* for several months. Allied losses were nine destroyers, one cruiser and one aircraft carrier. The German losses were relatively far heavier than these figures would suggest for their naval forces started off much weaker than those of the Allies. This was to be important when they were contemplating the invasion of Britain.

Three Allied landings took place in Norway. Two near Trondheim, in an attempt to recapture that vital port, failed. The third landing near Narvik succeeded in achieving its objective. On 27-28 May an Allied force of British, French, Poles and Norwegians recaptured Narvik driving the Germans in the direction of Sweden. However, on 10 May the German offensive in western Europe had started and by the end of the month things were going very badly for the Allies. It was decided to withdraw the force in Norway to try to halt the Germans in France. Norwegian resistance then inevitably quickly came to an end. By 10 June 1940 all Norwegian forces had ceased fighting; the government and King Haakon had resolved to continue the fight from London.

One shock for Hitler which partly resulted from the Norwegian campaign was the resignation of the British Prime Minister, Neville Chamberlain, after much criticism of his handling of the situation. Notorious for his appeasement policy before the war, he was replaced by the implacable enemy of Hitler, Winston Churchill. Churchill, who had not done too well as First Sea Lord during the

Norwegian campaign, headed a national coalition resolved to prosecute the war to a successful conclusion.

In France and the Low Countries the Allies were defeated by the same factors which defeated them in Norway: surprise, lack of air support, lack of armour, little or no coordination between national forces, apathy and subversion. They were not surprised by the attack on Holland, and even less so by the one on Belgium. They had proposed joint staff talks with Belgium but such talks were rejected.

The Allies did not expect the thrust to come where it did. They were expecting another move similar to the German plan of campaign in 1914, that is, across northern Belgium towards Paris. At Hitler's insistence the thrust was across Luxemburg, southern Belgium and the Somme Valley, with a simultaneous attack on Holland. The aim was to draw the British and some French forces into Belgium and then cut them off from the main French forces. The Germans could then outflank the French fortifications known as the Maginot line. Intensified German security regulations and able use of camouflage concealed the advance of the armoured units, and thus left the Allies in doubt as to which was the main thrust of the offensive. Once again the Germans used parachutists to capture strategic targets. An innovation was the successful use of gliders against strongly fortified positions in Belgium. They also gave the Dutch a taste of the aerial bombardment the Poles had suffered—though German writers today claim the destruction of Rotterdam was due to ' poor communications '. Five days of hard fighting were enough to cause the capitulation of the Dutch forces, though their government and monarch got away to Britain. The Belgians lasted two and a half weeks, capitulating on 28 May with their king at their head. Even with the same forces available, had these countries cooperated with each other and with the Allies before they were attacked the outcome could conceivably have been different.

Abandoned by their friends, the Allies lost no time in getting their troops out of this dangerous situation in which the Anglo-French units, which had gone to the aid of the Belgians, were cut off from the main French forces. On 26 May the order was given to evacuate Allied troops from the perimeter around the port of Dunkirk. An armada of vessels from large naval craft down to small civilian boats manned by volunteers swung into action. Against all expectations, in the nine days which followed, nearly 340,000 British and Allied troops were taken out. Most of their equipment was lost and the diversion of naval vessels from protecting other Allied shipping meant heavier losses in that direction. But the

F

successful evacuation was of the greatest importance to Britain both morally and materially. The lost equipment could be replaced, men could not have been.

One question which baffled the world at the time was how it was that the Germans could not prevent this evacuation. Some Germans argued that Hitler had actually allowed the British withdrawal to give the United Kingdom the chance to save face and then come to terms with Germany. This view rests on the fact that Hitler did halt the advance of German armoured columns for two days between 24 and 26 May. This decision undoubtedly gave the Allies the chance to organise some sort of defence around the evacuation base. Now we know that Hitler's order was in no sense motivated by any desire to placate the British. It was the result of Luftwaffe-Army rivalry, Hitler's own rivalry with his military men and the belief that, as the Allied forces were finished anyway, it was a good idea to regroup the Panzer units before going in for the final kill. Luftwaffe chief Hermann Göring felt the air force, a more National Socialist organisation than the army, should be given a greater share in polishing off the enemy than it had been given so far. Hitler was influenced by this intervention. General Gerd von Rundstedt, one of 12 generals promoted to field marshal in July 1940 for his activities in France, advised Hitler to halt the armoured units to give the infantry time to move up for he feared, if they were too far forward by themselves, they would be in danger of being overrun. Hitler agreed with him in his estimate of the situation. Further, he wanted to show his generals who was boss, for this view was not to the liking of some of them particularly those who hoped to be covered in glory by annihilating the British. The events at Dunkirk showed that the Nazi leadership overestimated (as have many other leaderships since) the role of air power. Their planes were not so very effective against the British Army, though it is true they were hampered some of the time by weather conditions, and they were up against R A F fighters operating from the British side of the Channel. One other factor aiding the British evacuation was that the Germans at first thought Ostend was the most important embarkation port and concentrated their efforts on bombing it.

With the bulk of the British forces out of France along with some of the French, and the rest of the French forces exposed and demoralised, the Germans made rapid advances into the interior of France. By 10 June they were over the Seine. Two days later the French government declared Paris an open city and fled to Tours. On 15 June it was on the move again. The following day the government resigned and Marshal Pétain, famous soldier of the 1914-18 war, took over the government. He immediately asked the Germans for an armistice. He also had to ask the Italians. On 11 June the Italians had attacked the staggering French in the south, no doubt in the expectation of cheap glory and spoils.

Hitler feared that if he dealt with the French too harshly their government would leave the country and attempt to fight on from one of the French colonies. This would probably have meant that the French fleet would sail for Allied ports and carry on against the relatively weak German Navy. Hitler was no doubt aware of the problems of trying to put the whole of France under German military rule. He therefore agreed to a French government continuing to rule in an unoccupied part of the country. This was roughly the south-east of the Republic, a largely agricultural area. Paris, the northern industrial region and the entire western coast were placed under German rule, though French local administration was to continue in these areas. As one would expect, French forces were to be demobilised and disarmed, their weapons and fortifications handed over in good order and the cost of the occupation was to be paid by France. More questionable was French agreement that their prisoners of war should be held captive in Germany until the end of the war, for was it not already over between the two countries? The French dishonoured their traditions by agreeing to hand over all German citizens wanted by the Gestapo. Worse still, they agreed that all Frenchmen caught resisting the Germans whether in France or anywhere else should be shot. On the vital question of the French fleet, still then in French hands, it was to be disarmed, but left under Vichy control. On 22 June 1940 the French signed the armistice agreement with Germany on the same spot where the Germans had been forced to sign in 1918. This was surely Hitler's greatest moment of triumph!

Some Frenchmen who had escaped from France were determined not to accept the authority of the pro-German 'Vichy French' government under Pétain. One of these was General Charles de Gaulle who had successfully commanded an armoured division. A day after the signing of the armistice he announced that, by agreement with the British, he was setting up a provisional National Committee to work for the recovery of national independence and to honour French alliances. The British government gave French servicemen, who did not wish to join de Gaulle, the chance to return home, but it decided on determined action against French naval vessels whose commanders intended to return them to Vichy France. When the commander of a French naval squadron at Oran, in French north Africa, refused to join the Allies or sail to a

French port in the West Indies, the British sank his ships as they lay at anchor.

OPERATION SEA LION—FAILURE OVER BRITAIN

On 16 July 1940 Hitler issued his Directive No. 16 which began with the words, ' As England, in spite of the hopelessness of her military situation, has so far shown herself unwilling to come to any compromise, I have decided to begin to prepare for, and if necessary to carry out, an invasion of England '. However, some months before the German leadership had started to think in terms of such an invasion. He had hoped that Britain would see reason and indeed on 19 July made a speech to that effect in the Reichstag, but at the same time he put in hand plans for an eventual invasion. Two days before his Reichstag speech the Army High Command ordered 13 picked divisions to places on the Channel coast for the first wave of the proposed invasion. And on the same day the Army Command completed its detailed study for a landing on the south coast of England. The main thrust was assigned to Field Marshal von Rundstedt. Within a few days the Germans expected to have landed 39 divisions by sea and two by air. The completion of Operation Sea Lion, as the invasion of Britain was code-named, would take about a month so Field Marshal Walther von Brauchitsch told Grand Admiral Raeder, head of the German Navy.

The British government and people took this invasion threat seriously and took what measures they could to prepare for it. Even before the fall of France the government decided to send out of the country all the gold in the banks. Shipments started to Canada on 24 June and by August gold and securities to the value of seven billion dollars had crossed the Atlantic—without apparent loss. Other measures included the setting up of the Local Defence Volunteers, later called the Home Guard, the establishment of a guerrilla-type organisation to operate behind enemy lines in the event of them establishing a bridgehead, and the evacuation of foreigners whose loyalty was questioned to Empire territories. Improvised fortifications were constructed in coastal and strategic areas, road signs removed and pronunciation-tests introduced for persons suspected of being enemy agents! That the situation was grim was admitted by the British Chiefs of Staff who reported at the end of May, ' Should the Germans succeed in establishing a force with its vehicles in this country, our Army forces have not got the offensive power to drive it out '. As well as their commitments at home, it should not be forgotten that the British forces had world-wide commitments.

Hitler knew the British Army must be in bad shape after the evacuation from France but he also realised that to launch a successful invasion the Wehrmacht would have to be in command of the air and the sea. He therefore took steps to bring this about, at the same time hoping that the British would be brought to their knees by bombing, blockade and radio propaganda. On 13 August the Battle of Britain began and on 17 August the Germans established an ' operational area ' around Britain, in which all ships were to be sunk without warning. In February 1940 the Germans commenced broadcasts from the New British Broadcasting Station. Others specifically aimed at Scotland, industrial workers and the ' Christian Peace Movement ' were operating from July.

The Battle of Britain began in August and lasted until the end of October 1940. There had, however, been German bombing raids before August and they continued, off and on, for most of the rest of the war. It was on 14 November, for instance, that the notorious attack which destroyed much of the centre of Coventry was launched. The German aim was to gain mastery of the air and to demoralise the population. To this end, they bombed radar stations, airbases, R A F control stations and aircraft factories. Later, in September, they turned their attention to centres of population. From the records available after the war it appears that had they concentrated their attacks entirely on the first set of objectives they might have been successful. Hitler ordered the change because of R A F raids on Berlin which started towards the end of August. These were not very effective but they boosted British morale and caused Hitler and Göring to lose face. The British raids had been ordered by Churchill in response to German bombing of the City of London on 24 August. This bombing was apparently a mistake. However, Hitler had thought before this of terror raids against Britain and from his early days had been a great believer in this kind of attack to demoralise the enemy ' masses '.

The Germans had certain obvious advantages in the Battle of Britain. Their morale was high due to their string of victories over the preceding year. Their bases were fairly close to the targets so that, by the standards of those days, they could send over heavy bomb loads. They greatly outnumbered the British in planes and crews. On the other hand, the British too enjoyed a number of factors in their favour. The British Spitfire was just that much better than the German Messerschmitt 109 fighter. Secondly, it was easier to pick up British pilots who bailed out as they were operating over home territory. Thirdly, the British were very well organised in groups and sectors and, due to the effective use of radar, squadrons could be quickly deployed where they were needed. Some would also claim that the British pilots were just that much better than their German opposite numbers but that claim is difficult to prove. Some Germans believe the opposite to be true because R A F fighter squadrons usually avoided combat with German fighters alone: being numerically weaker they were conserving their energies to deal with German bombers, a more essential task. Another reason for German defeat in the Battle of Britain was undoubtedly lack of determination on the part of Hitler. All the time he harboured the illusion that the British would crack and sue for peace. He overestimated the influence of air power in the same way that the Allies were later to do.

The fact that Britain did not crack in the summer and autumn of 1940 greatly strengthened the resolve of all those around the world who opposed Hitler. It influenced the decisions of the neutral states and helped Britain's friends in the United States. Finally, by holding out, Britain provided the base, as well as many of the men and material, for the future liberation of Western Europe.

AN EXCURSION TO THE BALKANS

One reason for Hitler's lack of decisiveness in dealing with Britain was that he had his mind on other things, on a possible attack on the Soviet Union. In July 1940—about the time of the start of the Battle of Britain—he announced to his military leaders his intention to attack Russia. The attack was to start in the following spring. If Germany could smash Russia, so Hitler believed, it could then finish off Britain for the British still counted on the Soviet Union. The invasion would begin in May 1941 and would last five months; then Russia would be smashed!

The Soviet-German agreements of 1939 had not changed much in relations between the two states. True there was increased trade, even trade in military and strategic goods—the Soviets got samples of German planes, tanks, artillery, even the plans of the *Bismarck*—and increased diplomatic activity, but the two dictators remained deeply suspicious of each other. Hitler was busy with his conquests on the field of battle, Stalin was trying to get as much as he could through diplomacy and, as far as small states were concerned, blackmail. Hitler was worried by Soviet advances in the Baltic but he needed Moscow's goodwill and strategic materials at the time and so could not counter such advances. Stalin could not be happy at the easy victories of a regime which had sworn to destroy Bolshevism. In June 1940, when Hitler had his hands full in France. Soviet troops occupied Bessarabia and North Bukovina in

Romania. Bessarabia had been seized from Russia at the end of the 1914-18 war, but Bukovina had never formed part of the Russian Empire. It was part of the Hapsburg Empire before 1919. Hitler feared the Soviets might try to take over the whole of Romania which was the main supplier of oil to Germany. Hitler managed to bring about a change in Romania in September to his own satisfaction, a pro-Nazi government being installed. German 'military advisers' then started to move into Romania. The Russians were naturally uneasy about this and about reports of German troops going to Finland. Officially these troops were on their way to Norway.

In November 1940 Soviet Foreign Minister Vyacheslav Molotov went to Berlin, at Hitler's invitation, to discuss with the Nazi leader future relations between the two countries. Both sides expressed the fears and suspicions outlined above. Molotov wanted clear agreement on specific issues rather than the vague general assurances mouthed by Hitler and his foreign secretary. Speaking to Hitler in a way that few had ever done before, Molotov demanded recognition of Soviet interests in Romania, Bulgaria and Turkey. Hitler urged the Russians to join the pact recently concluded by Germany, Italy and Japan. He claimed that the British were finished and that there would soon be pickings for all in the disintegrating British Empire. Molotov was not impressed, particularly as during his visit the R A F bombed Berlin. Later in the month Stalin made known his conditions for joining the pact with Germany, Italy and Japan. These included clear recognition that Finland, Bulgaria and the Straits, as well as the Persian and Arabian oil fields, were within the Russian sphere of influence.

We shall never know when Hitler decided irrevocably to attack the Soviet Union. We shall never know whether anything Stalin did or said influenced the decision at all. We do know, however, that shortly after Stalin informed him of his terms for joining the pact with the three totalitarian states Hitler issued Directive No. 21. This was on 18 December 1940 and was headed ' Operation Barbarossa '. In it Hitler talked of establishing ' a defence line against Asiatic Russia from a line running from the Volga River to Archangel '. This was to be achieved in a ' quick campaign ' of ' daring operations '. It was to commence in mid-May of the following year. The attack would be carried out with the assistance of Finland and Romania, and Sweden would have to be persuaded to permit the transit of German troops from Norway to Finland.

Hitler did not of course unleash his troops on the Soviet Union in May but in June 1941. What caused the delay? It resulted from the need to assist his faltering ally.

In North and East Africa the Italians suffered heavy defeats at the hands of much smaller British and Empire troops in late 1940 and early 1941. By May the British had forced the capitulation of the Italians in Abyssinia. In Greece, which had been invaded in October 1940, things were no better for the Italians. They were driven out by ill-equipped Greek troops to their base in Albania. German troops arrived in North Africa in February and quickly changed the situation. Simultaneously Hitler was preparing intervention in Greece. He had forced Hungary and Romania into the German camp in November. In March Bulgaria and Yugoslavia followed but a military coup in Belgrade reversed the position in Yugoslavia. Instead of dealing with the Greeks by an offensive through Bulgaria, Hitler now decided to finish off both Yugoslavia and Greece at one go. The German attack on Yugoslavia and Greece was launched on 6 April 1941. Yugoslavia was practically surrounded by the forces of the Berlin-Rome Axis and its troops were badly equipped. They were forced to surrender on 17 April. The Greeks, with a little British support, held out on the mainland four days longer. Anglo-Greek forces then tried to hold on to the island of Crete but were overwhelmed by superior forces and, above all, by superior airpower. But the bulk of the British troops managed to get away after inflicting heavy losses on the Germans.

By his onslaught on the Balkans, Hitler had prevented the British from getting a foothold on the European mainland, removed a threat to the, for Germany vital, Romanian oil fields, and eliminated the danger of an immediate second front after the start of the campaign in Russia.

BARBAROSSA

Hitler's plan to invade the Soviet Union must have been one of the most widely known secrets in military history. The United States State Department got the news from its legations in Bucharest and Stockholm and passed it on to Molotov. A British agent heard the news and Churchill immediately instructed the British ambassador in Moscow, Sir Stafford Cripps, to inform Stalin. This was in April. Stalin was warned by his own agents, Richard Sorge, who worked in the German Embassy in Tokyo, and the Schulze-Boysen organisation in Germany. Both these sources had reports in by March or even earlier. On 10 June a young German soldier, Communist Rudolf Richter, deserted to the Russians to give them the news. On the evening of 21 June another German soldier, Alfred Liskow of Kolberg, managed to get over to the Russians

and warn them. Finally, one hour before the invasion the German
N C O Wilhelm Schultz, a Communist mechanic from Eisenach,
reached the Soviets severely wounded but managed to get out his
warning before he died.

The rumours of the impending attack reached the world press.
The official Soviet reaction to these reports was to call them an
'obvious absurdity'. Up to the last last minute Stalin tried to placate
Hitler by diplomacy and prompt delivery of strategic goods. If Stalin
and the Communists had a completely unrealistic picture of the
other side, so, as we shall see, had Hitler, most of his generals, and
many political and military observers in all countries.

The conflagration which Hitler started in the early hours of
22 June 1941 was the most gigantic military operation in history
stretching along a 1,500-mile front. It was also, on Hitler's orders,
one of the most deliberately brutal—a result of his ideology and
aspirations in the East. Hitler and his colleagues had decided that
the Russians and the Ukrainians and the other peoples of the Soviet
Union were, like the Poles, fit only to be the slaves of the Germans.
He therefore sought to wipe out any of them who showed leadership qualities and was totally indifferent to the fate of the rest. As
he and most of his generals were completely confident of winning
an easy victory, they did not, at first, even try very much to conceal
their aims, nor were they concerned to make opportunist promises
in order to weaken resistance. Orders were issued not to treat Soviet
prisoners of war as other prisoners of war and to shoot certain
categories out of hand. The most notorious of these orders was the
Kommissarbefehl (Commissar Order) issued by the High Command
of the Armed Forces on 6 June 1941. This laid down that the
political commissars of the Red Army should be 'shot at once' as
representatives of Bolshevism. (These commissars were regular
uniformed and armed soldiers who could therefore expect to be
treated as normal P O Ws.) The German generals tried to justify this
and other such orders on the grounds that the Soviet Union had
not ratified normal international treaties which protected prisoners.
Yet the Soviet Union had requested its protecting power, Sweden,
on 17 July 1941, to notify the Germans that the Soviets would adhere
to the 4th Hague Convention of 18 October 1907 providing the
Germans did so. The Germans chose to ignore this. Finland, Italy,
Slovakia and Romania, on the other hand, let it be known that they
would respect normal international practice regarding prisoners of
war. Of nearly six million Russian troops captured by the Germans
only about one million emerged from the camps in 1945; most of
the others perished.

During the first few months of Hitler's campaign in Russia all seemed to be going well. Enormous advances were made which compared well with German successes on that front in World War I. In the areas of the U S S R acquired since August 1939 many people, who knew Stalinism but not yet Nazism, welcomed the Germans as liberators and this probably speeded their advance. So great were German victories that by the end of September Hitler was instructing the Army to prepared to demobilise some units so that the manpower could be used in industry. The Red Army, he concluded, was finished. Most Allied opinion agreed. In the early stages of the fighting many Soviet troops, when surrounded or out of ammunition or badly led, behaved just like the Poles, French, and even British, had done in similar circumstances: they surrendered in droves. Some, especially the non-Russians, deserted. But many Soviet troops resisted tenaciously even in hopeless situations. And as they recovered from the first shock and the chaos which followed, as they got battle experience and experience with new weapons the resistance grew. Most important of all, morale improved once they started to realise that even Hitler's crack units were not invincible. As early as the beginning of July, along the northern sector of the Finnish front, the s s Kampfgruppe 'Nord', with a Finnish and German Army division, suffered near disaster assaulting the Soviet stronghold at Salla. The five s s battalions employed in the attack were twice thrown back with heavy losses. As they attacked once again, the Soviets launched a counter-stroke which panicked them and sent them reeling back beyond their original lines. On this, and on the more usual occasions, when they pushed their opponents back, the Germans were suffering heavy casualties. General Franz Halder, Chief of the Army General Staff, noted in his diary on 8 October that German Army losses from the beginning of the invasion of Russia were 564,727. This was more than they had sustained on all fronts before 22 June. Generals like Halder had come to recognise, as he wrote on 11 August, 'we underestimated the strength of the Russian colossus'.

If the price was high so was the prize. By the beginning of October the Battle for Moscow had commenced. Moscow was not just the capital of a country, it was the capital of Bolshevism, it was the nerve centre of a highly centralised state, chief rail centre and a most important centre of arms production. In the autumn the German advance started to slow down. Apart from the stiff resistance the highly mechanised German forces suffered in the mud caused by the rain on the poor Russian roads. The mud changed to snow and the Russians could deal with it better than the Germans.

On 29 November the Germans of Army Group South were forced to withdraw from Rostov, the gateway to the Caucasus, suffering heavy losses. At the beginning of December Army Group North was held outside Leningrad. Outside Moscow the Germans were also held. Much of their equipment was useless in the severe weather conditions, men and animals became casualties of frostbite, supply trains became an easy target for partisans. In this situation the Soviet leaders brought up reinforcements. Some of these were poorly trained, poorly equipped, but very determined, Moscow factory workers. Many were well-trained and equipped troops brought in from Siberia. Under General Georgi Zhukov and General Ivan Koniev they went over to the offensive. Using ski and sledge troops, cavalry and massive artillery barrages, they forced the Germans back. The Wehrmacht only narrowly avoided a catastrophe similar to that of Napoleon's troops in 1812.

The day after Zhukov launched his 6 December counter-offensive, the Japanese made their surprise attack on the United States Navy at Pearl Harbor. Hitler's response to this new outbreak of hostilities was to declare war on the United States. The United States and the Soviet Union now became allies which meant not only American planes bombing Germany and American troops in action against the Germans in the West, but American supplies for the Red Army through Iran (which had been forcibly brought on to the Allied side by British and Soviet troops in August). The attack on Pearl Harbor also meant that the Japanese were too busy fighting Anglo-American-Chinese forces to attack the Soviet Union. At critical moments, therefore, Soviet troops could be moved from the east to the west.

DEFEAT IN THE DESERT

The first half of 1942 went well for the Wehrmacht. There were victories in Russia involving gigantic numbers of men and materials, and there were brilliant, but less significant in material terms, actions by General, later Field Marshal, Rommel and his Italian allies in Africa. The African successes came first.

Starting in January Erwin Rommel launched a series of daring thrusts designed to drive the British out of the Middle East, deprive them of the Suez Canal link with their empire, and link up with German forces in the Caucasus. On 20 June the strategic British fortress and port of Tobruk fell to Axis forces. Against the, as it turned out, sensible advice of the Italians, Hitler agreed to Rommel's continued advance into Egypt. At the end of June the German-Italian forces reached El Alamein in Egypt but there they were surprised by the stiff resistance put up by Commonwealth troops equipped with US supplies and occupying well-prepared positions. The British, from August led by General Montgomery, built up their forces until by mid-October they—150,000 British, Commonwealth, French and Greek forces with 1,114 tanks—were ready to do battle with the Axis. Rommel had 96,000 men and 500-600 tanks at his disposal. After 11 days of fighting the German commander decided, in defiance of orders, to try to pull back his forces. German military historians attribute Rommel's failure to the break-down of overseas supply lines, the irremediable weakness of Italian armaments, the increasing demands of the Eastern Front for Germany's remaining reserves, and the failure of the Italian fleet (in turn due to lack of fuel and air support). After taking his initial decision to withdraw Rommel hesitated on Hitler's orders. He subsequently lost most of his armour.

November was to be an equally black month for the Axis in Africa. Anglo-American forces under General Dwight Eisenhower went ashore at several points along the coast of (Vichy) French North Africa. There was little opposition, many French officers cooperating with the Allies. Hitler rushed troops to Tunisia to prevent Allied occupation and in the vain hope of expelling Eisenhower's force. The Germans were however overwhelmed. In May of 1943 the Army Group Tunisia was forced to surrender to the Allies. This surrender marked the end of the fighting in North Africa.

Even worse than the news from Africa in 1942-43 was that from Russia.

### STALINGRAD

On 2 February 1943 the last remnants of the once mighty German Sixth Army surrendered to the Russians at Stalingrad. Friedrich Paulus, commander of this army, and his staff, had already been taken into captivity on 22 January. Paulus had consistently refused Soviet demands to capitulate made after the Sixth Army was surrounded on 23 November. He refused because at first he had expected outside help. By Christmas 1942 all hope had disappeared but Paulus held on because of Hitler's order to do so, and because he (rightly) believed that by so doing he was holding down large concentrations of Soviet forces. Perhaps too he hung on because he had not decided his own fate. Hitler promoted him to field marshal on 22 January in the expectation that he would shoot himself. By continuing to resist after November the Field Marshal made inevitable the deaths of thousands of his troops in action, and the deaths of thousands more from hunger, frostbite and disease. In all about 90,000 men, led by Paulus and 24 generals, were taken prisoners. The high-ranking officers were given remarkably good treatment by the Russians, the other ranks, already weakened by their ordeal in sub-zero temperatures, suffered the long march to the camps and years of agony behind the wire. Few of them returned to Germany!

Stalingrad was a great railway centre, a key river port on the Volga and an important producer of tanks and guns. It had acquired some symbolic meaning for the supporters of the Soviet system for it was there that Stalin had defeated White guard attempts to capture it in the Russian Civil War in 1918. Then it was known as Tsaritsyn. Apparently, because of this, Hitler overestimated the psychological and ideological importance of the town for the Soviets.

The basic cause of the German failure at Stalingrad was under-estimation of Soviet military strength and morale. This was not just simply the result of ideologically-based prejudice. It was due to a failure of military intelligence and to the knowledge of the very heavy casualties sustained by the Soviet forces in the first half of 1942. After being pushed back from Moscow the Germans had regained the initiative in the spring of 1942. Hitler sought to capture the Maikop, Grosny and Baku oilfields. Wilhelm Adam, adjutant to the German Sixth Army, quotes Hitler as saying that without these sources of fuel the war was lost. In addition, by taking Sevastopol the Nazi leader intended to gain control of the Black Sea and event-ually reach Egypt by the back door. To the north, Stalingrad and Voronezh would be taken seizing industrial areas and making possible an attack on Moscow from the East. Sevastopol was under siege from December 1941. It fell in July 1942. The Germans did not reach Grosny but managed to take the wrecked fields at Maikop. In the north Voronezh was bypassed in July and panzer units pushed on to Stalingrad. Hitler had, by that time, committed the great blunder of aiming at too many objects simultaneously rather than concentrating his forces. At the beginning of the summer offensive in the south they stretched over a 800-km front. The length of this front was later greatly extended. Mounting losses forced the Germans to rely in certain key areas on Hungarian, Italian and Rumanian troops, who were poorly equipped and who had little interest in the war.

The factor which turned defeat into disaster was Hitler's order not to retreat, an order which had paid off in the previous winter when the German front was threatened with disintegration outside Moscow.

As we shall see, the battle of Stalingrad was not as decisive as was earlier believed. Still, it was important considering the size of the operation. In psychological terms it seems to have been decisive for both Germans and Russians. This was the first time in World War II that a German army had been destroyed with most of its high-ranking officers preferring life as prisoners of the ' sub-human Bolshevist-Jewish scum ' to death. It represented a severe blow to Hitler's prestige for he had claimed Stalingrad had fallen to his army and, worse still, he later promised to save the Sixth Army. Even hardened Nazis felt bitter, disappointed even stunned, by the Führer's failure to fulfil his pledge. What the Sixth Army felt towards the end was revealed years later when the last letters sent by them from Stalingrad were published. These had been confiscated at the time and analysed on the orders of the German High Command. Only 2.1 per cent of the letter-writers were positive in their attitude to the war leadership. Another 4.4 per cent had doubts and 57.1 per cent were regarded by the Wehrmacht experts as rejecting the war leadership.

### LIFE IN OCCUPIED EUROPE

By the end of 1942 National Socialist imperialism had reached the greatest extent of its expansion. Only Sweden, Switzerland, Spain, Portugal and Turkey remained precariously neutral, by making concessions to Germany, the rest of Europe lay at Hitler's feet. How did he see its future? How did he rule it?

Hitler's idea of a German Reich meant at least the Germany of 1914 with Austria and the Sudetenland added to it. This he actually carried through. He further expressed the view that the Baltic states and the Crimea would become part of the Reich. Finland would become a federated state and eventually the German-speaking part of Switzerland and Holland would be incorporated into Germany. The rest of Europe would be under German leadership and the vast areas of Poland, Ukraine and Russia would be colonies whose inhabitants would slave for Germany. Swiftly, on the heels of the Wehrmacht, came the Nazi officials who sought to make this nightmare a reality.

In the occupied East, rivalries developed between the different branches of the Nazi state, party and war machine. This hindered consistency in policy. Broadly speaking, the Nazis were most severe and reckless when they were winning, and a little less so when they were hard pressed or short of labour. Hitler's policy was to exploit these areas to the full for Germany's benefit and everything else was to be subordinated to this end. By various means he sought to destroy the educated classes of the East who were capable of resistance. Education for the subject peoples was to be reduced to the barest minimum, so were public health services. Cheap vodka, tobacco and contraceptives were to be made available to weaken resistance and keep the population down. The traditional imperialist policy of divide and rule was introduced, turning one nationality against another, one religious group against another and all against Jews and Russians. The policy of exploitation meant colossal exports of raw materials, food and manufactures to Germany at the expense of the indigenous population, reducing them to near starvation. It meant herding millions to work as forced labourers in the Reich. In December 1944 there were over two million of them at work in Germany. For most their status was little better than that of slaves. The third element in this policy was the use of extreme terror against the Eastern peoples. This was partly based on the Nazi view that they were subhuman or *Untermenschen*, partly to smash the growing resistance.

In western Europe the conduct of the Germans was somewhat better. This was particularly so in the early days of the occupation before the resistance movements were organised. Racial affinity and expediency also resulted in better treatment for countries such as Denmark and Holland. These considerations did not save them from immediate exploitation and eventual violence. The Nazis seized the gold and foreign currency holdings of these countries, charged exorbitant occupation costs, confiscated art treasures, paid for Wehrmacht supplies with near-useless paper money, and forced industrial and commercial undertakings into unequal partnerships with German concerns. These countries, like the nations of eastern Europe, were forced to provide millions of workers for the German war economy—over five million of them by the end of 1944. In addition, many of their soldiers, held as prisoners of war, were forced on to war production or farm work. On the whole, they received better treatment than those from the East though they, too, often suffered a great deal.

One of the best-known witnesses of this suffering was Dr Wilhelm Jaeger, a medical practitioner employed by the giant arms concern of Krupps. He recorded how he found French prisoners of war, slaving for Krupps, in a camp in Essen, who had been ' kept for nearly half a year in dog kennels, urinals and in old baking houses. The dog kennels were three feet high, nine feet long, six feet wide. Five men slept in each of them. The prisoners had to crawl into these kennels on all fours . . . There was no water in the camp '.

Any opposition to the occupation authorities was crushed as ruthlessly in western Europe as in the east. Potential opponents were rounded up immediately following the invasions. Later a system of concentration camps was established throughout occupied Europe. Thousands were sent to concentration camps in Germany under the *Nacht und Nebel* (Night and Fog) decree. Issued towards the end of 1941, this ordered that suspected resisters should not be tried in military courts in their own countries, which would give publicity to the resistance, but should be sent to Germany in secrecy and there isolated and possibly liquidated.

### THE FATE OF THE JEWS

The worst fate of all in Nazi-occupied Europe was that suffered by the Jews. The Polish Jews were conscripted to do forced labour by a decree of October 1939. About the same time they were required to wear a large yellow star with the word ' Jew ' on it. They were increasingly removed to ghettos. The first of these was set up at Lodz in April 1940. Later in the same year another was established in Warsaw; others followed. They were districts surrounded by walls or barbed-wire fences with their own internal administration. Their inhabitants were not allowed out except by special permission of the German authorities. They worked hard for the Germans but, in return, did not even receive subsistence-level rations. The result was death from slow starvation and disease. Into these ghettos were gradually crowded Jews from Germany and the occupied territories, the first Jews from the Reich being deported in autumn 1941. By the end of May 1943 Germany was declared ' free of Jews ', although this was not entirely correct.

With the invasion of the Soviet Union in June 1941 the anti-Jewish campaign reached a new intensity. So-called *Einsatzgruppen*, special units of s s and police, were formed to hunt and liquidate Jews, Communists, gypsies and other ' undesirable elements '. These units killed about one million people in mass shootings and by other methods.

The first camp equipped with gassing facilities was Chelmno in Poland which operated from December 1941. However, experiments with gas had been carried out at Auschwitz, set up May 1940, in the autumn of 1941. It was at the notorious Wannsee (West Berlin) conference in January 1942 that Reinhard Heydrich, on the orders of Hermann Göring, discussed with representatives of the various ministries the technical and organisational problems involved in removing the Jews to the East for liquidation. Adolf Eichmann, later executed by the Israelis as a war criminal, was present. It was at this meeting that the term ' final solution ' came to be used. In addition to Chelmno and Auschwitz, extermination camps were set up at Belzec, Sobibor, Treblinka and Maidanek. Killings of Jews and others continued in the many other camps, of which in April 1944 there were 20 main camps and 165 subsidiary ones. Heinrich Himmler, as head of the R S H A or Reich Security Main Office, was in charge of the camp system and the liquidations. Heydrich was, until assassinated by Czech patriots in 1942, his deputy. Though the figure of six million Jews exterminated is the one most widely quoted, we do not know exactly how many perished. It could have been less—or more—than that number. Rudolf Höss, commandant at Auschwitz until December 1943, later admitted that, during his service at this camp, ' at least ' two and a half million people were executed, and that a further half a million died from hunger and disease. Not all of these were Jews but that was in just one (the largest) camp.

Soon, due to enormous German losses on the Eastern Front, the extermination programme was competing for Jews with the forced labour requirements of the war economy, including the S S enterprises. Auschwitz became, not only the greatest ' factory of death ', but also the biggest employer of forced labour. How these ' lucky ' Jews were treated was once again recorded by Dr Jaeger. He was talking about a visit to a camp for Jewish women working for Krupps: ' I found these females suffering from open festering wounds and other diseases . . . There were no medical supplies . . . They had no shoes . . . The sole clothing of each consisted of a sack with holes for their arms and head. Their hair was shorn . . . The amount of food in the camp was extremely meagre and of very poor quality. One could not enter the barracks without being attacked by fleas . . .'

The question is often asked to what extent did the German people know of the bestialities of the Nazi system. Many Germans have denied all knowledge of the atrocities. If one examines the evidence impartially one is forced to conclude that any German had the means to know a good deal about the brutalities of Nazism but that few would have known the full horrors. No secret was made in 1933 of the widespread arrests of Communists and Social Democrats and later of Jews and others. No secret was made of the existence of the concentration camps. The notorious Nuremberg Race Laws were not secret and in many towns the populace saw the ill-treatment of Jews and sometimes the columns of prisoners on their way to the camps. In 1938 all Germany knew about the smashing up of the Jewish businesses, synagogues and homes. True, the Germans were told that the camps were there to re-educate political and other criminals. But did they not ask themselves why workmates, neigh-

bours and friends had disappeared? Why many died in these
' re-education camps '? Why the few who were released were afraid
of talking about their experiences? During the war millions of
Germans served on the Eastern Front: they could not help but see
what the ' New Order' meant in the countries concerned. Units of
the Wehrmacht took part in the shooting of hostages on all fronts.
The Germans who stayed at home saw the millions of slave labourers
clearing away rubble or labouring in the factories and on the farms.
Did they never ask themselves why these prisoners were in such a
pitiful condition? On the other hand, few Germans could have
known that their government was systematically exterminating
millions of Jews and the Nazi authorities tried to cover up the scale
of deaths in the camps. Any German with a minimum of thought
and feeling must have been aware that the Nazi system was barbaric.
Once they came to this conclusion, could they have done much
about it? This is a much more difficult question to answer. Given
the nature of the regime, resistance needed the opportunity, which
many did not have, and more courage than it is perhaps right to
demand of ordinary people. A few found both the opportunity and
the courage, though some of these did not realise fully the consequence of getting caught.

### THE GERMAN RESISTANCE

The first Aryan German to be executed for wartime resistance was
a communist working in the Junker factory in Dachau. He—his
name is unknown—refused to do air-raid protection work, was
reported by the works police, arrested and sent to the Gestapo in
Berlin. Himmler ordered his immediate execution. This was carried
out in Sachsenhausen concentration camp. Although most people
have heard of the July 1944 bomb plot against Hitler, the unknown
German worker is more typical of the German resistance than are
the officers of the July plot. The German workers, Communists and
Social Democrats who opposed Hitler were not attempting any
spectacular coup by assassination. They mainly sought to influence
their fellow Germans by leaflets, slogans on walls and secret
discussions. Sometimes they dared to ' go slow ' or even strike.
After the war started there were acts of industrial sabotage, help
for prisoners of war and slave workers. Among them were Bernhard
Bästlein, Franz Jacob and Theodor Neubauer who succeeded in
building up a Communist network in about a dozen towns. They
all died at the hands of the Gestapo, in 1944-45. Some German
workers found ways of resisting the Nazis in the armed forces. One
of these was Kurt Hälker who, as a member of a three-man group

in the H Q of the German Navy in Paris, provided the French resistance with arms and information and later joined them to use their weapons against the Nazis. Hälker survived to be able to tell his story to the author. Less fortunate was a man about whom we know little but who deserves mention. Anton Schmidt's name came up at the Eichmann trial in 1961. He was a Wehrmacht N C O, probably not a member of a group or party, who on the Eastern Front helped Jews to escape. We do not know what happened to him but some of those he helped reached safety and recalled his name for posterity.

In a separate category on the Left were the Communists who were prepared to carry out espionage for the U S S R as a means of defeating Nazi Germany. There was the group known as *Die Rote Kapelle* led by the Luftwaffe lieutenant Harro Schulze-Boysen and there was Dr Richard Sorge's group operating from the German embassy in Tokyo. Most of the members of these groups perished after doing valuable work for the Soviet Union. Finally, working with the Russians, were the officers and men who took part in the anti-Nazi ' Free Germany ' Committee. Among these the remnants of the Sixth Army were strongly represented.

Many more Germans than we in the past gave credit for, opposed the Nazis. And, like the Munich lawyer, Edgar J. Jung, and his ' Young Conservatives ', and the ill-fated Munich students Sophie and Hans Scholl, they were by no means always on the Left. That their numbers were considerable we know from the Gestapo files. In August 1942, for instance, 1,761 Germans were arrested for downing tools, 1,583 for illegal contact with foreign workers or prisoners of war. Another 1,210 more detained as ' Marxists ', 1,267 as ' reactionaries ' and 1,007 as ' resisters '. These were just the main categories of Germans arrested for political matters.

Despite the courage of the many groups and individual resisters the July plotters remain the most significant of the German opponents of Hitler.

The plot of 20 July 1944 was an attempt to kill Hitler and stage a military *coup d'état*. At its centre were military men who were in touch with a number of prominent civilians, the latter were to help form a government after the coup. The civilians included the Social Democrats Dr Julius Leber, who was to be Minister of Interior, Wilhelm Leuschner, Vice-Chancellor, Dr Theo Haubach, Information, and the Christian trade unionists Jakob Kaiser, deputy to Leuschner and Bernhard Letterhaus, Ministry of Reconstruction. The Conservative, former Mayor of Leipzig, Carl Goerdeler, was to be Chancellor and Ulrich von Hassell, former Ambassador to Italy, was to become Foreign Minister. A Catholic lawyer, Dr Josef Wirmer, was to take over Justice, Paul Lejeune-Jung, former Reichstag member, was designated Economics Minister. The provisional Head of State in this shadow regime was General Ludwig Beck. With the exception of Kaiser all the above-listed died in the purge which followed the failure of the plot.

The man who seems to have been the initiator of the July plot was Major-General Henning von Tresckow, Chief of Staff in Central Army Group on the Eastern Front. He was in contact with Goerdeler and other civilian and military opponents of Hitler. Tresckow, descended from a line of Prussian soldiers, had tried for some time to win over fellow officers for a coup. He had not been very successful. Many officers owed their positions to the rapid expansion of the forces carried through by Hitler. Their gratitude to him was strengthened by an oath of personal loyalty and by the Führer's brilliant victories up to the end of 1942. The Allied demand for unconditional surrender was a further factor helping to still the consciences of those shocked by the excesses of the Nazi regime. However, had they overthrown Hitler in 1943, by which time it was clear Germany had lost the war, they must have realised they could have got some kind of terms. At the very minimum they would have saved their people from the horrors of continued aerial bombardment, saved them from the horrors of occupation by undisciplined, angry and battle-weary troops, and saved the lives of their soldiers.

After many disappointments, Tresckow gained the active cooperation of a small group of important officers and the passive support of some others. Under the code-name 'Valkyrie' he worked out a plan for the military occupation of Berlin by the rebels. This was completed with the aid of Graf Claus Schenk Stauffenberg, a 37-year-old Wehrmacht colonel, who, after being severely wounded in Africa, became Chief of Staff in the supply section at the HQ of the Reserve Army in Berlin. Stauffenberg was for executing a coup as soon as possible. He realised that delay could only worsen Germany's position. He was aware too that the Gestapo was closing in on the plotters. Because of his position he was able to attend conferences with Hitler. He volunteered to make a bomb attempt on Hitler's life himself. Between 11 July and 20 July Stauffenberg prepared three attempts on Hitler's life. The first two, one of which might have succeeded, he abandoned. Tension mounted as his comrades in Berlin waited for news.

Rumours started circulating in Berlin, the result of vague messages from Hitler's HQ at Rastenburg. General Friedrich

Olbricht, Head of Supplies for the Reserve Army, chief military conspirator in Berlin in the absence of Stauffenberg, started the ' Valkyrie ' (Walküre) operation by issuing orders in the name of General Fromm. Friedrich Fromm was Commander of the Reserve Army. By the time Stauffenberg and Olbricht arrived at his office Fromm had heard that Hitler was not dead. Stauffenberg's bomb had exploded, killing or wounding several of those present. It might have killed the Nazi leader had not the case, in which it had been placed, been moved when Stauffenberg made his escape. Fromm refused to have anything to do with the attempted coup and was arrested by the conspirators. The rebels, including Beck, now with Stauffenberg, failed to take decisive action to control Berlin. They did not fortify themselves in their H Q, nor did they seize the radio station, telecommunications centres, Gestapo headquarters or airfields. They did not bring into action one of the few units they were sure of—the paramilitary police under S S General Graf Heinrich Wolf von Helldorf, a fellow conspirator. Their lack of resolve gave the only leading Nazi still in Berlin, Joseph Goebbels, Minister of Propaganda, a chance to act.

Goebbels showed considerable initiative. He knew from Rastenburg that Hitler was alive. He broadcast a message announcing this over the radio. He alerted Hitler's S S bodyguards stationed five miles from the centre of Berlin. He also got the guard's battalion led by National Socialist Major Otto Ernst Remer to move against the plotters in their Bendlerstrasse H Q. This exposed another weakness of Stauffenberg's men: they did not check the reliability of key officers *before* the coup. Remer's men were supposed to be taking over key points in Berlin for the conspirators.

As it became clear that Hitler was not dead and that the rebels did not even control Berlin, doubtful officers, such as Field Marshal Günther von Kluge, Commander-in-Chief West (France), and General Helldorf, dissociated themselves from the coup. This did not save them. Late on that evening of 20 July officers loyal to Hitler on duty at Bendlerstrasse, who had said little during the day but had smuggled in automatic weapons, rounded up Beck, Olbricht, Stauffenberg and others. They released Fromm who allowed Beck to shoot himself and executed the others the same night. He hoped to redeem himself in Hitler's eyes. Fromm was eventually executed by the Nazis.

The plot to save Germany had failed. The courage and patriotism of the rebels did not make up for their lack of competence and ruthlessness. Even so, they might have succeeded had not the great majority of Wehrmacht officers remained loyal to Hitler.

### THE BREAK-UP OF THE ROME-BERLIN AXIS

One of the first jobs Hitler had to do immediately after the bomb explosion at Rastenburg was to receive Benito Mussolini, the Italian dictator. One can imagine both dictators thinking that perhaps, after all, ' Providence ' had saved them for a higher purpose. Mussolini had had an escape which was almost as improbable as Hitler's.

Following up their successes in North Africa the Allies had invaded Sicily in June 1943. In the face of mass strikes in the industrial centres and imminent Allied invasion, the King of Italy and a majority of the Grand Council of the Fascist Party decided to get rid of Mussolini. They held the former dictator in custody and sought a separate peace with the Allies. An armistice was signed on 3 September and on the same day Allied troops landed in Southern Italy. The German forces in Italy were in a critical position and because of a Soviet offensive on the Eastern Front it was difficult to send many reinforcements. Whatever the reasons, the Allies did not exploit the opportunities open to them. The result was that Field Marshal Albert Kesselring, German Commander-in-Chief in Italy, was able to occupy two-thirds of the country, including the important industrial areas, and to disarm substantial Italian forces.

Not all the Italians were prepared to be disarmed. The Acqui Division stationed on the Greek island of Kefallinia were not. They were attacked and eventually overpowered. Then the 900 Italian prisoners were shot down in cold blood. This, and similar massacres, were carried through by the Wehrmacht, thus exploding the myth that only the s s committed war crimes. Both organisations were later responsible for crimes against Italian civilians. The Italian Navy avoided the fate of the Army and, together with the king and his government, made for Allied-held areas.

Even more dramatic than the occupation of Italy was the remarkable rescue of Mussolini by s s glider troops from a remote mountaintop hotel. The Duce was then set up as a head of the ' Italian Social Republic ' in the North. He became a German puppet and was eventually shot by Italian partisans who resisted the Germans and Italian Fascists.

### OPERATION OVERLORD

Urged on by Stalin and with growing confidence gained from the landings in North Africa and Italy, the Allies turned their attention to the invasion of north-west Europe. Britain became increasingly a vast arsenal as more and more American men and material evaded the German submarines. In 1942 the Germans had been sinking shipping faster than the Allies could replace it. In 1943 however the balance shifted very much in favour of the Allies, thanks to long-range aircraft carriers and radar-equipped vessels.

The Western Allies could also be reasonably confident because they knew the Germans could not draw on reserves from elsewhere. Since Stalingrad the Russians had taken an increasingly heavy toll of Germans. In July 1943 Hitler had launched his last great Eastern offensive. Seventeen panzer divisions and half a million men were flung against the Soviets at Kursk. This battle proved to be far more costly and far more decisive than Stalingrad. Now it was the Russians' turn to go over to the offensive, which they kept up to the end of the war. By the end of 1943 they were nearing the Polish and Romanian frontiers.

Despite the apparently good position of the Allies in June 1944 their invasion was faced with dangers which could have proved disastrous. There were the mine-fields to get through. There were the submarines. At key points along the coast there were German heavy naval guns. There was the weather to contend with: bad weather could have made landing men hazardous and landing heavy equipment even more so. The minefields, submarines and guns did not prove to be very dangerous. The weather was a more effective opponent. In the first month after D-day, the Allies lost 261 vessels destroyed or damaged by enemy action, as against 606 by the weather. A sudden gale, contrary to all meteorlogical experience, blew from 19 to 23 June, destroying landing craft and other vessels. In some respects too, the Allied forces were faced with superior weapons. The British Churchill and the American Sherman tanks were inferior to the German Tigers and Panthers. The quality of the German weapons did not make up for their lack of quantity. Nor did the determination of the s s units make up for their lack of numbers and reserves. From 6 June, the day of the landings, to 23 July, the Germans lost 2,722 officers and 110,357 non-commissioned officers and men, of whom no more than 10,078 had been replaced. Allied losses for the same period were around 117,000. All of them were replaced. Other German disadvantages were lack of air support, which for one thing impeded such reserves as were available due to the destruction of the railways, limited naval power, the growing resistance of the French underground, and lack of a clear plan of defence.

Once Eisenhower and Montgomery had successfully got their troops ashore on the Normandy coast it was only a matter of time before they broke out of the beachhead. By 25 August Paris was taken intact by the Americans and Free French. Some credit for this must go to the German commander General von Choltitz, who refused to obey Hitler's orders to blow up all the bridges and destroy the city. Less than two weeks later Brussels, the Belgian capital, was liberated by British troops and by 11 September the Americans had reached the German frontier. In the same month the Soviets occupied Sofia and reached armistice agreements with Bulgaria, Finland and Romania. The Germans also evacuated Estonia.

In 1944 the Nazis proved that they could be as ruthless as ever and that they were not yet beaten. In the East they crushed a rising of the Warsaw underground with the utmost vigour, after which, on Hitler's orders, the city was razed to the ground. The members of the Polish Home Army met the same fate as the Jewish resisters who, practically unarmed, had gone down fighting a year before rather than be deported like sheep to the slaughter house. The destruction of Warsaw made little difference to the military situation on the Eastern Front.

In the West the Germans virtually annihilated an Allied airborne expedition dropped at Arnhem and Nijmegen in Holland near the German frontier. It was hoped that this force would seize and hold important bridges across the lower Rhine until the main units arrived to outflank the German Siegfried Line. Failure to act on intelligence reports indicating heavy German troop concentrations, including two s s panzer divisions, led to disaster.

It was in the West that Hitler made his last big offensive of the war in the ' Battle of the Bulge '. His aim was, at a minimum, to gain time during which, as he thought, the Western Allies would fall out with the Russians and look for a negotiated settlement with Germany. His maximum aim was to knock the Allies off balance by a sharp, surprise thrust and drive them into the sea, again achieving the same political result. This was not as unrealistic as it sounded. After all, there were differences between the Soviets and the West, and Hitler had succeeded with similar offensives in 1940 and 1941. The Nazi leader greatly overrated his own strength and underestimated that of the Allies. Arnhem had given the Germans some renewed confidence and the Allies appeared to be in difficulties with their supply situation still being largely dependent on the port of Cherbourg. Realising that the enemy had overwhelming air superiority, Hitler planned the blow for December when the weather would interfere with aerial operations. He also sought to create the maximum confusion by using Germans dressed in American uniforms and equipped with American arms. To some extent this tactic succeeded. But many of the luckless Germans who later fell into American hands were shot, as was permitted under International Law.

It was on 15 December that the Germans attacked on a 70 mile front through Ardennes Forest. The Allies were certainly taken by surprise and initially the Germans had some success. American positions were overrun and the front appeared to be disintegrating. Yet the key communications town of Bastogne held against repeated German attacks and demands for its surrender. This gave the Americans time to regroup their forces. The weather which had been kind to the Germans changed and they soon felt the full force of the mighty Allied air fleets against which they were virtually powerless. Within a month the Germans had been driven back to their starting point losing some 120,000 men. The offensive had achieved nothing and had robbed Hitler of his last reserves so desperately needed on the Eastern Front. Like the other German offensives this one produced its atrocities. The most widely known of these involved the shooting of at least 71 unarmed American prisoners by the 1st S S Panzer Division near Malmédy.

### ' TERROR AND WANTON DESTRUCTION '

As mentioned above, Allied air superiority was of great importance in the success of the Normandy landings and in the battle of the Bulge. But this air superiority over the battle fields was only one aspect of the air war. Another was Allied attacks on targets within the Reich. As early as May 1940 93 R A F aircraft attacked industrial targets in the Ruhr and on 25 August the R A F made its first raid on Berlin. These first raids were more important as morale-boosters to the hard-pressed British than serious military operations. The early raids had been against key targets and had to be abandoned because of German air defences and, in the case of night raids, because of the inaccuracy of night bombing. This led in the course of 1941 to a shift of emphasis to general area bombing of the largest German towns. Though new inventions made precision bombing more feasible and daring precision attacks were mounted, the area of offensive reached devastating proportions after March 1943. One of the outstanding examples of these was the round-the-clock attack on Hamburg by 3,000 bombers between 24 July and 3 August 1943, causing great devastation and loss of life. Such raids were controversial. It was one thing to destroy aircraft and tank factories, blow up synthetic oil plants, blast dams and interrupt communications. It was quite another deliberately to destroy large residential areas, killing thousands of civilians. The idea was to ' bring home to the civilian population of Germany the horrors of war ', as one British M P put it to Sir Archibald Sinclair, Secretary of State for Air, who was ' in complete agreement ' with this formulation. Such attacks were opposed by an informed minority, men like the Bishop of Chichester, Dr Bell, and the Marquess of Salisbury. The majority of British people no doubt felt that the raids were a legitimate form of warfare against a foe who had introduced it, and who was known to be committing crimes against civilians under German occupation.

The most controversial of these attacks was that on Dresden in February 1945. Sir Arthur Harris, Commander-in-Chief of Bomber Command, ordered just over 800 aircraft to Dresden on 13 February 1945. In daylight on the next day 400 bombers of the U S Eighth Air Force took up the attack. Third and fourth attacks of 200 and 400 bombers finished off the destruction of this once beautiful town in central Germany. Churchill, putting it mildly, wrote in a memo of 28 March that the attack ' remains a serious query against the conduct of Allied bombing ', and implied it was an act of ' terror and wanton destruction '. It has never been established why the attack was made. In general the aim was to support the Russians by hindering the retreat of the Germans, causing chaos and depriving the Nazis of an almost intact city to which to evacuate their administration. The evidence seems to indicate that the Russians did not ask for the raid. In fact they were trying to restrict Allied bombing by establishing a ' bombline ' or ' air frontier '. They realised, if the bombing went on, they would inherit a desert. In the above-mentioned memo Churchill made the same point.

The military value of these raids is now in doubt. The German population did not crack, neither did the Wehrmacht. Production of war equipment was actually rising at the height of the bombing. Nevertheless the raids did tie up large numbers of German planes and men who otherwise might have been used against Allied ground forces and especially against the Soviets. The bombing of German fuel supplies was more effective as shortage of fuel did bring panzer units to a halt in the Ardennes offensive and in the battles on the Eastern Front in 1944-45.

THE FALL OF BERLIN

With the failure of the Ardennes offensive by February 1945 the end of the Third Reich came rapidly. Hitler was himself partly to blame for this. He might have withdrawn his still considerable forces from Northern Italy, Denmark, Holland and Norway, and concentrated them in the Reich. He might have attempted to defend the mountainous region of southern Germany and Austria—the so-called

National Redoubt—where the Nazis had built some fortifications. Instead he left his forces widely scattered. For the Ardennes offensive he had weakened the Eastern Front. After its failure he transferred units to the East. The armies of the Western Powers swarmed into Germany. Highly mechanised, they advanced at tremendous speed. They were anxious to get to Berlin. But they were not to head in that direction.

General Dwight Eisenhower thought in purely military terms. He felt that Berlin was not an important military objective. More important were the north German ports, and with their capture the isolation of German forces in Norway and Denmark, and the seizure of the 'National Redoubt'. Allied intelligence believed the Nazis would make a last stand in the mountainous area of south Germany and Austria—the so-called 'National Redoubt'. Bernard Montgomery, the British commander, wanted, for personal, patriotic, psychological and political reasons, to give priority to getting to Berlin. He, and Churchill, were convinced that once Berlin, the heart of the Reich, fell, German resistance would crumble. Montgomery further believed that it would make it easier to get on with the Russians if they were deprived of the prestige of capturing Berlin. Eisenhower feared the cost in casualties would be high, too high a price to pay for Berlin especially as it had already been decided that the area around Berlin was to be in the Soviet Zone, and that the city itself would be under joint allied occupation. When Eisenhower made his decision the Soviets were nearer Berlin than Western forces, and appeared poised to take it at any moment. After the war some writers and public figures criticised the Supreme Commander's decision claiming that had the West got to Berlin first, difficulties with the Russians would have been avoided. But at the time the Soviets were still regarded as allies, and it was believed they would be needed to help finish off the Japanese (no one knew then how effective the A-bomb was to be).

It was left to the Soviets then to take Berlin. They had halted on the Oder, the last main obstacle before the capital, and had been advancing in the south in Czechoslovakia and Austria. On 16 April 1945 they opened their last great offensive of the war against Hitler's Reich. The Soviet attack was preceded by what was the greatest artillery barrage of World War II. The Soviet force was opposed by Army Group Vistula under the command of General Gotthard Heinrici. Heinrici's men were the odds and ends of the once proud Wehrmacht: Luftwaffe personnel, administrative troops, police turned into infantry, units of the Volkssturm or Home Guard made up of old men and boys. There were soldiers who were on convalescent leave and those previously relieved of military service on health grounds. The whole army was strengthened by the remnants of the s s. It was welded together by fear—fear of what the Russians would do, fear induced by propaganda or knowledge of what the Germans had done in Russia, or what the Russians had done in areas they had already overrun. Those not impressed by such things were usually persuaded to remain by the sight of Wehrmacht officers and men hanging from lamp-posts—executed by the s s for alleged desertion.

The desperate courage of the Germans could not save Berlin from the reckless courage of the Soviets, from the armies of Marshal Georgi Zhukov and Marshal Ivan Koniev. Within days Soviet troops were nearing the centre of the city.

In the Nazi-held prisons s s murder squads were reeking their last vengeance on the prisoners still in their custody, July plotters, Communists, Social Democrats, deserters, those simply caught without papers, those who had uttered ' defeatist ' sentiments, and many others besides. Hitler and Goebbels, the Gauleiter of Berlin as well as Propaganda Minister, had refused to evacuate the population, who had to spend days, practically without food or water, in cellars, shelters and the Berlin Underground. For some these havens became their tombs. Whether on Hitler's orders or on their own initiative s s men blew up a tunnel running under an arm of the river Spree and the Landwehr canal. This was a rail link with four hospital trains and many Berliners sheltering in it. Many drowned. Hitler grew indifferent to the fate of his people and ordered a ' scorched earth ' policy. He had relied on ' wonder weapons ', such as the v1 and v2 rockets fired at London, from June 1944 to early 1945. Then he had expected a split in the alliance against him. All hope finally faded once it was clear that the death of President Roosevelt, on 12 April 1945, would not lead to a break-up of the Anglo-American-Soviet alliance. In these circumstances he resolved to kill himself. This he did together with his new wife Eva Braun on 30 April.

Hitler left Admiral Karl Dönitz at Flensburg, as President and Joseph Goebbels, in the Berlin Bunker, as Reich Chancellor. Himmler, who might have been given one of these posts, had deeply wounded Hitler by negotiating with Allied representatives behind the Führer's back. They did not respond. One of the first acts of Goebbels as Chancellor was to attempt the same with the Soviets. They were not interested and Goebbels, together with his wife and children, followed Hitler's example. Himmler killed himself shortly after his capture by the British. Göring was taken by the Americans and poisoned himself after being sentenced to death at the Nurem-

berg Trials. Not all the Nazis saw the end of the Third Reich as
their end. Martin Bormann, Hitler's deputy in the N S D A P, left the
Bunker in an attempt to escape, and, though some believe him dead,
is still being sought today. General Heinrici lived to tell, in peaceful
retirement, of the last days in Berlin. Nor need Goebbels have
sacrificed his family. Göring's and Hess' families spent the postwar
years in comfortable obscurity in West Germany.

The fate of the Berliners was a hard one. After years of bombing
and days of shelling they faced the horrors of collapse and conquest.
Many Soviet soldiers considered they had the right to plunder and
rape in revenge for Nazi bestialities in the Soviet Union. In the
closing stages of the campaign the Soviet armies had been aug-
mented by released P O ws who quite naturally hated the Germans.
The Soviet armies also contained many peasants who were astonished
to see the wonders of the big city and Asiatic troops, some of
whom had standards different from those of Europeans. Thousands
of German women committed suicide to avoid falling into Soviet
hands; some, at least, of the Nazis did the same. The overwhelming
majority did not. They survived and were to be surprised how
quickly things improved.

The last act of the Third Reich was the formal capitulation of
its forces to the Western Allies by General Alfred Jodl at Reims
on 7 May and by Field Marshal Wilhelm Keitel on the following
day to the Soviets in Berlin. Both signatories were later hanged at
Nuremberg for their war crimes.

# 6    Germany under Occupation

Having defeated and occupied Germany the Allies had to decide what to do with it. At several important wartime meetings the Allied leaders had discussed the matter. Their views changed somewhat according to the military and international situations, the venue and so on. They had to decide on the new Germany's frontiers, on the form the occupation would take, on the compensation Germany should pay, on the political future of Germany, the type of state or states it should construct, and the best means of preventing a recrudescence of Nazism, militarism, or the kind of nationalism which could endanger peace.

Meeting at Yalta, in the Crimea, in February 1945, Stalin, Roosevelt and Churchill agreed that 'the Eastern frontier of Poland should follow the Curzon Line . . . They recognise that Poland must receive substantial accessions of territory in the North and West . . . the final delineation of the Western frontier of Poland should thereafter await the Peace Conference'. In other words they were recognising the Soviet Union's acquisitions from Poland in 1939, offering Poland German territory in the west and in the north, East Prussia. The Western leaders lost some of their enthusiasm for Polish expansion at Germany's expense as it became clear that postwar Poland would be Soviet-orientated.

At the Potsdam conference in August 1945 the Anglo-Americans found themselves faced with a *fait accompli* by the Russians who had handed over to the Poles all the lands up to the Oder-Neisse Line. The conference decided to place all 'former German territories' east of a line running from 'the Baltic Sea immediately west of Swinemünde, and thence along the Oder River to the confluence of the western Neisse River and along the western Neisse to the Czechoslovak frontier, including that portion of East Prussia not placed under the administration of' the Soviet Union, 'under the administration of the Polish State'. This was 'pending the final determination of Poland's western frontier'. By this statement the Western Powers were recognising *de facto* Poland's new frontier with Germany even though, in later years, due to the Cold War, they and the West Germans were to emphasise the words 'pending the final determination '. But by agreeing that ' the transfer to Germany of German populations, or elements thereof, remaining in Poland, Czechoslovakia and Hungary, will have to be undertaken ', the Western Powers were making it very difficult to argue in favour of a new revision of Germany's frontiers at Poland's expense. With the loss of the Oder-Neisse territories the Germans forfeited 24 per cent of the entire area of 1937 Germany. The conferences did not deal with Germany's western frontiers. The re-establishment of Austrian independence had been declared an Allied aim by the foreign ministers of the Soviet Union, Britain and the U S A in Moscow on 1 November 1943.

In an agreement of 12 September 1944, signed in London, Britain, U S A and the Soviet Union agreed that the Germany of 31 December 1937 should be divided into three occupation zones, an eastern, a north-western and a south-western. Berlin would be divided in a similar way and would be ruled by an Inter-Allied Commandatura. The Russians would receive the eastern zone but it was not decided, due to Anglo-U S rivalry, which zones the two Western Powers would receive. This matter was cleared up by an agreement of 14 November under which Britain was assigned the north-west and the U S the south-west. On the same day the three powers decided Germany would be ruled by an Allied Central Council. They also made provision for a French zone to be carved from the Anglo-U S zones. It was later agreed, against some opposition from Stalin, to give France a place on the Central Council.

The Yalta communiqué recognised Germany's obligation to pay compensation to the Allied Nations. The nations to receive priority treatment would be those ' which have borne the main burden of the war, have suffered the heaviest losses and have organised victory over the enemy '. Reparations could be exacted from ' the national wealth '—equipment, machine-tools, ships, rolling stock, investments abroad, etc—from ' annual deliveries of goods from current productions ' or by ' use of German labour '. Potsdam went into greater detail about reparations. It laid down that the U S S R and Poland were to receive their share from the Soviet Zone and from German foreign investments, and the Anglo-Americans and other nations from the Western Zones and German foreign investments. The conference further granted the Soviet Union the right to substantial reparations, partly in exchange for raw materials and food, from the remaining intact steel, chemical and machine-making plant, in the Western Zones.

What kind of political future could the German people expect? The Potsdam communiqué assured them that ' it is not the intention of the Allies to destroy or enslave the German people. The Allies want to give the German people the chance to prepare itself to rebuild its life on a democratic and peaceful basis '. Once it had achieved this Germany would once again be able to take its place among the nations. Potsdam implied a united Germany, except for the territories east of the Oder-Neisse Line, in that it spoke of the economic unity of Germany, equal treatment for all Germans, and the setting up of ' a few, important, central German administrative departments '. This was somewhat in contrast to earlier discussions of the ' Big Three '. They had toyed with various schemes for the division of Germany into several states. The most controversial of these was that advocated by U S Secretary of the Treasury, Henry Morgenthau. He wanted boundaries to the east similar, but not as favourable to Poland, as those which came into existence in 1945. Secondly, he wanted the internationalisation of the Ruhr and the Kiel Canal area. Thirdly, France should get the Saar and the adjacent territories bounded by the Rhine and the Moselle Rivers. Finally, he advocated the establishment of a North German state including much of old Prussia, Saxony and Thuringia, and a South German state comprising Bavaria, Wuerttemberg, Baden and some smaller areas. The plan also demanded that the Ruhr ' should not only be stripped of all presently existing industries but so weakened and controlled that it can not in the foreseeable future become an industrial area '. Morgenthau's proposals never became official policy despite Churchill's and Roosevelt's signatures on the plan at the Quebec Conference in September 1944. The plan did though influence future policy towards Germany.

How did the Allied leaders intend to, in the words of Potsdam, ' assure that Germany never again will threaten her neighbours or the peace of the world '? By complete ' disarmament and demilitaris- ation of Germany and elimination or control of all German industry that could be used for military production '. To this end all German military, semi-military organisations, even veterans' organisations ' shall be completely and finally abolished '. All Nazi organisations were dissolved, all Nazi or militarist propaganda banned, all Nazi- inspired laws abolished, all war criminals brought to justice. Further, all Nazi members ' who have been more than nominal participants in its activities and all other persons hostile to Allied purposes shall be removed from public and semi-public office and from positions of responsibility in important private undertakings '. On the positive side, German education and the judicial system, administration and local government were to be reconstructed according to democratic principles. Democratic parties were to be encouraged and, ' Subject to the necessity for maintaining military security, freedom of speech, press and religion . . . [and] . . . the formation of free trade unions shall be permitted '. The Germans were allowed ' average living standards not exceeding the average of the standards of living of European countries ' (excluding the U K and the U S S R).

## ' IN DARKEST GERMANY '

Those Germans who had the time, energy or interest to read the text of the Potsdam agreement might have thought the terms could have been a lot worse, hard though they were in certain respects. Most Germans were concerned with the struggle for personal survival. But most ordinary German manual and office workers, farmers, housewives and pensioners were not afraid of being classed as ' more than nominal participants ' in Nazi organisations. Their struggle for survival was concerned with homes, food, jobs and keeping their families together. In the Germany west of the Oder-Neisse Line 20 per cent of all homes had been destroyed. This was made worse by the fact that certain key towns—Berlin, Cologne, Dortmund, Dresden, Düsseldorf, Essen, Hamburg, Magdeburg, Stuttgart, among them—were more than 50 per cent destroyed. In addition, homes had to be found for the millions of Germans pouring in from Eastern Europe. Germany had a housing problem before the war started. In 1939 there was a shortage of about one million homes. In 1948-49 West Germany alone had a shortage of five million homes. The poorer sections of the population were hit harder than the rest. It was the central districts of Berlin, Dresden and Hamburg which had been so heavily bombed rather than the outer, middle-class, suburbs. The problem was increased by the movement of wartime evacuees back to their former places of residence. Some middle class people lost their homes, in most cases temporarily, to the occupation forces.

The Germans had lived well for most of the war. Food and loot had been available from the occupied territories, and the German economy had not operated as a total war economy for considerable periods between 1939-45. In the last months of the war the situation changed. After the end of hostilities the Germans learned what many Europeans had already learned—what it feels like to be hungry. Production of agricultural products went down. The region which became the Anglo-U S Zone produced, on average, 16.1 million tons of potatoes in the years 1935-38, in 1945 only 12.3 million tons and in 1946 no more than 11.2 million tons. The respective figures for rye, in million tons, were: 2.7; 1.5 and 1.7. The wheat harvest fell in these years from 2.2 million tons to 1.3 millions. Milk pro-

H

duction dropped from 12.9 million tons in 1935-38 to 7.4 millions in 1947. Meat and butter supplies were also greatly reduced. Yet in this area there were 4.3 million more people to feed! The situation was worst in the British Zone which was predominantly industrial. Britain was forced to buy wheat in North America and then export it to the British Zone. In his book *In Darkest Germany*, Victor Gollancz, the British Left-wing Jewish publisher, showed great compassion towards the Germans and revealed their plight. He found that in Cologne only 11.7 per cent of children between 6 and 12 years old had completely normal weights, 29.5 per cent were definitely below normal. Gollancz found a similar situation in other towns in the British Zone. Though conditions were bad in Germany it is as well to remember that they were also bad in neighbouring Holland, not very good in the towns of France and Italy, and extremely bad in Poland, the western U S S R, Yugoslavia and other parts of Eastern Europe.

Those German men who had survived the holocaust, and who had either avoided being stuck in P O W camps or who were lucky enough to secure early release, were worried about their jobs. Many factories which had missed being bombed were candidates for demolition or removal as reparations. The reparations hit the Soviet Zone hardest. There, everything from complete factories, sometimes with their key managers, workers and technicians as well, to (some) railway lines were removed to the U S S R. The French Zone was also heavily burdened by reparations. This zone had little industry but its rich forests were exploited in the French interest and its agricultural produce was required to feed the French Army.

More important for France was control over the industries of the Saar, an important centre of the German iron and steel and coal industries. By unilateral actions the French started to reorientate the economy of the Saar towards that of France. Under pressure, the U S A and Britain, but not the Soviet Union, accepted this process. By the end of 1947 a pro-French government was installed in the Saar and the Landtag ratified a constitution proclaiming the Saar's independence of Germany and making it economically part of the French Union. At the time this solution brought the people of the Saar many material advantages. Had the original reparations plans been carried through they would have hit the British Zone very heavily. As it was, as the Cold War got under way, and partly due to it, a more friendly attitude towards the Germans developed, and as a result of the pleas from German businessmen and trade unionists to their renewed contacts in Britain and the U S, these plans were whittled down. American policymakers had also to consider the effect of reparations on demands for u s aid and, in turn, on the American taxpayer. Some firms were put out of business as rivals, others escaped because some Allied firm had an interest in them. The removal of machinery and installations ended completely in April 1951 in the Anglo-American Zones.

The preservation of family units was not easy in the immediate postwar years. First of all there was the obvious difficulty of maintaining contact with one's relatives in the armed forces. As Germany lost the war this became more and more difficult. After the capitulation one could not know what would happen to those taken prisoner. Millions were retained to work in various European countries, some were in the United States and Canada. It took time for contact to be re-established. The large-scale evacuations were another factor causing family members to lose touch with each other. The breakdown of the railway system and the restrictions placed on Germans moving from one zone to another, contributed to the same result.

## THE NUREMBERG TRIALS AND DENAZIFICATION

The trials and punishment of war criminals was not a new thing. After the 1914-18 war a few trials were carried through by the victors and there had been demands to ' hang the Kaiser ', though these had come to nothing.

This time the Allies were determined to punish the leaders of an evil regime whose innumerable crimes were official policy rather than isolated cases resulting from the over-enthusiasm of a few junior officers. It was hoped the trials of the surviving leaders of the Third Reich would make clear to the Germans, in the words of Potsdam, ' the terrible crimes committed under the leadership of those whom in the hour of their success, they openly approved and blindly obeyed '. Further, they would serve as a warning to future generations. The trials would also demonstrate the determination of the new United Nations' Organisation to act as an effective guardian of international peace and morality, for the Tribunal, which was to conduct the trials, was originated in a u n commission, set up early in 1943. The Tribunal sat at Nuremberg from 20 November 1945 to 1 October of the following year. It dealt with three classes of crimes: crimes against peace, war crimes and crimes against humanity. Accused were the surviving Nazi leaders. Göring, as mentioned above, was sentenced to death but managed to commit suicide. Hanged were: Joachim von Ribbentrop, Hitler's Foreign Minister; Field Marshal Wilhelm Keitel, Chief of High Command; Ernst Kaltenbrunner, Chief of the Gestapo; Alfred Rosenberg, Nazi ideologist and Commissioner for Eastern Europe; Hans Frank, Governor of Poland; Wilhelm Frick, Minister of Interior; Julius Streicher, the most prominent Nazi anti-semite; Fritz Sauckel, head of the slave labour programme; Artur Seyss-Inquart, Governor of Holland; General Alfred Jodl, Chief of Operations of the High Command. Luckier were: Walter Funk, Head of the Reichsbank; Rudolf Hess, Deputy Führer of the N S D A P, who, following his abortive attempt to negotiate with the British in 1941, had spent the rest of the war in British captivity; Admiral Erich Raeder, Commander of the German Navy. They received life imprisonment. Baldur von Schirach, Hitler Youth Leader, and Albert Speer, head of the armaments' programme, only received 20 years each. Baron Konstantin von Neurath, first Nazi Foreign Minister and later Protector of Bohemia and Moravia, was awarded 15 years' imprisonment and Admiral Karl Dönitz, Hitler's successor as Head of State, 10 years. Martin Bormann, Hitler's deputy, was sentenced *in absentia* to death and, as mentioned in the last chapter, is still being sought. Franz von Papen, deputy Chancellor in 1933 and later Ambassador to Turkey, Hjalmar Schacht, one-time President of the Reich Bank, and Hans Fritzsche, an official in the Propaganda Ministry, were found not guilty. These three were later sentenced by German courts but served little time in jail.

Other trials were held at Nuremberg by the Americans alone. The most notable of these were against ' cannon king ' Alfred Krupp, prominent lawyers, and the chemical concern of IG Farben. The defendants were found guilty and sentenced to long terms of imprisonment but they were released quite soon in an American attempt to win over West German opinion.

In 1950 General Lucius D. Clay reported, in his capacity of U S High Commissioner for Germany, on the progress made in punishing leading Nazis. Of the 24 most important, he reported, six were executed, six were still serving sentences up to life, and eight had died or committed suicide. The fate of one was obscure and three were still at liberty. Of the 42 persons who held the rank of Gauleiter or regional party and administrative chief, eight were executed, ten had committed suicide or had died; one was shot by the Nazis themselves; 11 were still jailed or interned; while the fate of four was unknown; eight were known to be at liberty, some of these had already served their sentences.

Apart from trials for crimes Germans were liable to denazification procedures. The occupying powers were officially concerned to remove all former Nazis from positions of power or influence. The difficulty was to define the term 'Nazi'. There had been eight million members of the Nazi party and many others who had been members of its affiliates. On the other hand, there were those who had not been members of the Party but who had played a more active role in its crimes than most members. Millions of Germans, particularly in the U S Zone, were required to fill in long questionnaires (*Fragebogen*) about their activities between 1933 and 1945. This could be followed up by a trial before a denazification court. The courts, run by the Germans themselves, placed defendants in one of several categories from 'free of Nazi connections' to 'bearing major responsibility'. They could deprive defendants of their civic rights, fine them or send them to a labour camp.

These courts or tribunals came in for a good deal of criticism. There were great variations in their activities, not only between zones of occupation but even within each zone. Connections helped. Those incriminated Germans who had something to offer the occupying power could often work their passage. Soon all the Allies were prepared to intervene on behalf of experts of various kinds. Little Nazis who had no such expertise to offer often got worse treatment than more prominent Nazis who had. One of the most notorious examples of this is that of Heinz Felfe. He was an officer of the S D, the S S Security Service, as such he was arrested by the Allies. By 1946 he was working for the British intelligence services. They helped to get him denazified and recommended for the German police. To their credit the West Germans, including Dr Gustav Heinemann, now West German President, then Minister of Interior, would have nothing to do with him. The Gehlen organisation, then an intelligence agency run by former Wehrmacht General Reinhard Gehlen for the Americans, recruited him. He became prominent in that organisation and remained so after it became the official West German intelligence agency, B N D. For ten years, however, he was working as a Soviet agent in Gehlen's organisation.

It was not only the occupying powers who intervened on behalf of incriminated persons. The Catholic Church was an influential friend to many of them. In ministries and government agencies they later repaid the Church in kind.

## THE RETURN OF POLITICAL LIFE

It is perhaps remarkable that Germans, despite the many mundane yet essential jobs they had to do to ensure their own personal survival, should have any energy left for anything else. Yet thousands of Germans found the energy to take part in political activities once again when the occupation authorities licensed political parties.

The Soviets were the first to allow political activity in their zone. In June and July 1945 they licensed four parties in their zone: C D U, L D P D, S P D and K P D.

On 17 June, 35 persons signed a manifesto of the Christian Democratic Union in Berlin. Among the more significant signatories were: Andreas Hermes, former Centre Party politician and former Reich Finance Minister; Jakob Kaiser, a Christian trade unionist connected with the anti-Nazi opposition; Heinrich Krone, a former Centre Party Reichstag member, and Ernst Lemmer, another Christian trade unionist and former member of the Reichstag. Other important personalities at the meeting were: Dr Hans Lukaschek, former Mayor of Breslau; Otto Nuschke, former Reichstag member; Dr Walther Schreiber, one time Prussian Minister of Trade. Like Lemmer, Nuschke and Schreiber were members of the small, middle-class, middle-of-the-road Democratic Party in the Weimar Republic. Protestant Bishop D. Otto Dibelius also took part in the deliberations. Of the 50 or so leading members, 21 were former Centre Party members, about the same number were former Protestant Conservatives, and 8 or 9 were former members of the Democratic Party. They were united in their view that the old Conservative and old denominational parties should not be reestablished. They retained their earlier anti-Marxist and pro-Christian ideas. They wanted to break down denominational barriers and were even prepared to accept members not tied to a particular church provided they recognised 'the Law of natural ethics'. On economic policy they proposed state ownership of mineral wealth and state control of 'monopolistic key undertakings'. Further, they recognised the place, indeed importance, of the worker in the community, and advocated a united trade-union movement.

Partly unknown, because of communications' difficulties, to the Berlin founders of the C D U, other Christian groups were setting up similar groups in other parts of Germany. In Cologne a meeting took place on 17 June attended by 18 former leading officials of the Centre Party. They decided not to reform their old party but to work for unity with local Protestants. Dr Leo Schwering, a librarian and for many years member of the Prussian Landtag, was asked to draft a programme. What emerged was a vaguely Christian Socialist draft. More strongly Christian Socialist were the Hesse C D U based on Frankfurt and greatly influenced in those early days by Dr Walter Dirks. In northern Germany, Schleswig, Hamburg and Bremen the C D U won over a greater number of Protestants and took up a more clearly Conservative position than in the Rhineland, Hesse or Berlin. In Bavaria where they called themselves the

Christian Social Union, they were more traditional right-wing clerical in their orientation. There they were also predominantly Catholic.

Who were the mass of members of the new Christian party? In Hamburg, in June 1946, 12 per cent of them were workers, 32 per cent white-collar employees, 10 per cent civil servants, 8 per cent professional people, 14 per cent housewives and 2 per cent unknown. Politically, they were a varied lot. Of the first thousand Hamburg members one was a former Communist, 20 were former Social Democrats, 171 were former Centre Party members and another 5 had belonged to small Christian groups. On the right, 41 had belonged to the moderate Conservative, German People's Party, 36 were from Hugenberg's Nationalists and 254 were former Nazi party members. Of the former Nazis, 36 had held some position in the party. It is difficult to say to what extent the political composition was similar to that of other areas. It is probable that it was similar to other C D U organisations in North Germany, less so to those in other parts. The social composition of the Hamburg party was similar to those of Christian Democratic groups in other urban areas except that, in North Rhine Westphalia, the working class was more strongly in evidence. In South Germany and in Schleswig Holstein the farming community was strongly represented.

Gradually, in the British Zone the local groups of Christian Democrats came together and formed, in February 1946, a party on a zonal basis. Dr Konrad Adenauer, Centre Party politician for many years before 1933 Mayor of Cologne, who had not taken part in the founding of the party, was elected chairman. In the American and French Zones it was not yet possible to set up zonal organisations.

One memorable event in the early history of the C D U was the adoption of the so-called Ahlen Economic Programme by the British Zone Christian Democrats in February 1947. This programme showed the relative strength of the Christian trade unionists in the party at the time. It contained the words, ' The capitalist economic system has not proved suitable to the political and social life interests of the German people . . . The content and goal of the social and economic reorganisation can no longer be capitalistic power and profit-seeking, but only the welfare of our people '. The programme was to have little practical significance for the C D U.

Throughout Germany the remnants of the old Liberal parties found the courage to start up their groups again. In Berlin they founded the Liberal Democratic Party of Germany. In Würtemberg they called themselves the Democratic People's Party (D V P). In Hesse they were the Liberal Democrats and in Bavaria the Free Democrats. The term Free Democratic Party was the one which

gradually gained complete acceptance in the Western Zones. Led
by such former Reichstag members as Theodor Heuss and Reinhold
Maier they had more pronounced Liberal, *laissez-faire* views on
economic matters than the C D U, and feared the harmful influence
of the Church in politics. They were very largely a middle-class party
and much more Protestant than Catholic.

The Social Democrats were the oldest German party, a party
which had survived persecution before 1900, a party with a large
number of trained cadres. The Nazis had done their best to stamp
it out and a considerable number of Social Democrats had been
murdered, but it was only to be expected that when the Third
Reich collapsed the S P D would raise its head again.

In May 1945 Social Democrats in Berlin started to discuss the
re-establishment of their party. By 15 June they were ready to issue
their programmatic appeal to their countrymen. In their appeal
they called for ' Democracy in the state and in the (local) community,
Socialism in the economy and in society '. They wanted an ' anti-
fascist, democratic regime and a parliamentary democratic republic '.
They advocated the nationalisation of the banks and insurance
undertakings, mineral resources and the fuel economy, and the
breaking up of the great estates. Significantly, they called for the
unity of the working class and warmly welcomed an appeal of the
newly refounded Communist Party. Among the Berlin group were
the two survivors from a committee of 12, which had been given
the task by the last Executive Committee of the old S P D, to carry
on the fight in Germany. (The Executive Committee itself had fled
abroad.) These survivors were Max Fechner and Richard Weimann.
With them were former Reichstag's members Otto Grotewohl and
Gustav Dahrendorf, Annedore Leber, wife of July resister Julius
Leber, and a number of functionaries of the old S P D. They
established a *Zentralausschuss* (Central Committee) with Fechner
and Grotewohl as chairmen, and sought contact with their comrades
in other zones.

As it turned out, the key figure in the other zones was another
former member of the Reichstag, Dr Kurt Schumacher. Schumacher,
whom the Nazis had released from concentration camp in 1943 as a
very sick man, lived with his sister in Hanover. A man of magnetic
personality and great will power, he set about refounding a S P D
organisation in Hanover a few days before the American arrival
in April 1945. Convinced of his own mission, Schumacher was not
prepared to accept the leadership of the Berlin Social Democrats.
At the time this was academic, for the occupying powers would not
allow organisations embracing all four zones.

A third group of Social Democrats could claim, legally if not morally, that they and they alone, were the true surviving leaders of the Weimar S P D. These were the remnants of the old Executive or Vorstand who had maintained a Social Democratic organisation in London. This group included Hans Vogel, a S P D Chairman, who died in 1945; Executive member Erich Ollenhauer, Fritz Heine and Erwin Schoettle. By the time they were allowed to return to Germany Schumacher had established himself in the Western Zones and the Berlin group were about to unite with the Communists. The Londoners therefore joined Schumacher.

As already mentioned, the Grotewohl-Fechner group had called for working-class unity, this could only mean unity with the Communists. This was bitterly opposed by Schumacher. Why did the Berlin group want unity with the Communists? Firstly, because they believed that the division of the working class in 1933 had assisted the rise of Nazism. Secondly, shared experiences of persecution under Hitler had brought some of them closer together. Thirdly, the Communists seemed to have learned from past mistakes: they no longer called for a Soviet Germany but for a democratic republic; the Communist International had been disbanded during the war which was taken to mean Communist parties would now operate independently of Moscow; the first appeal of the re-established German C P, of 11 June, was politically moderate. Finally, Social Democrats and Communists had common origins as Marxists.

The K P D had been preparing for its re-establishment in Germany longer than any of the three other parties. Of course, officially, it had never ceased to exist. Communist emigrants had carried on its activities from Moscow between 1933 and 1945. Some of these returned on the heels of the Red Army and immediately set about their allotted political tasks. They quickly established their authority over the survivors of those who had remained in the Reich. Ernst Thälmann, party leader until Hitler gained power, had been murdered in a concentration camp. His place was taken by veteran Communist and former Reichstag member, Wilhelm Pieck. Thirteen of 16 signatories of the 11 June appeal had spent the Hitler years in Moscow. They included, apart from Pieck, former Reichstag members Walter Ulbricht, Bernard Koenen and Edwin Hoernle, the writer Johannes R. Becher, Spanish Civil War veteran Anton Ackermann, his wife Elli Schmidt, two Landtag members, Hermann Matern and Gustav Sobottka, and Michael Niederkirchner, Martha Arendsee, Otto Winzer and Hans Mahle. All the other three had been in concentration camps, one, Ottomar Keschke, a former Reichstag member, for 12 years. Franz Dahlem had an impressive record: member of the Reichstag, member of the Central Committee of the K P D, had served in the International Brigade and then in concentration camps. Hans Jendretzky, the third man, had been a member of the Prussian Landtag.

### THE S E D

The line of the new K P D was to avoid immediate fusion with the Social Democrats. The Communists wanted to build up their own position first and hoped that, even under their own steam, they would be stronger than the socialists. They over-estimated their own strength. The ranks of the Communist cadres had been decimated by Hitler's, and to a lesser extent Stalin's, murder squads. Rank-and-filers, in Germany as elsewhere, had been disillusioned by the sudden switches in Stalin's policies. Many ordinary Germans had been influenced by Goebbels' anti-Soviet hate propaganda and horrified by the behaviour of Soviet troops. And the expulsion of millions of Germans from their homes east of the Oder-Neisse Line did not seem to have anything to do with Socialism or 'Leninist norms'. Still, the Communists had been right when they had warned, 'Hitler means war', and they were obviously the favourite of the Russians. Many of the old supporters re-registered and were joined by some young idealists and, no doubt, by a good many opportunists. But despite help from the Soviets: transport, buildings, printing presses, paper, money, prestige; the K P D found it difficult to match the growth of the Social Democrats. In November 1945 the German Communists received a shock which was to help them to change their minds on the unity issue. The Austrian Communists, who were also being aided by the Soviets in their zone, were severely defeated in the first postwar elections. In addition, they knew that some of the Social Democrats who had originally favoured unity were having second thoughts. So Pieck and Ulbricht decided to act quickly to bring about a Socialist Unity Party which would replace the two existing working-class parties.

In spite of some doubts the leaders of the Berlin-based Social Democrats expressed their approval of such a party and announced their intention to put the matter to a Reich's conference of the party. They were under a good deal of pressure from the Soviet Military Government who made it clear they wanted this party established as quickly as possible. Some of the rank-and-file officials of the S P D, led by Franz Neumann, urged their leaders to put the issue to a vote of the entire party. This Grotewohl and his colleagues refused to do. With the help of the Western Powers, and encouraged by Schumacher, Neumann succeeded in carrying through the referendum in the Western Sectors of Berlin. There a great majority of members voted, and voted against an immediate fusion of the two parties. They did however vote for fraternal cooperation between the two. Having suffered something of a moral defeat Grotewohl had no difficulty in getting his way at a conference called to decide on unity. The delegates were drawn mainly from the Soviet Zone.

On 21 April 1946 the Socialist Unity Party (S E D) was established. Its joint Chairmen were Pieck and Grotewohl, its joint Secretaries were Ulbricht and Max Fechner. Its writ ran only in the Soviet Zone and East Berlin. In West Germany the S P D and the K P D continued to exist as rivals. In Berlin the S P D was reconstituted and delivered a sharp blow to the S E D in October 1946. In elections for the Berlin city council held in all four sectors the S P D gained 48.7 per cent of the vote as against the S E D's 19.8 per cent. The Christian Democrats won 22.1 per cent and the Liberals 9.4 per cent.

Meanwhile, in the Western Zones of Germany Kurt Schumacher pushed ahead with the building up of a strong S P D. He had come to terms with the Londoners and in May 1946 the first party conference of the West German Social Democrats was held. Schumacher was elected Chairman, Ollenhauer his deputy. The party came out strongly in favour of democracy but also for Marxism and Socialism, including extensive socialisation of industry.

By April 1946 the German working class was once again as bitterly divided as it had been in the Weimar Republic. This time though its division was in no small measure a result of the divisions among the major world powers and their differences were to divide Germany.

## CURRENCY REFORM AND THE BERLIN BLOCKADE

As we have seen, Western policy towards Germany was not entirely consistent. During the war the punitive element had been strong. As the anger of war subsided it started to become more compassionate. There were those who recognised that the Germans could not be won for democracy on empty stomachs. Some Allied statesmen —Churchill was one of them—very soon concluded that a policy of generosity ought to be pursued because the West would need the Germans as allies against the Soviet Union.

No one can say with complete confidence what Stalin's policy was in the war and postwar years. He too had favoured a punitive policy. He too wanted the Germans as allies. Most experts agree he wanted to create a defensive line of Soviet-orientated states in Eastern Europe. Further, that he wanted to extract from Germany the greatest possible amount of reparations. This was understandable in view of the Soviet Union's enormous losses in men and material, the extent of which the West did not fully appreciate in 1945. If Stalin ever planned a Communist Germany he did not adopt policies designed to bring this about. The annexation of German lands, the reparations, the use of German P O Ws and civilians as forced labourers, the behaviour of Soviet troops, were not calculated to win the hearts of the Germans. Stalin possibly soon came to realise that any attempt to communise Germany by generosity was bound to fail as the Americans did not want a Communist Germany and they could outbid the Russians any time in generosity. Force was another possibility but so long as America remained in Germany this too was out of the question. The early setting up of a non-Communist German government could not be attractive to the Soviets especially if the issues of reparations and Germany's frontiers had not been settled. But the four powers failed to agree on these issues. Perhaps Stalin would have acted differently had he received a large reconstruction loan which he had mentioned to the Americans at the end of the war. The loan was not forthcoming. Russia and the West were separated by 30 years or so of mutual suspicion.

The Western Allies, unable to get agreement with the Soviet Union, initiated measures to rehabilitate their zones economically and unite them politically, thus they set in motion the division of Germany.

The first American move was the offer made in July 1946 by the U S Secretary of State, James F. Byrnes, to merge the United States Zone in economic affairs with that of any other Ally willing to join. The British, desperately short of funds, agreed before the end of the month. By so doing they virtually forfeited their right to pursue their own policy in the British Zone. The Soviets rejected the Byrnes' plan and so, for a time, did the French until the U S and Britain agreed to their Saar plans. In March 1947 the ' Truman Doctrine ' was enunciated. President Truman guaranteed the active support of the United States to all peoples resisting internal subversion or external aggression. Initially help was to be given to Greece, Iran and Turkey under pressure from the Soviet Union. The Truman Doctrine was followed in June of the same year by the announcement of Marshall Aid which came after a winter of economic, social and political crisis in Western Europe. General George Marshall in a speech at Harvard University, declared that if the nations of Europe would agree on a combined plan for recovery, the United States would finance it. Although Marshall Aid did not explicitly preclude Soviet participation, the terms were such that it was rightly anticipated that the Russians would not accept them. An intrinsic part of the Aid plan was that the economic recovery of Germany was the key to the recovery of Europe.

It was only to be expected that any policy aimed at the economic rehabilitation of Germany should include a reform of the currency. Once again, as in the 1920s, the German currency was rapidly becoming worthless. Some were saying that Germany was under the dictatorship of the cigarette for it had become a universally accepted unit of value. The practice of barter was widespread. Anything could be obtained on the black market at greatly inflated prices, little was obtainable over the counter in the shops. The Western Allies, therefore, carried through a change of currency in June 1948. Ten old Reichmark had to be handed over for one new Deutsche Mark, though each adult German was given first 40 and then, two weeks later, another 20 new Marks. The reform hit small savers the hardest. Owners of land and property got away with little damage. Cash suddenly became short and the shop windows, equally suddenly, became full in order to attract it. For some time the Western Powers expressed the hope that the Soviets would allow a single currency for the whole of Germany, a currency issued on a quadripartite basis. Had the Russians agreed they would have been greatly weakening their power over economic, and political, policy in their Zone. Of course they did not oblige and announced that the new currency would not be permitted to circulate even in the Western Sectors of Berlin. Marshal Vassili Sokolovsky, from 1946 to 1949 Commander-in-Chief of Soviet forces in Germany, in making the announcement, rather enigmatically described the Western Sectors as being part of the Soviet Zone.

There is some doubt about the Western Allies' intentions regarding the introduction of the Deutsche Mark to West Berlin. But they did soon introduce it declaring on 25 June that both the Deutsche Mark and any ' East ' Mark would be valid in their part of Berlin.

As part of their reaction to the Marshall Plan and to the six-nation (the Benelux countries and the Western Powers) London conference of March 1948, which allowed the West Germans to draft a constitution, the Russians restricted travel between their Zone and West Germany. This policy was introduced from 1 April. In reaction to the currency reform they extended the restrictions to freight movements between Berlin and the West. The prospects for the West Berliners looked bleak. The Western Sectors were largely dependent on West Germany for their food and fuel, some electricity and gas was supplied from the Soviet Sector.

The right of access to Berlin by the Western Allies had not been laid down in any formal treaty. This is not as surprising as it might

seem. The Soviet Union had recognised the right of its Western
partners to sectors in Berlin which would automatically seem to
imply the right of access. In any case, the Four Allies had not
intended that the four zones should be sealed off from each other.
Still, as Russian pressure mounted, the lack of any agreement on
access proved embarrassing. Luckily, there was a quadripartite
document covering Western use of three air corridors to Berlin
from Bückeburg, near Hanover, Frankfurt and Hamburg. From
June 1948 to May 1949 these were the only lines of communication
between West Berlin and West Germany. If the Russians aimed at
driving the Western Powers out of Berlin either to seal off their
zone, or give themselves control of the future capital of a united
Germany, or merely to demonstrate their capacity to humiliate the
West, the blockade of Berlin was a good gamble. Never before had
a city been supplied by air, let alone one of 2.4 million people. The
Russians had gained experience on the effects of blockades from
Leningrad. They had watched the failure of the Luftwaffe to supply
the Nazi Sixth Army at Stalingrad, and, in general, World War
II had demonstrated the weaknesses as much as the strengths of
air power.

The success of Operation Vittels—as the Americans called the
Air Lift—surprised the practitioners as much as it must have
surprised Stalin. It was estimated that to keep Berlin alive required
a minimum daily transport of 4,000 tons. On the record day, in
April 1949, 13,000 tons were lifted into Berlin. The Western Powers
had been fortunate when the sectors were originally allocated, in
that they got the best airports including Tempelhof. For whatever
reasons, the Russians did not withdraw from the Four-Power air
control body regulating traffic to and from Berlin. Nor did they
interfere with the radio beacon situated in their sector used for
guiding Allied aircraft. And, after one of their fighters had caused
the crash of a British airliner, they ceased ' buzzing ' Allied planes.

The blockade was ended by the Four-Power New York agreement of 4 May 1949 under which the Soviet Union agreed to rescind
the restrictions it had imposed, and the Western Powers likewise
withdrew restrictions they had placed on communications between
their zones and East Germany. This was confirmed at the Four-
Power conference in Paris in the following month. The Paris conference achieved little else. Like the earlier Four-Power conferences in
1946 and 1947, it was unable to resolve any of the fundamental differences between the Powers on Germany.

The blockade over, Berlin was to remain divided politically. After
being harassed by Communist-organised demonstrators, the non-

S E D majority of the Berlin city council had decided in September 1948 to transfer their meetings to the West Sectors and to carry through fresh elections in December. They were not permitted to hold the elections in East Berlin where a separate administration was set up. As Berlin's police and university were also Soviet-orientated, a separate police force and the ' Free University ' were established in West Berlin in August 1948 and May 1949 respectively. The Western administration was headed by Ernst Reuter, who had been a K P D official briefly in the early 1920s, and then until 1933 and again after 1945 a Social Democratic politician. His opposite number in East Berlin was Friedrich Ebert, son of the first (Social Democratic) President of the Weimar Republic, himself a member of the Reichstag for the S P D. In 1946 Ebert had gone with Grotewohl into the S E D.

## TOWARDS TWO GERMAN REPUBLICS

Starting as early as the summer of 1945 the administration of Germany was gradually structured by the Allies into Länder. Some of these, such as Bavaria, Hamburg and Hesse, in the West, and Mecklenburg, Saxony and Thuringia, in the Soviet Zone, were based on traditional German states. Others, such as Bremen, emerged because of Allied needs, in this case the need for a port for the Americans. There was also the need to remove Prussia from the map which was formally done by an Allied decree in February 1947. In all, 11 Länder were established in the West and five in the smaller area of the Soviet Zone. In addition there was Berlin. In the U S Zone a *Länderrat* (Council of States) was established in 1945 to serve the state governments as a coordinating organ for those interstate activities which could not be dealt with properly by individual states. The existence of the Länder later influenced the drafting of the West, and to a lesser extent the East, German constitution. The constitutions of these administrative units tended to reflect the ideas of the occupying power in whose zone they were.

In other respects too the evolution of political and economic structures in the zones resembled the views of the Allies of what was good for the Germans rather than what a majority of Germans would have wanted had they been entirely free to decide for themselves. This was truer of the Soviet Zone than the others, but it happened in the Western Zones to a greater extent than is commonly supposed.

In the Soviet Zone a number of important reforms which probably had the support of the great majority, and the active opposition of very few, were pushed through. On the other hand, Stalinist measures were introduced which made a mockery of the words democracy and socialism. The first big reform which started in 1945 was the redistribution of the land. The Junkers, the great landowners who had been such an important pillar of the German Army, and who, although they were more likely to be Nationalists than Nazis, had played an important part in undermining the Weimar Republic, had their estates confiscated. War criminals and Nazi activists suffered the same fate. Up to 1 January 1949 just over 7,000 properties of over 100 *Hektar* and another 4,200 of less than 100 *Hektar* were taken over. From these and public land, holdings were found for nearly 120,000 landless peasants and farm workers; nearly 90,000 refugees from the area east of the Oder-Neisse; 169,000 workers and craftsmen. Additional land was found for 80,000 small farmers, and 45,000 tenant farmers. Finally, about 40,000 farmers received forest land. This measure, which amounted to a social revolution in the agricultural areas, had one serious economic drawback. The smallness of the holdings, lack of machinery and, in some cases, lack of skill of the new proprietors, resulted in a fall of productivity on the land. It meant less food was available for the towns or for export to other parts of Germany. But in 1945, considering Germany's past, it seemed the right thing to do. In any case, the Soviets were soon thinking in terms of collective farms, and Social Democrats, who had long advocated such a measure, advocated Scandinavian-type cooperatives to counter the economic drawback. A much less thorough land reform was carried out in the Western Zones, where the political and social problem of the large estates was not as great.

Another fundamental reform in the Soviet Zone was the confiscation of all private banks which were then re-organised as Länder and provincial banks. This measure was introduced in July 1945. More important still was order No. 124 of the Soviet military authorities issued on 30 October 1945. It confiscated all German state property; all property belonging to leading N S D A P officials, leading members and influential followers; property of the military authorities and organisations; property of all forbidden societies, clubs and associations; property of other Axis states or their citizens; the property of individuals on special lists drawn up by the Soviet military authorities. Although some aspects of this reform were later criticised, especially property on the ' special lists ', there is no doubt that the great majority of Germans in the Soviet Zone agreed with the measure. Social Democrats, as well as Communists, all over Germany were calling for similar measures and a great many Christian Democrats shared their view.

In the Western Zones the Americans saw to it that similar measures were not implemented there. On 1 December 1946 the people of Hesse had agreed by 1,081,124 votes to 422,159 to a clause in the Land constitution nationalising the mines, power stations and the iron and steel industry. In August 1948 the parliament of North-Rhine Westphalia nationalised the mines in its Land. In 1947 nationalisation measures had been passed by the parliaments of Bavaria and Schleswig-Holstein. All these measures were set aside by the Anglo-Americans. The U S Military Governor, General Clay, claimed these were matters which could only be dealt with by a German national government but he confided in a colleague: ' If we can thus defer the issue while free enterprise continues to operate and economic improvement results, it may never become an issue before the German people '. The British were pledged to the public ownership of these industries but because of their financial dependence on the U S A deferred to Clay's views. As we shall see in the next chapter, the British did permit the introduction of codetermination which is generally regarded as one of the achievements of West Germany.

In the field of education too reforms were on the agenda. The Russians and their German helpers sacked the great majority of teachers in their zone because of their Nazi pasts. The Russians set up a German Administration for Education in the summer of 1945 to reorganise the education system. All five Länder of the East Zone adopted the Law for the Democratisation of the German School in 1946. It was to rid the schools of the old ideology, break the educational privileges of the old propertied classes, bridge the differences between urban and rural schools, and raise academic standards in the schools. The prewar *Volksschule* was replaced by a *Grundschule*. After eight years in this new basic school pupils went on to a four-year secondary school or received vocational training. Fees for secondary schools were abolished and would-be students from working-class homes were given preference at university. Workers and Peasants' Faculties were also set up to help those who did not have the necessary entry requirements.

In the American Zone the basis for school reforms was the list of recommendations made in September 1946 by a U S Education Mission, headed by George F. Zook, the President of the American Council on Education. The chief proposals were a comprehensive school system, a common six-year elementary school, increased emphasis on social studies and cultural subjects, improved teaching aids and library facilities and, educational exchanges. The U S Military Governor followed up Zook's mission, in January 1947,

I

by requiring the Länder in its zone to submit proposals for the reorganisation of education in their areas. Their proposals should be based on 15 principles laid down by the U S Military Governor. These called for equal educational opportunity for all, free tuition, free textbooks and materials, school attendance between 6 and 15 and compulsory part-time education from 15 to 18. As it turned out, most progress towards these goals was made in Bremen, some in Hesse and little in Bavaria. In the British Zone, as in the U S, most progress was made in the Social Democratic-ruled areas, particularly Hamburg. On the whole progress was less dramatic in the West than in the East and many Germans interested in education were depressed by the re-establishment of denominational schools in many areas of West Germany.

In the two halves of Germany organs of two central German governments were gradually evolving. In May 1947 an Economic Council was created for the Anglo-American Zones or Bizonia as they became known. Its job was to formulate and promulgate ordinances on economic matters subject to the approval of an Anglo-American board. Members were to be selected by the regional parliaments or Landtage on the basis of proportional representation. In 1948 a Council of States (*Länderrat*) was added. Its members were mainly the Prime Ministers of the individual Länder together with their chief ministers. The Economic Council became a kind of shadow lower house of parliament with the Council of States becoming a shadow upper house. What about a shadow cabinet? This was known as the Administrative Council and was also created in May 1947. A German High Court was established in February 1948. Although the Western Allies set up these institutions with the help and advice of German politicians and experts, they themselves played an important part in shaping these bodies which, in turn, influenced the form the new West German state was later to take.

In Soviet Germany the occupying power had, by 1946, established 15 central administrative bodies which dealt with matters usually handled by the ministries of a modern state. At first they were merely advisory but by 1947 they had been invested with considerable authority. After the establishment of Bizonia the Russians launched a Permanent Economic Commission in their zone. Two-thirds of its 25 members were appointed by the military administration and the rest by the trade unions and farmers' organisations. The new body took over economic affairs from those of the fifteen central administrative bodies which had been concerned with them. By building up strong administrative organisations packed with reliable people the Soviets were reducing the importance of parliaments and elections in their zone. And, as Austrian experience was to show, even had it come to a non-Communist all-German government, the Russians could have gone on for some time exercising influence in certain spheres, because of the way they had built up the administrative machine in their zone.

It has already been mentioned that the London six-nation conference in February 1948 agreed that the West Germans should start drafting a constitution. At a meeting on 1 July at Frankfurt the Western Military Governors presented the German Minister Presidents (or Prime Ministers) of the Länder with three documents. The first empowered them to convene a constituent assembly by 1 September to draft a democratic, federal constitution. The second document authorised the Germans to investigate the possibility of boundary changes among the Länder. In the third document the Allies set out the powers to be reserved by them in order to further carry out the purposes of the occupation. The Minister, Presidents— five S P D, five C D U, one F D P—not wishing to prejudice the chances of re-establishing German unity, wanted to emphasise the temporary nature of the new part-state. So it was agreed that the constitution-drafting body should be called a Parliamentary Council rather than a Constituent Assembly. It was further agreed that the Council would not draw up a Constitution (Verfassung) but a Basic Law (Grundgesetz).

The Parliamentary Council met at Bonn on 1 September 1948 and comprised 27 members of the C D U/C S U, an equal number of S P D members, five from the F D P and two each from the Centre Party, the Communists and the German Party. The delegates were elected by the Landtage roughly proportionate to population. As the two major parties were equal, the C D U favouring, the S P D opposing federalism, and the three mini-parties had no united approach, the F D P was able to exercise a disproportionate amount of influence. This party tended towards centralism rather than federalism. But the Americans, and their influence was strong, argued for a decentralised, federal, system. General Clay feared the S P D was inclined towards a strong central government because it wanted to be able to raise enough revenue to pay compensation for its nationalisation programme—which he opposed! After a good deal of argument, some of it bitter, the Basic Law was approved by the Council on 8 May 1949 and by the Military Governors four days later. In the same month it was ratified by all the Länder except Bavaria. However, as two-thirds of the Länder had ratified it, Bavaria accepted the verdict of the others and joined the federation. Again after a good deal of argument, the Council decided on Bonn as temporary capital. This did not please the S P D for Bonn was (and is) a stronghold of the C D U and did not have the space or style of a capital. It was, though, convenient for Dr Adenauer who had lived all of his life just outside the sleepy, Beethoven town.

The constitution made provision for a bicameral system with a popularly elected lower house, the Bundestag, and an upper house, Bundesrat, to represent the Länder interests. The upper house is one of the most powerful in the world and is in effect a continuous meeting of Land ministers who vote in accordance with instructions of their governments. The federal government is required to submit all its legislative drafts to the upper house before they go to the lower one, and most bills passed by the latter need the approval of the former. The Chairmanship of the Bundesrat devolves in turn on a representative from each of the Länder. The Länder send delegates roughly in accordance with the size of the population of their Land. Each has a minimum of three, those with populations between two and six millions send four, those with populations of over six millions nominate five delegates. The Federation was given exclusive authority over such things as currency and coinage, weights and measures, posts and telecommunications, and later, after West Germany had regained its sovereignty, foreign affairs and defence, etc. The Länder were granted exclusive legislative authority over a fairly limited range of subjects: education, culture, religious affairs, police, local government, internal administration.

The fathers of the constitution tried to learn from the mistakes of Weimar especially in respect of the Presidency. They got away from the directly-elected, strong President. Under the Basic Law the President is elected for five years by the Federal Meeting (*Bundesversammlung*). This consists of the members of the lower house and an equal number of delegates elected by the state legislatures on the basis of proportional representation. The Bonn President has less power than the Weimar President had. He cannot on his own authority appoint or dismiss a Chancellor, select Cabinet Ministers, dissolve the Bundestag, or declare a state of emergency. The Chancellor, on the other hand, was strengthened as compared with his predecessors under Weimar. According to the Basic Law the Bundestag may express its lack of confidence in the Chancellor only by simultaneously electing a successor and submitting to the President a request for the dismissal of the former Chancellor. After the bad experience of Weimar the framers of the Bonn Constitution decided to throw out the referendum as a legitimate part of democracy. Finally, as a result of the Weimar experience, the Basic

Law makes provision for banning parties considered to be operating against the democratic order. Article 21 (paragraph 2) states: ' Parties which, by reason of their aims or the behaviour of their adherents, seek to impair or destroy the free democratic order or to endanger the existence of the Federal Republic of Germany are unconstitutional.' The basic Law did not regulate the details of elections to the Bundestag but, here too, as we shall see, Bonn tried to learn from Weimar. The Basic Law claimed that its framers had acted for all those Germans who were prevented from taking part. According to Article 146 the Basic Law would lose its validity on the day a constitution, freely arrived at by the German people as a whole, came into force.

In the Soviet Zone the military authorities and the German pro-Soviet leaders attempted to match the efforts in the West at constitution-making. There the constitution of 1949 resulted mainly from discussions in three German People's Congresses (*Deutsche Volkskongresse*) between 1947 and 1949. The People's Congress movement had been called into life by the S E D in an attempt to lead the discussions on a future German Constitution. Apart from Communists, and a few pacifists and neutralists, the movement attracted little support in the West. Even in the Soviet Zone the C D U was not at first prepared to cooperate. But its two Chairmen, Ernst Lemmer and Jakob Kaiser were forced to resign, after which the party became more cooperative. The Liberal Democrats sent delegates. In March 1948 the second People's Congress met and elected a People's Council, a kind of shadow parliament. The Communists gradually gained complete control of this body both by purges of the C D U and the L D P D, and by the setting up of two pseudo-bourgeois parties in 1948, the National Democratic Party (N D P D) and the Democratic Farmers' Party (D B D). Both were under the control of Communist cadres from the start. The practice of allowing ' mass organisations '—trade unions, the Free German Youth, Democratic Women's League, League of Culture, Farmers' Mutual Assistance—to send delegates to the People's Congress further increased Communist influence as all these bodies were under Communist control.

In May 1949 the people of East Germany were asked to elect delegates to a third People's Congress. The electorate were presented with a single list of candidates which they could either accept or reject. The S E D had vetted all the candidates through the Anti-Fascist Democratic Bloc to which all parties had to belong. All the mass media campaigned for the official list and no open opposition was possible. It is therefore not surprising that 95.2 per cent of the electorate voted and of these 66 per cent approved the official list. The Congress then approved the Constitution and elected a new People's Council. On 7 October the Council formally constituted itself as the provisional People's Chamber (*Volkskammer*). Meeting as the People's Chamber it unanimously approved a Law on the Constitution of the German Democratic Republic.

The Constitution approved by the People's Chamber need not detain us long for it was not carefully observed in the years which followed. Its preamble asserted that it was 'the German People' who 'have given themselves this constitution'. Article 1 proclaimed: 'Germany is an indivisible democratic Republic; its constituent parts are the German states. The Republic decides on all matters essential for the continued existence and development of the German People as a whole.' The text did not indicate the area in which the constitution was valid. The People's Chamber was the highest organ of the republic, its deputies, subordinated only to their consciences, were elected at universal, equal, and secret elections every four years. Provision was also made for a second chamber to represent the interests of the Länder. This was the *Länderkammer*. The Prime Minister was to be chosen from the largest party represented in the *Volkskammer*. He could not be dismissed until a successor had been found for him. The President's functions were largely ceremonial. He was elected by joint-session of the two parliamentary chambers. Berlin was proclaimed capital of the German Democratic Republic (D D R) but due to the Four-Power status of the city, the Berlin representatives in the People's Chamber had only non-voting status.

*Total crap!*

# 7    Adenauer's Germany

The election of 14 August 1949 to the first Bundestag did not yield a decisive result. The Christian Democrats pulled slightly ahead with 7.3 million votes (31 per cent). Schumacher's Social Democrats gained 6.9 million votes (29.2 per cent) and the F D P 2.7 millions (11.9). The Communists must have been disappointed with their 1.3 million votes (5.7 per cent) thinking back to their millions in the Weimar Republic. Another 21.1 per cent of the votes were given to seven or so other parties and independents such as the remnants of the old Centre Party, the Bavarian Party, the Right-wing groups like the German Party (D P) and the German Rights Party (D R P).

The result was not too bad for the S P D considering the difficulties it was up against. It was cut off from many traditional centres of Social Democracy—Berlin, Erfurt, Halle, Leipzig, Magdeburg, Dresden—now in the Soviet Zone. The Christian Democrats benefited from the greater proportion of Catholics in the Federal Republic as compared with the Weimar Republic. This ensured them a mass basis for their party. They also got help from the Catholic Church. The American and French military authorities favoured the Christian Democrats and gave them discreet support. Moreover, the Christian Democrats could claim they, together with the F D P and the D P, by holding office, were partly responsible for the Western Zones improving economic and political situation. Since June 1947 these parties had headed the Economic Council of the Western Zones.

The indecisive result of the election left some room for manoeuvre. But Dr Adenauer was a better negotiator (or intriguer) than Dr Schumacher and had already worked with the F D P and the D P. He managed to prevail over the Left-wing members of his party in this matter. The result was that Adenauer mobilised mass Christian Democratic support for Prof. Theodor Heuss, who was elected Federal President. In return he proposed Adenauer for Chancellor. Remarkably, the proposal was carried by one vote—Adenauer's own! Few would have predicted in 1949 that the 73-year-old

Adenauer, presiding over a precarious coalition, would rule for 14 years and become one of the most influential world statesmen. It looked very much as though Bonn would follow Weimar with frequent changes of government.

Dr Adenauer's government faced problems which seemed at least as great, if not greater, than those which faced, and defeated, the governments of the Weimar regime.

There was the problem of unemployment. This was actually getting worse. By the end of 1948 it reached 760,000. During the whole of 1949 it mounted month by month increasing to 1.56 millions by the end of the year.

This problem was complicated by the refugees from the lost territories and from the D D R. In 1950 16.4 per cent of the population of West Germany were from the lost territories, while another 3.3 per cent came from the D D R. On past experience unemployed and refugees added up to political extremism. German industry also faced great problems. It had been disrupted by demolitions, reparations and the division of Germany. Certain branches of industry in which Germany had been leading—aviation for instance—were forbidden. In any case, the interruption of production meant that markets were no longer assured. As well as the unemployed and the refugees, the war victims had to be cared for. In 1952 there were over 1.5 million war disabled in West Germany.

ECONOMIC RECOVERY

Anyone acquainted with the term ' economic miracle ' automatically associates it with West Germany, even though, since the Federal Republic's remarkable economic development there have been others—Italy, Japan, U S S R, and to a lesser extent, East Germany and Spain. Certain figures make clear the extent of Federal Germany's ' miracle '. The gross national product of the Republic rose by 61 per cent between 1953 and 1960, compared with 37 per cent on average in the O E E C countries (roughly the West European states), and 21 per cent in the United Kingdom. In terms of living standards, as measured by the volume of private consumption, West Germany had a 58 per cent rise, in the same period, as against 34 per cent in all O E E C countries and only 25 per cent in the U K. To the extent that non-military government expenditure helped to raise living standards, this aspect of living standards rose more rapidly in West Germany than in Britain. Such expenditure per head increased in the Federal Republic by 71 per cent, but by only 39 per cent in Britain.

How was all this possible? Dr Erhard, Minister of Economic

Affairs between 1949 and 1966, and as Director of the Economic Administrative Office of the Anglo-u s zones, the man responsible for carrying through the currency reform, denied there was any miracle. He claims the upsurge was due to the ' honest efforts ' of the West German people who had been given, by him, the opportunity of using ' personal initiative and human energy '. Undoubtedly the ' honest efforts ' of the West Germans meaning hard work and long hours, was an important factor in getting that part of Germany on its feet again. No doubt too, Dr Erhard's policy of freeing the economy from many inherited controls helped. But there were other, even more decisive factors. Marshall Aid was one of these. West Germany was the fourth largest recipient of such aid which was particularly useful for buying new machinery and raw materials from the u s a. Secondly, Germany had reached a low ebb economically with a great deal of pent-up demand which helped to get the economic resurgence under way. Thirdly, although West Germany had occupation costs to pay, it did not have the heavy burden of armaments in the early years. Later on fairly large sums were put aside for defence but the productive capacity of the nation was not involved and could go on producing goods for export. Because of world-wide rearmament following the outbreak of the Korean war West German goods were in even greater demand. Nor was West Germany burdened with military expenditure abroad, except to a very minor extent, with its devastating effect on the balance of payments. On the contrary, Allied troops in the Federal Republic have helped to swell its ' invisible exports '. West German taxation policies have also been designed to encourage high investment. Taxes on the higher income brackets were relatively unprogressive. There were premiums for savers, subsidies for industry and exemption of overtime from tax which encouraged the practice but aided employers in keeping down the cost. Another very important fact was the situation on the labour market. West Germany had more than one million unemployed until 1955, and more than half a million until 1959. The Republic's rate of unemployment was higher than that of the u k until 1960. This obviously reduced the power of the trade unions to press wage demands. The unions had been hit initially by the currency reform which destroyed their cash reserves needed to finance industrial disputes. In addition, the union leaders were responsible men who were prepared to moderate their policies in the general interest. Codetermination in industry made it easier for them to sell a policy of moderation to their members. Reformed trade union structure made it easier to avoid interunion friction and unofficial strikes. Finally, though the Federal Republic had to contend with a flood of refugees from the East, these refugees represented an educated labour force. Many of them, especially those from the D D R, were highly skilled workers, technicians and managers.

## CODETERMINATION

Demands for some form of codetermination, workers participation in management, as well as public ownership were first heard in Germany in the nineteenth century. With the advent of the Weimar Republic they achieved some, very limited, recognition. These gains were destroyed by the Nazis but stronger demands were made by socialists. Social Democrats, Communists and trade unionists after 1945. As we have seen, these demands were in keeping with the views of the British Labour Government, which was responsible for the main industrial region of West Germany, but it had to defer to American proprivate enterprise policies because of financial dependance on the United States. The British had, however, pushed through certain reforms in 1946 and 1947 which were to be the basis for future German legislation. The Americans were more concerned with decentralisation of German heavy industry and under their influence measures were passed in the Anglo-American zones— Law No 56 in the United States Zone and Decree No 78 in the British—in February 1947, aimed at decartelisation. In the years since West Germany regained its independence this has been largely reversed.

In the early days of the Occupation, German industrialists fell over themselves to get agreement with the trade unions to try and avert complete nationalisation or worse. By the time the Federal Republic had been established the workers in the iron and steel industries had experienced codetermination and were determined to keep the gains they had made and, if possible, extend them. But the employers had regained their confidence and were hoping their friends in parliament would help them to rescind the Allied measures. They were supported by the F D P, the D P and the right wing of the Christian Democrats. In addition, the syndicate of Benelux investors in Germany made representations in Bonn against codetermination together with the American National Association of Manufacturers and the French High Commissioner. The unions prepared strike action to enforce their demands that the arrangements in the iron and steel industry should be recognised and extended to the coal and chemical industries. Only after hard bargaining was a crisis averted.

The Corporation Law of 30 January 1937 recognised three governing bodies of an industrial corporation: the general stockholders' meeting, the supervisory board of directors (*Aufsichtsrat*) and the managing board of directors (*Vorstand*). The Vorstand is elected by the *Aufsichtsrat* and carries on the day-to-day business of the enterprise. The Co-Determination (*Mitbestimmung*) Law of 10 April 1951, laid down that the *Aufsichtsrat* of every public company in the iron, steel and coal industries should consist of 11 members, of whom five were to be representative of the shareholders and the other five nominated by the employees. One of the shareholders' nominees must not be a shareholder or official of an employers' association. The five employees' representatives must include one manual and one salaried employee of the enterprise nominated by the Works' Council (*Betriebsrat*) after consultation with the trade unions, two nominated by the appropriate trade unions after consultation with the Works' Council, and one other who must not be a trade union official or an employee of the enterprise. The eleventh is elected by the other ten. Under the same law one member of the *Vorstand*, in all there are three members, who is the Personnel Director (*Arbeitsdirektor*), is nominated by the appropriate trade union. His appointment must be confirmed by the Work's Council.

A second law of July 1952 decreed that at least one-third of the members of the *Aufsichtsräte* of all joint stock companies, other than those covered by the earlier law, must be nominees of the employees. Against union wishes the law does not provide for trade-union representation from outside the enterprise on the *Aufsichtsrat*. The same law established work's councils in all enterprises employing at least five people who are 18 or over and having at least three employees over 21. The councils, elected by secret ballot for two years, must be representative of the various trades of wage-earning and salaried staff. The councils discuss everything from complaints from individual employees to holiday arrangements, technical training, proposed mergers and changes in the nature of the enterprise.

There are many problems for the unions connected with codetermination: divided loyalty is just one of them. More important, as new concentration has developed in the economy in the 1950s and 1960s, the unions have found themselves without representation on the new boards running the holding companies.

## RECOGNITION AND REARMAMENT

The government which took office in October 1949 was not master in its own house. Some relief was given under the Petersberg Agreement of 22 November 1949 between Dr Adenauer and the

Western High Commissioners (as the former Military Governors were now called). Bonn was permitted to carry on consular relations with foreign countries and participate in international organisations, and was given concessions in the question of demolitions. In return the Chancellor agreed to West Germany joining the Ruhr Authority, set up to control the industries of the Ruhr and dominated by the Western Powers. The New York conference of September 1950 brought new progress for Bonn. West Germany could take up diplomatic relations and its rights to speak for the whole of Germany was recognised. West Germany and West Berlin were given a security guarantee by the Western Powers and the Länder were allowed to set up paramilitary security police. The Federal Republic was granted important concessions regarding its industries. Restrictions on shipping and shipbuilding were lifted, it was permitted to produce artificial rubber and synthetic petrol and the situation of the chemical industry relieved. In 1951 the Republic was recognised as a full member of the Council of Europe and in the same year joined France, Italy, Belgium, Holland and Luxemburg in establishing the European Coal and Steel Community. The Community sought to create a common market for coal and steel by the elimination of restrictions in the trade in these products between the six countries. The treaty setting up the community meant the end of the Ruhr Authority, nullified the main advantages to France of the customs union between France and the Saar, and led to the lifting of the ceiling on German steel production. In July of the same year Britain and the Commonwealth, France and the U S A ended the state of war with West Germany. In September the Foreign Ministers of these three countries declared in favour of the integration of a democratic Germany into a European Community on the basis of equality, the abolition of the Occupation Regime and the cooperation of West Germany in the defence of the West.

These aims were to be realised in May 1952 with the *Deutschlandvertrag*, which ended the Occupation Regime, and the signing of the European Defence Community (E D C) agreement in Paris. At its most basic the E D C was designed to overcome the dangers of a rearmed, nationalist Germany, by creating a European Army, with a West German contingent, attached to the political institutions of a united Europe, with a European Minister of Defence. The E D C never became a reality because the French parliament failed to ratify it. West German rearmament was, however, achieved through the deliberations of conferences in London and Paris in September-October 1954. It was agreed to set up the West European Union which meant extending the Brussels (Defence) Treaty of 1948, signed by Belgium, France, Luxemburg, Holland and Britain and later joined by Italy, to include the Federal Republic. It was recommended that West Germany be admitted to N A T O. There were no hitches with the new plan and the Federal Republic regained its sovereignty in May 1955 and was admitted to the North Atlantic Treaty Organisation in the same month. Under the agreements West Germany renounced the right to manufacture on its territory (though not that to acquire or control) atomic, bacteriological and chemical weapons. It further undertook never to use force to achieve reunification or the modification of its frontiers. There was to be no new German General Staff even though Bonn would raise 500,000 men for N A T O. For their part the Western Powers once again expressed their recognition of the Federal Republic as the only ' freely and legitimately ' constituted German regime and therefore the only government entitled to speak for the German people in international affairs. They reaffirmed their view that the question of Germany's frontiers would have to await a peace settlement between a government of a free and united Germany and its former enemies.

Another important agreement of Adenauer's first term was that concluded with Israel and the Conference on Jewish Material Claims Against Germany to pay compensation for the Jewish victims of Nazism. This was in 1952. When it was debated in the Bundestag it met opposition from 238 members, including two Ministers; 402 members, mainly the S P D and part of the C D U, supported it. Indeed, the mere outlining of the development of the Federal Republic's foreign relations in these years wrongly ignores the really bitter debate which took place in the Federal Republic about these issues. We must now look at this debate and see how it affected West Germany's politics from 1949 onwards.

It was widely believed outside Germany that the Social Democratic Party of Kurt Schumacher, and after his death in 1952 of Erich Ollenhauer, was a pacifist party opposed to all rearmament. Although this was the view of many rank-and-filers, it was never the view of the leaders or official party policy. As Schumacher explained in 1950: ' The difference of opinion is not one between those who want to rearm and those who are absolute pacifists . . . the big difference is between those who simply want to push through rearmament under the present conditions, and those who reject rearmament unless certain national and international conditions are agreed to.' At the Dortmund Conference of the party in 1952 the Social Democrats set out their conditions for agreeing to rearmament. They were: that an effort be made to establish a European security system within the framework of the United Nations; that the efforts to achieve German reunification be just as strongly continued; that the treaties requiring military obligations of the Federal Republic could be dissolved by the Federal Government if these were found to hinder the reunification of Germany and such treaties should not be binding on a future government of a re-united Germany; that all participants are equal and receive equal treatment so far as defence measures are concerned.

For the Social Democrats then, German reunification remained more important than German rearmament. Schumacher himself was from the area beyond the Oder-Neisse Line, Adenauer was from the Rhineland and was accused of being a separatist in the 1920s. Their backgrounds coloured the views of these two politicians on the reunification issue to some extent. Schumacher also differed from Adenauer in that he saw the danger of Communism in social and economic terms rather than military ones. If the Federal Republic adopted progressive social and economic policies it would not be ripe for Communist infiltration. On the other hand, hurried rearmament brought with it the danger from the militarists who would once again wield tremendous power. Against this Adenauer was a keen protagonist of *die Politik der Stärke*, the policy of strength, meaning military strength. If the West became strong enough it could 'roll back the Iron Curtain'! Once the West became strong enough it could, he said in March 1952, 'conduct reasonable conversations with the Soviet Union'. He did not understand that the Soviet Union was getting stronger too. Once the Soviet Union broke the U S monopoly of nuclear weapons in 1949 a decisive weapon was virtually neutralised. Even then the Russians did not relish the thought of a strong, Western-orientated, German military force, backed by enormous economic and scientific power. Just what they were prepared to give up to allay this nightmare we do not know, but in 1952 they made an offer which, though belated, looked attractive and might have been serious.

In its note of 10 March to 1952 to the Western Powers the Soviet Government called for a peace conference between the nations whose forces had fought against Germany and 'an all-German Government'. The Soviet Union was willing to offer the Germans complete freedom for German industry to expand and export, German national land, sea and air forces 'which are necessary for the defence of the country', German arms production sufficient to equip such armed forces, German membership of the U N O, full civil rights for all former officers and men of the German armed forces and for all former Nazis, except for those in prison as a result of court action. In return Germany would give up the territories east of the Oder-Neisse Line, it would not join any coalition or military alliance directed against any state which had fought against Germany, and all organisations opposed to peace and democracy would be banned on German territory. The note also called for the removal of all foreign troops and bases from German territory within one year of the signing of a peace treaty. None of these conditions was really so harsh. Even the one concerning anti-democratic organisations was similar to a clause in the West German Basic Law, though it might have meant, in addition to the banning of outright neo-Nazi parties, the winding up of refugee organisations. This could have represented a political advantage for the C D U and F D P.

One vital point the note did not mention: how the 'all-German Government' was to be formed. Was it to be the result of all-German elections? In a later note of 9 April the Soviet Government agreed to all-German elections being carried through under a commission made up of representatives of the Four Powers. Neither the Western Powers nor the West German Government were prepared to accept the Soviet conditions of German neutrality or recognition of the Oder-Neisse Line. An American note of 25 March demanded that the 'all-German Government ought to be free both before and after the conclusion of a peace treaty to enter alliances which are in line with the principles and aims of the United Nations'. According to the Western view N A T O was such an alliance. Further, the American note stated that the frontiers of Germany must be decided at a peace conference, not before. In a memorandum presented by Dr Adenauer to President Eisenhower of the United States on 29 May 1953 the Chancellor expressed the view that 'no German Government would ever be in a position to recognise the Oder-Neisse Line', though Germany tried to solve the problem of its frontiers in a new spirit of international co-operation.

The majority of people in leading circles in Bonn and other Western capitals regarded the Soviet notes as merely a means to hold up Western defence planning and were therefore not prepared to go beyond repetition of well-known Western views. The Social Democrats, on the other hand, though by no means convinced the Russians were sincere, wanted the West to examine the Soviet proposals carefully. In this they were backed up by small groups of neutralists in the Federal Republic. The most significant of these was one led by Dr Gustav Heinemann, who as a leading Protestant churchman had risen to the post of Minister of Interior in Dr

Adenauer's first Cabinet. Heinemann resigned in 1950 in protest against the setting up of paramilitary police formations.

## ADENAUER RE-ELECTED

The election of September 1953 was fought by the Social Democrats to a great extent on the issues of German reunification and defence. They accused the Federal Government of having failed to make serious attempts to bring about German unity. And they claimed that the policy of Western integration of the Federal Republic reduced it to a position of inferiority and one-sided foreign control. A majority of West Germans did not appear to share this opinion. Many of them had as much fear and hatred of the Russians as the Russians had of them. Though they did not want war, they believed only a show of strength would make the Soviets vacate the D D R and the lost territories. Many of them were impressed by what had already been achieved for West Germany in international affairs. Once again Germany's voice counted and even if foreigners did not love the Germans, they respected them. More Germans still were impressed by the apparent economic miracle at home. True, the prices in the shops were still high, hours of work were long, there was a great housing shortage, and there were about 12 million West Germans living on pensions or welfare payments of one kind or another, quite apart from the unemployed. Yet despite all this there had been a change for the better. The bulging shop windows, the buzzing economic activity throughout the Republic and the export records offered hope.

Of course, it must not be forgotten, that even if the situation had been entirely different the C D U/C S U would have had the mass support ensured by Church backing. The Social Democrats suffered too from the high proportion of women voters—a result of two world wars. In Germany, as elsewhere, women, and especially older women, tend to be more Conservative than men. Many of the younger male working-class, who form a natural reserve of voters for Left-wing parties, had been killed in the war. The Christian Democrats fought a hard campaign, calling the S P D the party of Marxism and claiming 'all Marxism leads to Moscow'. The S P D suffered from two other factors. Firstly, its much-respected leader, Dr Kurt Schumacher, had died in 1952, and there had been little time for the new leader, a sincere but not very charismatic figure, to establish himself. Secondly, in June 1953 strikes and demonstrations had broken out in the D D R and had been put down by Soviet tanks and this tended to convince voters that Adenauer's policy of strength was the only valid one in dealing with the Russians. The turnout of voters rose from 78.5 per cent in 1949 to 85.8 per cent in 1953. Undoubtedly, the higher turnout brought ' unpolitical ' voters to the polling stations where they voted C D U/C S U.

The Christian Democrats gained 45.2 per cent of the vote as against 28.8 per cent for the S P D and 9.5 per cent for the F D P. The S P D actually increased its vote in absolute terms and, therefore, the number of its members of the Bundestag. The small parties did not do as well as in 1949. One of the reasons for this was the stiffening of that part of the electoral law designed to eliminate small parties. In 1949, in order to gain representation in the Bundestag parties either had to win a constituency directly, by getting the highest number of votes in that constituency, or had to secure a minimum of five per cent of the votes in any given Land of the Republic. These votes were then distributed according to the principle of proportional representation. Under the new law parties had to gain five per cent of the votes throughout the Federation. This made it more difficult for parties which were confined to particular Länder. The Bavarian Party was the main one of these. It did not secure renewed representation in the Bundestag. The Communists also failed to get back gaining only 2.2 per cent of the vote. The German Party won only 3.2 per cent of the vote but gained a number of constituencies due mainly to electoral alliances with its partners in the government. The Centre Party returned three members in 1953 through an alliance with the C D U. One new party to secure representation was the B H E, the Refugee Party. Founded in 1950 in Schleswig-Holstein it soon became a force throughout the Federal Republic. It was mainly concerned with the problems of the refugees and demands for a return of the Sudetenland and the territories beyond the Oder-Neisse Line. It won 5.9 per cent of the vote and 27 seats.

Excluding the West Berlin members, who were elected by the parliament of West Berlin, the C D U/C S U had won half the seats in the Federal Parliament. This was something new in German politics. Dr Adenauer renewed his coalition with the F D P and the D P and brought the Refugee Party into government as well. The Bonn Cabinet took on a more distinctive Right-wing flavour.

RESTORATION

The new Minister who personified this more Right-wing flavour was Dr Theodor Oberländer. A member of the B H E, he became Minister of Refugees. Oberländer was an ' Eastern expert ' of the Nazi party and a member of the S S; he was later forced out of office by world public opinion after East German revelations about his past. The

K

Minister of Interior, Gerhard Schröder, was a former Nazi member; Heinrich Lübke, Minister of Agriculture, was later to be in trouble because of his wartime activities; Hans-Christoph Seebohm, Minister of Transport, became notorious for his utterances on behalf of the Sudeten Germans; Viktor-Emanuel Preusker, Minister of Housing, had been in the S A and S S; Waldemar Kraft, Minister for Special Assignments, was ex-S S. Over a third of the Cabinet, therefore, had doubtful pasts,

People started to talk about a ' restoration ' of the Nazis. And indeed the early 1950s saw a massive reinstatement of former officials of the Third Reich and pensions for those who could not be given their old jobs back. In 1952 Dr Adenauer admitted in the Bundestag that two-thirds of the senior officials in the Federal Republic's Foreign Service were former Nazi party members. The same was true of many of the other ministries. Among the more notorious cases were those of Dr Hans Globke, Adenauer's chief personal adviser, who was co-author of the official commentary on the Nazi Nuremberg Race Laws; Friedrich Vialon, a State Secretary whose signature was found on decrees about the disposal of the belongings of Jews earmarked for extermination; and Franz Thedieck, State Secretary, who had the special task in occupied Belgium of ' maintaining close cooperation with the S S ', and during whose service 25,000 Belgians were deported to Auschwitz.

Pensions for ex-Nazis, including convicted war criminals (pensions which often compared very well with those of Hitler's victims) were another feature of the restoration. Admiral Erich Raeder was granted a monthly pension of 2,246 D M (about £180 or $550 at that time). The widow of Heydrich, Himmler's deputy responsible for occupied Czechoslovakia, received 1,000 D M per month (about £80 or $200). Anton Kassler, former commandant of Sachsenhausen concentration camp, was paid 6,000 D M (£500 or $1,500) as a kind of resettlement grant. There were very many other similar cases.

Another shocking aspect of the restoration in the early 1950s were the many Nazi doctors who had experimented on patients in concentration camps who found their way back into well-paid official positions. Here one of the worst cases which came to light was that of Dr Hertha Oberheuser. She had been sentenced to 20 years' imprisonment by a U S court for crimes committed in the women's concentration camp at Ravensbrück. She was released in 1952 and was recommended for preferential treatment by the West German Ministry of Labour and found employment in an Evangelical Church hospital. Later she set up a private practice near Kiel. In 1958 the British Medical Association felt obliged to protest against this and similar cases saying, in a resolution, that this was a ' cynical affront to the honour, morals and high ideals of the true practice of medicine throughout the world '.

The problem of what to do with the millions of ex-Nazis was a very difficult one. No democratic society can afford to have for long a large group of its citizens who harbour a deep sense of grievance, reject the system, and feel outside it. They could soon become the basis for a new extremist party. Moreover, many of those who had voted for the Nazis, and many who had joined the party, did so solely because they despaired of Weimar's ability to solve the problem of mass unemployment, defend Germany's frontiers and regain Germany's legitimate place in the world. It is doubtful whether the mass of them were highly conscious anti-semites. Many others joined the Nazi party solely to keep their jobs, or because one stood a better chance of getting a job with a party card in one's pocket. Other Germans, who may or may not have been in the N S D A P, were appalled by revelations about Nazi atrocities, but felt that Germany had paid the price in the mass aerial bombings and the expulsion of millions of Germans from their homes in the East. They therefore felt there should be no more emphasis on Nazi crimes and no more prosecution or purging of, to them, German ' war criminals '. Dr Adenauer was conscious of all these considerations and this prompted him to a generous policy towards former Nazis. No doubt this paid off in votes. As the above cases show, what might have been conceived as a policy based on political realism and Christian charity became a potentially dangerous policy of over-indulgence towards the ex-Nazis.

MISSION TO MOSCOW

No doubt feeling increasingly confident of his own diplomatic skills and under considerable presure both from the S P D and from his own coalition partners, the F D P, Dr Adenauer decided to negotiate directly with Moscow. He was further encouraged by the more friendly attitude towards the outside world of the Soviet leaders since the death of Stalin in 1953. In May 1955 Austria had regained its independence by a state treaty which led to the withdrawal of the four occupation forces. Austria, however, paid a price Adenauer had not been willing to pay—neutrality. (However, Adenauer's supporters argued that a solution which worked for tiny Austria would never work for mighty Germany.) The Soviet leaders also patched up their quarrel with President Tito of Yugoslavia, a quarrel started by Stalin in 1948. Chancellor Adenauer visited Moscow after these two events in September 1955. He took with him representatives of the opposition led by Prof. Carlo Schmid. He wanted to discuss with the Soviets the question of German reunification and the return of German prisoners-of-war. Little progress was made on the major issue but Adenauer got a promise on the second and it was not long before thousands of Germans, some of them war criminals, were allowed to return home. Bonn and Moscow decided to establish diplomatic relations which shocked some of Adenauer's political friends. The Chancellor insisted that this did not imply any weakening on Bonn's part and he forced the Russians to accept a note stating that the Federal Republic still did not recognise any of the territorial changes made since 1945. Close on the heels of Adenauer's delegation was one from the D D R. It regained the formal sovereignty for that part of Germany with the right to enter into diplomatic relations with other states. Thus Moscow had diplomatic relations with both German states. If other nations did the same it would make it very difficult for Bonn to claim convincingly that it was the only real German state and the only one entitled to speak on behalf of all Germans. To counter this threat Bonn thought up the Hallstein Doctrine. Though apparently it was formulated by diplomat Wilhelm Grewe, it was associated with the name of Walter Hallstein, State Secretary of the Foreign Office who later became President of the Commission of the European Economic Community. The Doctrine was quite simply that recognition of the D D R by any state would be seen by Bonn as an unfriendly act and Bonn would not have, or would break off, diplomatic relations with such a state. This happened in 1957 with Yugoslavia after she had recognised the D D R. Due to the power of its purse Bonn managed to prevent the nations of the Third World from recognising East Germany. But it could not prevent the East Europeans from recognising Herr Ulbricht's regime and by maintaining the Hallstein Doctrine, West Germany kept itself out of Eastern Europe until late into the 1960s.

Dr Adenauer's failure in the East was overshadowed by new successes in the West. At a conference of the Foreign Ministers of the six countries of the Coal and Steel Community, held at Messina in Sicily in May 1955, proposals were discussed for further advances towards European economic integration. This led in March 1957 to the Rome Treaties signed by the six nations. The first of these set up the Common Market through the progressive reduction and elimination of tariffs and quota restrictions between members, harmonisation of economic policies, and the consolidation of the external tariffs of the six into a single tariff system, applicable to imports from outside the Community. The Treaty seemed to offer the rapidly expanding German industry golden opportunities in a large market. German farmers were later to grumble about the effects of the Treaty on them. The second Treaty provided for the coordination of nuclear research and power projects within the Community.

Another outstanding success for the Federal Republic in this period was the return of the Saar to Germany. This was effective from 1 January 1957 following a referendum in October 1955 in which 67.7 per cent of the Saar people voted for a return to Germany. As the author remembers, German hearts swelled as the barriers between the Federal Republic and the Saar came down.

## ABSOLUTE MAJORITY

During Dr Adenauer's second term of office from 1953 to 1957 the Federal Republic had regained its sovereignty, become a member of NATO, joined the Common Market and been reunited with the Saar. It was an impressive record. The Chancellor could also claim he had tried to reach agreement with Moscow, even taking Social Democrats with him to help, and if he had failed there it was not his fault.

In home affairs, although the Federal Republic was a land of sharp social contracts, unemployment had fallen from 7.5 to 3.4 per cent and some highly desirable social legislation had been passed. The most important measure was the new system of retirement pensions introduced in 1957. Instead of the pensioner receiving a flat-rate payment, which declines as the cost of living rises and which is well below what the wage earner received during his working life, the West German pension is wage-(or salary-) related, and account is taken of the cost of living. This put the Federal Republic ahead of most other countries in this respect. Ironically, West Germany took the idea over from Social Democratic Sweden and the German Social Democrats had done much to make the scheme popular in Germany, but it became law under Dr Adenauer's auspices. The Federal Republic also had a very good house-building record, completing well over half a million houses per annum from 1953 onwards. Once again some of the best results were achieved by Social Democratic-controlled Länder authorities, Bremen, Hamburg, West Berlin, for instance. All this contrasted with the harder life in the 'Socialist' DDR and in the months before the election of September 1957 Adenauer's propagandists tried to link, in the public mind, the 'Socialist' SPD with the 'Socialist' DDR. At one point the Chancellor actually accused some Social Democratic officials of receiving funds from East Germany—a charge he withdrew *after* the election. More legitimately C D U propagandists could claim that in 1949 the S P D had favoured 'planning' rather than a 'free' economy and that they had been proved wrong on this.

Remarkably, despite his apparent successes, Dr Adenauer was not so very popular in 1956. In August of that year public opinion research bodies indicated that within 12 months the proportion of the population favourable to the Chancellor's policies had fallen from 59 to 37 per cent, and according to a poll of July 1956 only 34 per cent of West Germans wanted Adenauer to serve for another four-year term, while 44 per cent believed he should retire. These polls were confirmed by local and Länder elections later in the same year.

One factor in the Chancellor's unpopularity was growing working-class opposition to him. 1956 saw a long and bitter metal-workers' strike which was one of the few really big labour disputes in postwar West Germany. The Bonn coalition was also in disarray. The Free Democrats had not been too happy with the Chancellor's foreign policy. They disagreed when Adenauer had acquiesced in the 'Europeanisation' of the Saar in 1954-55 and again they sympathised with the S P D's view that Adenauer's foreign policy made German reunification more difficult. Early in 1956 some Free Democrats in North-Rhine Westphalia revolted against continued alliance with the C D U. They formed a coalition in West Germany's most important Land with the S P D. This in turn lost the Chancellor his two-thirds majority in the Upper House which could impede constitutional amendments. An angry debate broke out in the F D P which led to all the party's ministers in the Bonn coalition leaving the F D P to form the Free People's Party (F V P). Already in the summer of 1955 a split had developed in the Refugee Party and though its two ministers remained in the government, the party itself went into opposition.

In the autumn of 1956 when the situation seemed far from rosy for Dr Adenauer the Russians once again came to his aid. The Hungarian Revolution of October 1956, smashed by the Soviet armed forces, brought panic-stricken German voters behind the Chancellor. Right up to the election the C D U/C S U exploited this event. In a highly professional publicity campaign, made possible by millions of marks from industrial concerns, the Christian Democratic slogan was 'No Experiments'. Believing, as the Secretary-General of the C D U Dr Bruno Heck put it, that 'The electorate wants a ruler type', the Christian Democrats released a 'Big Brother' poster. This widely distributed poster depicted Adenauer as a serious, sun-bronzed, fair-haired, father figure with penetrating blue eyes which appeared to follow the passer-by. It is believed it helped to convince the women. A majority of valid votes, 54 per cent, were cast by women, and a majority of these went to the Christian Democrats. In other respects too the trends of 1953 continued. The turnout of voters rose from 85.8 per cent to 87.8 per cent. The Christian Democrats were helped by the return of the predominently Catholic Saar a majority of whose population voted C D U. For the first time in German parliamentary history one party, the C D U/C S U, received a majority, 50.2 per cent, of the votes. This gave them 270 seats. The S P D gained 31.8 per cent and 169 seats. Their votes had been swelled to some extent by Dr Heinemann's supporters who had disbanded their own party to join the S P D. The Communist Party had been banned in September 1956 and its voters had undoubtedly turned to the S P D in great numbers. The F D P was reduced to 7.7 per cent and 41 seats. No other parties gained representation in the Bundestag.

## CRITICAL VOICES

The election results might lead one to believe that critical voices had no place. This was not the case. The cultural scene has not been as exotic as it had been in Weimar but there are those in the theatre, the cinema, among the writers and the journalists who have carried on the critical traditions of the 1920s.

Germany is the classic land of political cabaret and to be sure after 1945 such night clubs were opened in the major cities of West Germany but, the experts say, they have not achieved the standards of the pre-1933 clubs. Wolfgang Neuss of West Berlin is the best-known exponent of this art.

The West German cinema has suffered from lack of finance and competition from television and foreign films. Split up into a number of small companies, it has had to cater for the less discriminating cinema patron. Most of its production has been comedies about rural Bavaria, the so-called *Heimat* (homeland) films, cowboy and detective dramas, and rather superficial war stories. A few directors have shown greater courage, among the better known of whom are Wolfgang Staudte and Bernhard Wicki. Wicki, born in Switzerland, made a number of pacifist-inclined films—*The Bridge, Children, Mothers and a General*—and a socially-critical film, *The Miracle of Malachias,* completed in 1961.

Obviously many German writers have been concerned with the events between 1933-45 and there has been a ready market for such literature. Novels about the experiences of ordinary soldiers, which exposed the horror of war, included: Remarque's *A Time To Live And A Time To Die*, Helmut Kirst's *08/15* (and other books), and Heinrich Böll's stories of the Eastern Front. In his *Stalingrad* and *Berlin* Theodor Plievier, an emigrant in Russia who later went West, tried to show life on both sides. Carl Zuckmayer examined the morality of the 'non-political' general in *The Devil's General*.

Few writers have dealt successfully with the reality of post-war Germany. The most outstanding of those who have is Heinrich Böll. Born into a Catholic, working class family, in Cologne in 1917, his 'heroes' are those without wordly ambition, the down-at-heel, the war widow, the tenement-dweller. He criticised the priests of his church who were more concerned with saving the young serviceman from the prostitute than from the prostitution of service for Hitler.

Equally original, and equally famous is Günter Grass. In 1959 he published his strange, off-beat, novel, *The Tin Drum*, about a nasty-minded dwarf from Danzig, through whose eyes we see a panorama of the long German nightmare since the 1920s. The book provoked extreme reactions. Grass, only sixteen when the war ended, belongs to the younger generation of more aggressively critical writers. Rolf Hochhuth and Uwe Johnson are among the better-known members of this generation. Hochhuth caused anger and praise for his play *The Representative* in which he bitterly attacked the Catholic Church, and in particular the Vatican, for not condemning Nazism more clearly. Johnson, an emigrant from the D D R, has been concerned with the effects of the partition of Germany in his *Two Views* and *Speculations About Jacob*.

Highly critical about the state of West German Society Grass and Hochhuth have supported the S P D. Böll, though a Catholic, has attacked the S P D for its drift to the Right. He has been even more critical of the Christian Democrats.

Given the situation in the West German press it is remarkable that any journalist would chance his arm to strike at authority. The largest newspapers—*Bild Zeitung, BZ, Die Welt,* etc., are the property of one man. The Hamburg 'press lord' Axel Springer was responsible in 1967 for 39 per cent of the circulation of daily papers and over 9 per cent of all periodicals. He has been strongly criticised for pro-cold war, anti-S P D line of his publications. Despite Herr Springer's power, liberal, critical, even some radical, opinions find their way into significant publications in West Germany. Among the 'quality' dailies there are the *Süddeutsche Zeitung* and the *Frankfurter Rundschau* representing the liberal tendency. But up to 1970 both had lower circulations than Springer's *Die Welt* and the more conservative *Frankfurter Allgemeine Zeitung.* In the popular sector there were no radical papers. Unorthodox views are also found in the highly respected weeklies *Die Zeit* and *Der Spiegel,* and in the illustrated magazines *Stern, Quick* and *Konkret.*

West German television producers and journalists have also been prepared to voice independent and critical opinions over the years —often to their cost! The documentary programme *Panorama* put out by the North German Broadcasting Corporation (N D R) established itself in the 1960s as a serious, yet popular, commentary on world events. But many of its leading staff were removed for offending the Christian Democrats and other interests.

In East Germany no such critical voices were heard. There, writers, directors and artists had to fall in line with the S E D's interpretation of what were suitable themes and how these themes should be handled. The results were that little new of value was produced. Though such eminent writers as Anna Seghers, Arnold Zweig, Stefan Heym, Ludwig Renn, Johannes R. Becher, and, above all, Bertolt Brecht, had chosen to reside there, their output was small. Many writers preferred to avoid contemporary problems keeping to the (safer) horrors of the Third Reich. Some of those who have successfully confronted post-war reality, Wolf Biermann and Christa Wolf, have had their difficulties. One who has not is Dieter Noll whose *Adventures of Werner Holt* achieved success in the 1960s, though the most popular part of this work dealt with the Nazi period. For its cultural image the D D R has had to rely on the high technical achievements of the Berliner Ensemble, which mainly stages the works of Brecht, its orchestras, and occasional documentary films such as those by Walter Heynowski and Gerhard Scheumann on the Congo and Vietnam.

## THE S P D AT BAD GODESBERG

Naturally the defeat of 1957 was a staggering blow to the S P D and, as is usual after such defeats, many discussions were held to see how the party could make itself more attractive to the electorate. Particularly active were those who claimed the party had lost because it was too negative, appeared as a narrow, old-fashioned, class-war party, talking in terms of Marxism, and public ownership which confused it in the public mind with the East German S E D. Further, it was said that the party was too ambivalent on defence (an important consideration for many electors) and not friendly enough to the churches in a country where religion, especially the Catholic religion, was still important.

The S P D had in fact been slowly changing its views over the

years. Though it called for the common ownership of coal, iron
and steel and energy, the Dortmund Programme of 1952 was neither
a thorough-going Socialist programme nor was it couched in class-
war terms. At one point it called for help for middle-class enterprises.
The S P D was changing because Schumacher had encouraged the
recruitment of middle class members who knew little of Marxist
traditions and less of working class life. These included Prof. Karl
Schiller, Prof. Carlo Schmid and Helmut Schmidt, among others.
Secondly, some of those who had been emigrants—Willy Brandt,
Erich Ollenhauer in the Anglo-Saxon countries or Scandinavia were
impressed by the empiricism of their socialists as against the Marxism
of continental socialists. On the other hand, they were put off
ideology by experience of Nazism and Communism. The latter also
reduced their enthusiasm for nationalisation. As far as religion was
concerned, as early as 1946 at Hanover, Schumacher had proclaimed
that it did not matter how a man came to socialism—through Marx
or the Sermon on the Mount. The declaration of the Socialist International at Frankfurt in 1951, signed by the S P D, incorporated this
idea. There was no hard evidence that the S P D had lost votes
because it had advocated public ownership of the basic industries,
or because it was thought to be Marxist and anti-religious. But
successive defeats won a majority of the party leaders for a thorough-
going attempt to improve the party's image.

One of the most prominent of these was Herbert Wehner who had
been a fairly senior Communist in the Weimar Republic. The
programme adopted by the Bad Godesberg conference in 1959 by
324 votes to 16 was designed to do just that. The programme calls
for a ' free partnership ' between the S P D and the churches, says
that Socialism is rooted in Christianity, calls for the protection and
encouragement of private ownership of the means of production,
and proclaims the S P D's positive attitude to national defence.
Within a matter of months S P D leaders were calling for a united
front on national questions.

The S P D was obviously preparing its campaign for the 1961
election. Its Chancellor candidate was Willy Brandt, since 1957 the
world-famous Lord Mayor of West Berlin. This time it was going in
for a promotion campaign of American style and dimensions. Brandt
tried to play the German Kennedy, the latter having become U S
President in January 1961, and made a fairly convincing job of it.
This time too a crisis was to work in the Social Democrats' favour.
This was the renewed crisis over Berlin which started with a
Khrushchev speech threatening the Western position in West Berlin
in 1958 and ended with the building of the Berlin wall by Walter

Ulbricht's regime in August 1961. The building of the wall exposed not only the weakness of the East German regime (it was erected to stop East Germans going West), but showed up Adenauer's claims that the *Politik der Stärke* would lead to German reunification. Another matter which had dented the Chancellor's image was his statement in April 1959 that he would like to stand as Federal President on the retirement of Theodor Heuss in that year. Adenauer was by then 83 years old and said he would give the Presidency the influence it deserved!

When the votes came to be counted in September 1961 they indicated that *Der Alte*'s (as Adenauer was nicknamed) popularity was on the wane. The C D U/C S U's share fell to 45.3 per cent and 242 seats. The S P D increased its share to 36.3 per cent and 190 seats, and the Free Democrats jumped to 12.7 per cent and 67 seats. They were the only parties to be returned to parliament. The Free Democrats had gained from the promise made by their leader, Dr Erich Mende, that he would not serve in a Cabinet which Dr Adenauer led. This party also gained for its more positive and flexible stand on German reunification even though it had for years been in government with the Christian Democrats. No doubt too it gained votes from disillusioned middle-class voters who still could not bring themselves to vote for a 'working-class party', the Social Democrats. It is possible that had the S P D given a clearer alternative to the Christian Democrats on national issues it might have gained more ground still.

Dr Mende kept his promise but once again a coalition was formed between the C D U/C S U and the F D P. The Free Democrats, however, got Adenauer to promise that he would retire within two years. Before the Chancellor finally retired he was to face one more great political crisis.

### THE SPIEGEL AFFAIR

Adenauer's last crisis concerned action taken against the news magazine *Der Spiegel*, one of the Federal Republic's two leading weeklies. Although not associated with any political party *Der Spiegel* had often criticised various aspects of government policy and had been an outspoken critic of the Bavarian Franz-Josef Strauss since he had taken over the Defence Ministry in 1956. The magazine attacked what it considered to be the Minister's personal deficiencies as well as his policies. In its edition of 10 October 1962 *Der Spiegel* published an article attacking the performance of the *Bundeswehr* (armed forces) as revealed in the N A T O exercise 'Fallex'. A police raid, which reminded the public of those of the 1920s and early

1930s, was made on the offices of the magazine in Hamburg. Leading journalists were arrested either in their offices or homes, one, Conrad Ahlers, was arrested by Spanish police while on holiday. The authorities claimed the article was treasonable because it contained military secrets. The proceedings against Ahlers and Rudolf Augstein, the publisher, who was detained in prison for 14 weeks, were given up in 1965 for lack of evidence. The S P D and the F D P alleged that the authorities, in particular Herr Strauss, were guilty of unconstitutional action. Eventually, in 1966 the Constitutional Court divided evenly on that issue. But the resignation of five F D P Ministers in November 1962 caused a political crisis which forced the Defence Minister from office.

Herr Strauss's departure was more agonising because West German Christian Democracy was going through a deep crisis. For years there had been tension between the more socially-orientated, more working-class, ' Left wing ' of the C D U typified (until his death in 1958) by Karl Arnold, Prime Minister of North-Rhine Westphalia from 1947 to 1956, and the business wing of the party. The latter group had gained the ascendancy by the early 1950s but the Left remained strong enough to force through certain social legislation. The crisis of the early 1960s was of a different nature. With Dr Adenauer's retirement not far off personal rivalries increased. Dr Erhard, Economics Minister, creator of the ' economic miracle ', had surrounded himself with a group of supporters. But they were opposed by the ambitious Herr Strauss who could whip up Bavarian patriotism to support his claims. Strauss also cloaked his ambitions in a vague ideology. He became known as a German ' Gaullist '. His position was supported by Baron von Guttenberg, Wilhelm Grewe, Heinrich von Brentano, who was Foreign Minister from 1955 to 1961, and others. Dr Adenauer also inclined to this view. Very roughly the group stressed Europe's role in economic, political and military terms but, unlike President de Gaulle, they advocated a tough line with the Soviets. Erhard and Dr Gerhard Schröder, Minister of Interior 1953-61, Foreign Minister 1961-1966, looked more to the U S A and the ' Atlantic Community '. As the United States under President (1961-63) John Kennedy, were pursuing a more conciliatory policy towards Moscow, Erhard and Schröder were prepared for small concessions in that direction.

Dr Adenauer's last journey as a statesman was his visit to Paris in January 1963 to conclude a Franco-German Treaty of Friendship. During the visit, the French President questioned Britain's qualifications for entry into the Common Market. As a result when ratifying the Treaty, the Bundestag insisted on inserting a preamble which reaffirmed the West German desire to maintain the Atlantic alliance and admit Britain to the European Community. Nevertheless, the Franco-German Treaty must have given great satisfaction to many ordinary Germans. It gave another boost to the German ' Gaullists '.

# 8   Ulbricht's Germany

By the time the German Democratic Republic was set up in October 1949 control by elements subservient to Moscow had been virtually secured. Parliament consisted only of representatives of the five official parties and the ' mass organisations ' and was thus a rubber stamp. The parties and the mass organisations had been purged of most leaders who might have displayed any independence, and, in any case, their organisations were held firmly within the corset of the National Front. The radio, cinema and most of the press were under the control of the s E D, as were the police, education and the economy. Apart from the Soviet secret police, an East German security police was being built up. This work was completed with the founding of the Ministry for State Security—*Ministerium für Staatssicherheit*—in February 1950. In all spheres the tendency was towards centralisation. For instance, in July 1952 the Länder were abolished and replaced by 14 weak districts or *Bezirke* subject to central authority.

Despite all these measures unorthodox views were still sometimes heard. Representatives of the churches criticised various aspects of official policy as did members of the c D U and L D P D. C D U Chairman Otto Nuschke spoke out, at his party's congress in November 1949, against single-list elections. Such elections were nevertheless carried through in October of the following year. They followed what was by that time standard practice in Eastern Europe. There was not only a single list with one candidate per seat, but no opposition was permitted. The mass media exhorted the electorate to vote greatly over-simplifying the issues, large numbers of agitators went round urging the reluctant to go to the polling stations, and in some cases they were marched there *en bloc*. On arrival all they had to do was to collect their ballot paper, fold it and put it into the box. Only those wishing to cross out names of the National Front candidates needed to go to the cubicles provided. By so doing they were drawing attention to themselves and it is not surprising, therefore, that few availed themselves of the opportunity. It might be wondered why the regime bothered with such manifestly unfree elections. Yet every regime wishes to appear to be based on the popular will and by showing they can force their citizens to conform, authoritarian systems demoralise their opponents. The Communists also regard their elections as a means of popular education for the ' campaign ' lasts for several months, during which the regime's immediate and long term aims are discussed.

Another question which needs clarification is why those in effective control of East Germany maintain five political parties when all have the same aims, methods and policies, and are not allowed even the slightest degree of autonomy. Once again there is the need for window-dressing; five parties look better than one, for there is then the illusion of choice. Secondly, a one-party state might have reminded the East Germans too much of the Third Reich and led them to conclude the regimes were similar. Thirdly, the four ' allied ' parties help to win for the regime supporters who would not want to join the S E D, officially a Marxist working-class party. As its name proclaims, the Christian Democratic Union seeks to win Christians for its objects, which since its sixth party congress in October 1952 have been, ' in the spirit of Christian responsibility, to mobilise all our energies in the struggle for Peace, Unity and Socialism '. Such a party would cater for the tiny handful of genuine Christian socialists or pacifists prepared to cooperate with the Communists, the very much larger group of middle-class business and professional people and some pastors, who try to save what they can of their old values and way of life, and those who feel they need to indicate some degree of acceptance of the regime but do not want to get too deeply involved. Further, the continued existence of this party has meant that many of the original members, who joined before the fate of the C D U became clear, could be ' trapped ' in their party and utilised for the regime. Finally, there are those who have been ordered into this party by their S E D superiors.

The membership of the other ' bourgeois ' parties is largely made up of the same type of people with the same reasons for joining, except that the N D P D was set up to win over former nominal Nazis and officers for the regime, and the L P D aimed more at the non-church orientated middle class.

The ' bourgeois ' parties of East Germany have also served as bridges between the D D R and bourgeois groups in West Germany and other countries. The L D P D, for example, has had exchanges with the Free Democrats of West Germany and with the British Young Liberals, the C D U with Left-wing Catholic groups, and so on. The S E D would find it difficult to make these contacts.

The years 1948-53 were in very many respects grim years in Eastern Europe. They were the years of Stalin's purges, forced industrialisation and intensified class struggle. East Germany fitted into this general pattern. First there were purges in the Christian Democratic and Liberal Democratic parties designed to remove those who still showed independence. Then came similar moves in the Socialist Unity Party.

In September 1948 the Unity Party's executive committee announced decisions which were to bring East Germany into line with what was happening in the rest of Eastern Europe. In June of that year the Communist Information Bureau or Cominform, made up of the Communist parties of Eastern Europe (excluding the S E D) and those of France and Italy, expelled the Yugoslav party. It was claimed the Yugoslavs had ' pursued an incorrect line on the main questions of home and foreign policy, a line which represents a departure from Marxism-Leninism '. The Yugoslavs were further accused of ' seceding from the united socialist front against imperialism, have taken the path of betraying the cause of inter-national solidarity of the working people, and have taken up a position of nationalism . . .' Tito's main ' crime ' was his refusal to subordinate the interests of Yugoslavia to those of the Soviet Union, and his refusal to imitate the Russians in every sphere. Stalin feared that Tito would find friends and allies in the other countries of the Soviet bloc. He therefore unleashed a purge which was to lead to the deaths of leading Communists throughout Eastern Europe. The Socialist Unity Party could not for long remain uninfluenced by this development especially as East Germany was under Soviet military rule at the time. The September decisions of the S E D executive represented its recognition of this. The executive called for a ' struggle against nationalism, the slandering of the Soviet Union and Peoples' Democracies, and against the theory of a special " German road to Socialism " '. Another executive decision was the establishment of a party central control commission, similar to that of the Soviet C P, to supervise party members and, if necessary, to discipline or expel them.

The S E D four-day conference of January 1949 was another decisive step along the road to changing the nature of the party. The conference demanded that the S E D must become a ' party of a new type ', in other words, a Leninist or Moscow-type organ-isation. It would accept Leninism including Democratic Centralism, as well as Marxism, and abolition of the parity principle under which former K P D and former S P D members were equally represented at all levels, and become an élite party. In future would-be members had to serve for one or two years, depending on their social back-ground, before they could become full members. The conference decided on the setting up of a Politburo to lead the party, this too was on the Soviet model.

In July 1950 the third congress of the S E D was held. It introduced a Soviet-style constitution for the party including the replacement of the executive committee by a central committee. Walter Ulbricht, widely regarded as Moscow's chief agent in East Germany, was elected secretary general of the party—the key position in any Communist state. Another change in the S E D agreed at this congress was the change in structure. Henceforth, party members would belong where possible to a unit at their place of work rather than where they live, though residential units were not abolished. This again was in line with the K P D and Soviet tradition.

In August 1950 the first major purge in the S E D took place. Stalin had linked ' Titoism ' with ' Trotskyism ' and both with ' Social Democratism '. In other words, roughly speaking, anyone who voiced doubts about Soviet actions in Germany, or about the wholesale adoption of Soviet methods, norms or terminology, could find himself accused of ' Titoism ' or ' nationalism '. Anyone who criticised bureaucracy was in danger of being labelled a ' Trotskyite ', or anyone who resisted the destruction of internal party democracy or wanted the trade unions to act as trade unions could be dubbed a ' Social Democrat '. Stalin also regarded the Zionist movement as an international conspiracy working on behalf of United States imperialism, and sent out his emissaries hotfoot to the capitals of Eastern Europe to purge ' Zionists '. Almost anyone of Jewish background was under suspicion.

Those purged in August 1950 fell, it was said, due to revelations at the (notorious) Rajk trial in Hungary. The more important victims included Paul Merker, a senior official in the Ministry of Agriculture, Leo Bauer, editor-in-chief of the East German radio, Lex Ende, editor-in-chief of the S E D newspaper, *Neues Deutschland*, and Willi Kreikemeyer, director general of the D D R railways. In December 1952 Prof. Leo Zuckermann, head of D D R-President Pieck's Chancellory, was accused of Zionism, but he reached West Berlin before he could be arrested. More ' Zionist agents ' were ' exposed ' in the following month in the V V N, the League of Victims of National Socialism. In May 1953 two members of the Central Committee of the S E D were expelled from the party for allegedly giving away information about illegal party work at the time of Hitler. One man not in the S E D purged at this time was Georg Dertinger, East Germany's Foreign Minister, and deputy Chairman of the C D U. He was accused of enemy activity against the D D R.

L

Terrible though these purges were, involving the disgrace and harsh imprisonment of many of those ' exposed ', the situation in the D D R did not degenerate in the way it did in the rest of Eastern Europe. There dozens of life-long Communists were brutally treated, humiliated at show trials and executed. In the D D R, on the other hand, virtually all those removed survived to he rehabilitated after the death of Stalin, though by no means all of them got positions equal to those they had lost. It is also only fair to mention that Western intelligence agencies have continually sought to infiltrate East German bodies.

### SOCIALIST CONSTRUCTION

Given that Germany was not being treated as an economic whole, the East German leaders were in a difficult position. Their part of Germany was not, as is often commonly supposed, without industry. But its industries were mainly light industries—textiles, consumer, goods, automobiles, office machinery and light engineering products of all kinds, optical equipment, electrical goods and chemicals. Most of these were dependent on raw materials or parts from other areas of Germany. Attempts to replace these from within the D D R meant heavy, in some cases, uneconomical, investments. Another disadvantage suffered by the Soviet Zone/D D R was the heavy dismantling by the Russians. Their zone suffered about twice as much as the Western zones. In addition, the Russians demanded goods from current production which were, in many instances, not traditional manufactures of this area; fulfilment of these demands required heavy investments which held down living standards. The East German economy suffered further from loss of key workers, technicians and managers to the West. Some did not want to work for a ' socialist ' regime, some, in the early years, feared being forced to work in the Soviet Union, many did not appreciate being forced into political activities after working hours, even more sought better living standards and a more relaxed atmosphere in the West. Between 1945 and 1961 just over 3 million Germans whose homes were in the Soviet Zone/D D R migrated to West Germany. During the same period some 2.7 million Germans from the lost territories, who had been quartered in the Soviet Zone/D D R, moved West. Of course, many of these were not employed in industry.

In order to try to make their state independent of West Germany the D D R leaders, starting with the first five-year plan of 1951-55, invested large sums in the energy and iron and steel industries. Dismantling cost the Soviet Zone 85 per cent of its very limited steel rolling capacity. The area is poorly endowed with hard coal and its brown coal capacity was reduced by about 40 per cent by dismantling. The extraction of the relatively plentiful brown coal was given priority and a great many technical problems were solved in order to enable it to be used in the metallurgical industry. But production costs remained high in that industry and heavy dependence on brown coal is a factor in the relatively high costs of East German industry as a whole. The most publicised project in the brown coal industry is the ' Schwarze Pumpe ' complex near Hoyerswerda started in 1955. In the iron and steel industry the most important project is that at Eisenhüttenstadt on the East German-Polish frontier. Supplied with coke from Poland this is an entirely new project and new town which was known as Stalinstadt from March 1953 to after the 20th congress of the C P S U in 1956. The D D R's efforts to build up its steel industry are indicated by the following figures:

Per capita Production of Rolled Steel (*in kilograms*)

|       | D D R | Federal Republic |
|-------|-------|------------------|
| 1946  | 5     | 50               |
| 1958  | 70    | 300              |
| 1964  | 170   | 430              |

Despite East Germany's progress in this field it remains a very large importer of steel.

Another industry which commanded large investments was shipbuilding. This hardly existed in what is now the D D R before the war and suffered greatly from dismantling. It was built up largely to provide reparations for the Soviet Union, and since the end of reparations has been dependent to a considerable extent on orders from the U S S R.

All these reparations and investments in slow-maturing projects required sacrifices, great sacrifices of the East German people. Living standards did not rise in the way they were doing in the Federal Republic in the early fifties. This became widely known in East Germany through the West German radio, letters from friends and relatives in the West, and Western visitors. Naturally dissatisfaction spread. Often in those years and since, the author has heard ordinary East Germans comment: ' We work as hard as they do. We are no less skilled. Why should we be worse off than they are? Are we alone responsible for the war?' In 1952 new sacrifices were imposed. It was announced that the D D R would build up its own ' national armed forces ' as well as the basis of Socialism. This was proclaimed as the East German response to the Federal Republic's signing the European Defence Community Treaty a few weeks before. The D D R already possessed certain paramilitary forces which were officially part of the police. These were re-organised and expanded. An intensive recruitment campaign was launched. Officially this was voluntary but a good deal of pressure was used to persuade the reluctant. As a result of the war and migration to the West the D D R was short of labour and the expansion of the ' People's Police in Barracks ' caused further strain on the nation's resources. The new forces had to be housed, fed and equipped. Only by new burdens could the necessary means be found.

The Economic Plan for 1953 sought to find the means by a great increase in the productivity of the labour force and by a new wage structure based, to a much larger extent than before, on piece work. In April 1953 food prices were increased and in May it was announced that the work ' norms ' for industrial workers would be raised, which meant more work for the same money.

One would have thought such measures alone would have given the state and party officials enough to do as they involved reorganisation, paper work and much propaganda activity. But at the same time due to the decision to commence socialist construction the class struggle was being intensified. More nationalisation measures were being put into effect, a collectivisation drive in agriculture got under way, there was more discrimination against students from non-working-class homes, the intelligentsia lost some of their privileges, and the churches came under increasing pressure. These measures were largely self-defeating because they led to more East Germans going West which in turn caused greater difficulties in every sphere of society.

REVOLT IN JUNE AND THE ' NEW COURSE '

Since the death of Stalin in March 1953 the Soviet leaders had been taking stock of their inheritance and had reversed some of his policies. Early in June they advised the Politburo of the S E D to do the same in the D D R. Most of the discriminatory measures were then rescinded but confusion remained about the work norms of the industrial workers. Did the ' New Course ' cover them?

On 16 June about 80 building workers on the main ' Stalinallee ' site in East Berlin went on strike against the higher norms. The next day strikes and demonstrations took place in many parts of East Germany. In some places they were orderly and peaceful, in others not so peaceful. Some were concerned solely with economic grievances, others demanded the resignation of the government and free elections. In East Berlin, where violence did take place, demonstrators were joined by West Berliners, some of whom were undoubtedly agents for Western organisations. R I A S the Radio in the American Sector (of Berlin) was of key importance in spreading news of the strikes and so encouraging further strikes and demonstrations. The 'revolt' soon ended when Soviet troops took up key positions in the towns throughout the D D R and martial law was proclaimed. Although they admitted that their 'mistakes' were an important cause of the strikes, the S E D leaders sought to show that the events of 16-17 June were part of a plan for their overthrow worked out by Western intelligence agencies. They have failed to offer much hard evidence of this. In West Germany the events of those days became known as the People's Revolt, which in fact they were not. Most of those involved were workers, few members of other social classes took part. Secondly, the extent of the strikes is generally widely exaggerated. Research carried out for the West German Ministry for All-German Affairs indicates that 372,000 workers downed tools. The same source estimates that there were some 8 million workers in the D D R at that time which, if correct, means that about 4.5 per cent of the D D R's industrial workers stopped work. East German estimates worked out higher! From their accounts the percentage would be 5.5. Nor did the rising end in a blood bath. Western estimates put the number of those killed at 21. The number of wounded was higher.

The June revolt shook the East German leaders and their supporters. They resolved to continue the New Course appeasement policy. They also looked for scapegoats. One of these was Max Fechner, Minister of Justice, who was condemned for 'hostile activities'—he had upheld the right to strike—and imprisoned. Rudolf Herrnstadt, editor-in-chief of *Neues Deutschland*, was removed together with Security Minister Wilhelm Zaisser, and the Secretary of the S E D Berlin organisation, Hans Jendretzky. Herrnstadt was given a post in the state archives, Fechner and Jendretzky were later rehabilitated.

### THE 20TH CONGRESS AND WOLFGANG HARICH

In the years after 1953 the D D R's policies and priorities were influenced to a great extent by the more conciliatory attitude of the Soviet leaders to the West, an attitude summed up in the term 'peaceful coexistence'. On their own account though they attempted to 'build socialism' at home and gain recognition abroad. They remained somewhat uneasy about their position fearing a Soviet sell-out. This was particularly so in 1955 when the Soviet Government joined the Western Powers in signing an Austrian Peace

Treaty and withdrawing from that country. In that same year West Germany established diplomatic relations with Moscow without making any concessions on the question of the recognition of the D D R or Germany's post-war frontiers.

For Herr Ulbricht in particular the second half of the fifties was worrying. 1956 brought the 20th Congress of the Soviet Communist Party with Khrushchev's dramatic anti-Stalin speech. Ulbricht, as a man who had served Stalin faithfully, could not be sure he would not be sacrificed on the altar of ' de-Stalinisation ' and coexistence. Perhaps luckily for him, the Hungarian revolution came in October 1956 and there were troubles in Poland. Both were partly the result of ' de-Stalinisation ', both frightened the Soviet leaders. Ulbricht appeared to have things under control in East Germany, so why not leave well alone? The D D R did not entirely escape the consequences of the 20th Congress. The East German leaders made statements in line with Moscow's reappraisal of Stalin. Streets, institutions and Stalinstadt, named after him, were renamed. His books and photographs of him were removed. Those purged by Stalin's edict were rehabilitated.

The official de-Stalinisation measures were not regarded as adequate by some party intellectuals. Dr Wolfgang Harich, lecturer at the S E D's own school and editor of the official journal of philosophy, became spokesman for such individuals. Harich was in touch with circles in Poland, Hungry and Yugoslavia as well as the West German Social Democrats. He wanted intellectual freedom, more say for the workers, a more positive role for the East German parliament, more emphasis on raising living standards and the revitalisation of the S E D together with a refurbishing of its ideology. The East German leaders obviously feared his influence for he was arrested, brought to trial in March 1957 and sentenced to ten years' imprisonment. He was, however, released in autumn 1964.

' OVERTAKE THE WEST '

By the time of the 5th Congress of the S E D in 1958 Walter Ulbricht could feel more confident than before. He had got those who might have opposed him, the most senior of whom was Politburo member Karl Schirdewan, removed from the party leadership. In the Politburo he was surrounded by colleagues who, apart from Otto Grotewohl who died in 1964, remained with him throughout the sixties. East German living standards remained lower than those prevailing in West Germany, but they were tolerable and improving. His government seemed to be winning the confidence of the D D R people. The numbers going West was declining. In 1959 ' only '

143,917 left, the lowest figure since 1949. Internationally Ulbricht had the backing of the Soviet leader, N. S. Krushchev, who attended the congress. The colossi of the world communist movement, the U S S R and China, were at one, and Soviet space achievements helped to convince comrades they were on the winning side. The optimism of the congress was indicated by Ulbricht's promise that by the early 1960s the D D R's per capita levels of consumer consumption would outpace those of West Germany. This promise was to prove totally unrealistic. The congress endorsed the introduction of polytechnical instruction in schools which aimed at giving school children some knowledge of elementary technology and the factory or agricultural system at an early age. And, for those who wished to go on to higher education, the new edict laid down a year's compulsory practical work in the economy. This was in line with Soviet education. Like earlier S E D congresses, the fifth made a number of proposals on the German issue. These included a defensively rearmed, neutral, united Germany, based on the frontiers of 1945, which had emerged from a confederation of the two German states.

### THE BERLIN WALL

The optimism of 1958-59 did not last. Measures aimed at 'the comprehensive construction of Socialism', including virtually total collectivisation of the land and more nationalisation, led to economic difficulties and both to an increase in the number of refugees going West. This in turn increased the strains and stresses of East German life and produced yet more refugees. Mr Khrushchev's ultimatum, which amounted to a demand that the Western powers recognise the D D R or suffer interference with their position in West Berlin, created uncertainty and further contributed to the outflow of people from the D D R. In some cases too West German firms, short of labour with a booming economy, recruited East German workers with promises of higher wages. With just over 199,000 of his citizens lost in 1960 and a further 155,000 in the first eight months of 1961, Herr Ulbricht was forced to take drastic action. On 13 August 1961 the Eastern part of Berlin was sealed off from the Western part and the construction of the Berlin Wall begun. In addition, the frontier with West Germany was strengthened. Even so, another 50,000 or so East Germans managed to cross to the West by the end of the year. The Wall is a scar bisecting a great city. It is physically ugly, morally uglier still. Up to the end of 1968 over 60 people died while attempting to cross it. Altogether, at least 137 people were killed trying to reach West Germany from the D D R during this period.

# 9    East Germany in The Sixties

Many East Germans feared that the closing of the Republic's Berlin frontier in August 1961 would lead to repression and renewed austerity. Their worst fears were not realised. Those caught trying to get to West Germany were jailed, and there was some toughening of the official attitude to certain 'pampered' groups, such as building workers, who had earned very high wages by East German standards before the Wall. But, on the whole the regime was a little less hard than before. East Germany was on the verge of a mild 'thaw' which was to last until the end of 1966.

The main features of East German life in the 1960s were the spreading of prosperity, more genuine discussions between the rulers and the ruled on important, though mainly non-political matters, coupled with continued rigidity in political and intellectual affairs. The prosperity and a greater measure of international acceptance have helped in the consolidation of the regime.

THE NEW ECONOMIC SYSTEM

Under Mr Khrushchev cautious reforms of the Soviet economic system associated with the name of Professor Yevsei Liberman were introduced in 1962. In 1963 the Sixth Congress of the Socialist Unity Party announced similar reforms for the D D R. Among the principal authors of the East German reforms were Erich Apel, who had studied and worked in the Soviet Union, and Günter Mittag.

The reforms were given the rather ponderous title of the New Economic System of Planning and Managing the Economy. The main ingredients of the new system were: the restoration of profit as a measure of economic utility and stimulus to growth; less rigid planning and more power for the directors of the 80 'socialist trusts' (v v b's) into which the major part of industry was divided; a more creative role for the banks with a discriminatory credit policy designed to reward or penalise the 'socialist trusts' according to their varying performances; more emphasis on quality as against mere quantity of production, and concentration on the products best suited to East German skills, capacities and raw materials. The congress decisions meant greater concentration on the traditional patterns of industry in this part of Germany.

When they heard the news the East German people were no doubt somewhat sceptical. This was by no means the first shake up of the D D R's economic system. Each new change had been heralded as progress, and each time they had been bombarded for months by the mass media with the details of the new changes, exhortations to study them and promises of better times. The promises and forecasts made at the last congress in 1958 regarding living standards had proved hollow. This time there were fewer specific promises and the results were more convincing.

Of every 100 households in East Germany in 1958 only 5.1 had television sets, whereas in 1965 the number was 48. In 1958 only 2.1 per cent had refrigerators, but in 1965 the figure was 26. Washing machines were found in 1.6 per cent of households in 1958. By 1965 the figure had risen to 28 per cent. By this time more East German homes possessed television sets than did the homes of Austria, France, Italy and Switzerland. The progress they still had to make is indicated by a comparison with the situation in Britain in 1965. In that year 39 per cent of British homes were equipped with refrigerators, 56 per cent with washing machines and 88 per cent with T V. In the second half of the sixties further progress was made in the D D R. By 1969 48 per cent of East German households had fridges, the same number washing machines and 66 per cent television receivers. But despite this progress the party leaders had still not redeemed their 1958 pledge to provide their people with more consumer goods than the West Germans. And although East German architecture had recovered from the stultifying effects of Stalinism by the time of the Sixth Congress, and many respectable, even pleasing buildings of contemporary design were erected in the following years, the housing situation remained critical by the end of the sixties. The modest housing targets were still not being fulfilled.

In other respects too East German living standards lagged behind those of the advanced nations of Western Europe. Private motoring started in earnest in the 1960s but by 1970 the D D R remained one of the most undermotorised industrial countries in the world. The standard and variety of clothing available in the shops left much to be desired compared with that found in neighbouring Western countries. This situation resulted to a considerable extent, from very large exports of textiles and clothing. And despite the growth of foreign travel in the 1960s, many East Germans felt bitter about the fact that they were unable to holiday in Western countries or even in Yugoslavia. The only people who really felt deprived, however, were the old age pensioners and they were allowed to journey to West or emigrate if they so desired.

On the positive side, most East Germans, including all industrial workers, got a statutory five-day week in September 1967, and this was something enjoyed by most, but not all, British or West German workers. They also receive relatively long holidays. Their health service, which suffered from the emigration of doctors in the 1950s, had recovered and was of a high standard; and educational opportunities, especially in technological and applied science subjects, were to be commended. Sports facilities were good but the DDR had fewer swimming baths than the Federal Republic. In the Mexico Olympic Games of 1968 the DDR finished fifth in the unofficial medals table. West Germany, with more than three times the population, was placed eighth.

### HAVEMANN, THE INTELLECTUALS AND THE CHANGING ÉLITE

The new interest in economic reform from 1963 resulted in a modicum of academic freedom in East German universities. This was especially true for those engaged in teaching or researching in subjects essential for the New Economic System—economics, mathematics, statistics, and the newly discovered cybernetics and sociology. Just how limited this freedom remained, however, was indicated by the case of Professor Robert Havemann.

Havemann joined the Communist Party in 1932 and was later sentenced to death by the Nazis for his anti-regime activities. His researches were regarded as so important—he is a physical-chemist —that the sentence was not executed. After the war he was in trouble with the Americans in West Berlin for his opposition to US nuclear arms. He was appointed to a chair at the Humboldt University of East Berlin and eventually became a member of the East German Academy of Sciences. Apparently it was a series of lectures given by Havemann in the autumn and winter of 1963-64 which got the professor into trouble again. These lectures, later published in West Germany under the title *Dialektik ohne Dogma?* by the Rowohlt Publishing Co., amounted to a call for democracy in the DDR. 'What is necessary, what is a condition of life for Socialism, and what was lost during the period of Stalinism, is Democracy. Socialism cannot be achieved without Democracy'. Havemann claimed he was speaking as a good Leninist. The professor also attacked capital punishment, still a penalty in the DDR in 1970 though rarely used, arguing, 'In the last resort the death penalty is only demanded in order to be able to kill political opponents'. He showed even greater courage by attacking academic colleagues who, without any knowledge of the natural sciences, rejected 'Western' scientific theories because they did not fit in with their own dogmatic view of Dialectical Materialism. Such people had discredited Dialectical Materialism and the DDR. They were still at work. Their theories were still being widely publicised in the DDR even though the Soviet Union had discarded them.

Havemann's courage was rewarded by his removal from the university and his expulsion from the Academy of Sciences. He was given research work. His plight brought support from the American Nobel Prize Winner, Linus Pauling, who urged the East German Academy President, Prof. Werner Hartke, a former Nazi party member, to 'take immediate action to revoke the unjust and improper dismissal of Professor Havemann'. Pauling himself had been awarded an honorary doctorate of the Humboldt University.

Professor Havemann was a popular lecturer at the Humboldt University. Yet neither his removal nor other events of the 1960s caused much opposition among East German students. Can we conclude then that they, unlike their West German colleagues, were supremely content? This was not the case. True, in certain respects, East German students were in a better, or rather a different position from students in the Federal Republic. The great majority of them, unlike those in West Germany, received monetary grants and they were likely to have been more carefully selected. As a higher proportion of East Germans were studying science and technology they were less involved in controversial issues than their colleagues in the arts and social sciences. East German courses were more vocation-orientated and the DDR's students were more likely than West German students to know that they had secure jobs to go to. Moreover, Ulbricht's students could feel that their state, as the friend of those idols of student rebels the world over, North Vietnam, the Arabs and Castro's Cuba, was more worthy of support than the Federal Republic.

Yet East German students had their grievances. At least some of them were known to feel overburdened by compulsory subjects—Marxism, maths, Russian and a second foreign language, and sport—which all students were required to do. Some ached from the strain of too much extra-curricular activity for the SED or from what were, officially, voluntary vacation shifts on farm or building site or in the Republic's factories. It would have been surprising too if all were satisfied with their material conditions. Most East German students, if they could have experienced them, would certainly have regarded the living and working conditions of British counterparts as luxurious. Most East German students regretted the lack of opportunity to travel to western countries. Some of the idealistic and more sensitive minority no doubt shared some of Robert Havemann's preoccupations. This was shown during the Warsaw Pact countries' invasion of Czechoslovakia in 1968 when a few young people, including the sons and daughters of prominent S E D members, issued leaflets and daubed slogans denouncing the action. But the majority of East German students were probably no different from the majority elsewhere. Concerned with successfully completing their studies, and embarking on their careers, they had little taste for politics. The Berlin Wall and the fate of earlier opposition to the regimes of Eastern Europe had helped to convince them that making the best of what they had was preferable to fighting a hopeless cause.

Between 1952-70 over half a million students had graduated from East Germany's universities and technical institutions. They were to a great extent responsible for the D D R's recent achievements and of these they were proud. Their collective and individual successes gave them a common consciousness. Many of them occupied positions of responsibility which they might not have gained had they lived in the Federal Republic. Such positions became available after early postwar purges, and the flight of senior colleagues to the West, or were created by expansion. In some cases, those holding such positions knew they had been favoured as students because of their working-class background. These factors, as well as fear of the secret police and growing alienation from the West welded the D D R's élite to the system. This should not be taken to imply that the members of this new mass élite were uncritically behind the regime—far from it—but they were unlikely to want to put their hard won gains in jeopardy by attempts to bring about sharp and sudden changes in the D D R. Their attitude depended on a number of factors including the satisfaction of their material expectations and their degree of participation in decision making.

This postwar generation of technicians, managers and members of the professions is gradually taking over the top positions from the older generation. The latter were, except for the salvaged remnants of the prewar bourgeois intelligentsia, often old Communist all-round functionaries rather than the academically trained specialists.

We can see the advance of this new generation in the Central Committee of the Socialist Unity Party. By 1964 well over 90 of the Committee's 181 full and candidate members could be placed in the category of the specialists. At the very top of the Party, in the Politburo, which is formally elected by the Central Committee, the old generation still dominated in 1970. Remarkably, this had changed but little by the mid-1970s, Walter Ulbricht apart. Who were the members of the Politburo, the rulers of the German Democratic Republic in 1970?

Walter Ulbricht, aged 77, had held the key position of first secretary of the S E D since 1950. He thus had more experience of power than any other Communist leader except for China's Mao Tse Tung and Enver Hoxha of Albania. As Chairman of the Council of State since the death of President Pieck in 1960, Ulbricht was head of state. He started life in a working-class home in Leipzig and, on leaving school became an apprentice cabinet-maker. Conscripted into the army he opposed the 1914–18 war and became a founder member of the German Communist Party. By the early 1920s he was a full-time Communist official and by 1923 a member of the Central Committee. In the years which followed he served the Soviet Union, as the 'first Socialist State', faithfully, living in the U S S R from 1933 to 1945. The Soviets rewarded him with their support. This was the basis of his success. It was nonetheless remarkable that he should have survived so many major upheavals, so many twists and turns of Soviet policy.

Apart from Walter Ulbricht, the most experienced East German politician was Willi Stoph. Born in 1914, he joined the K P D in 1931. He was a truck driver in the German Army during the war, but his official biography credits him with 'illegal anti-fascist activity' between 1933-45. A former Defence Minister, he had been Prime Minister since the death of Herr Grotewohl in 1964, as well as member of the Politburo and of the Council of State. Erich Honecker was widely expected eventually to replace Ulbricht as S E D secretary, as he was Ulbricht's deputy. Born in 1912, the son of a miner, he became a K P D member in 1929, and spent ten years in prison under the Nazis. Hermann Matern, a veteran Communist, and Friedrich Ebert, former Social Democrat and son of the President of the Weimar Republic, were long-standing members of the Politburo. Both were well into their seventies and becoming less active in politics. Herbert Warnke (68), head of the trade unions, and Prof. Albert Norden (66), in charge of propaganda, could also be considered nearing the end of their careers. Of the younger members, Dr Günter Mittag (born 1926), a member of the Council of State, and one of the authors of the New Economic System, was the most prominent.

The members of the Politburo were a fairly homogeneous group. All, except Albert Norden, the son of a Rabbi, were from working-class backgrounds, and most were in the pre-1933 working-class movement. Contrary to common belief, few spent the war years in Moscow; most were either emigrants or in jail.

A NEW DEAL FOR WOMEN

As mentioned above, to some limited extent, the rulers of the DDR had attempted to start a dialogue with their people. There was something like a genuine discussion on educational reform in the 1960s and on the Family Law of April 1966. Many feminists in West Germany and other countries regarded the new law as a great step forward in the fight to achieve full equality for women. The Family Law obliged both partners in marriage to do their share in educating any children they had, and in doing the housework. Both had the duty to contribute towards the maintenance of the family, though ' a spouse who has no income or means contributes through housework towards the upbringing of the children '. The Law broke new ground in respect of property. The property that each partner had on marriage remained their own, as did any gift acquired during the marriage. Property of any kind obtained during the marriage by work became the joint property of both. This implicitly rewarded women who spent their time as housewives and mothers. Another ' advanced ' feature of the Family Law was that it did not grant the wife the automatic right to be kept by the husband. In most situations she would have that right—as a full-time mother, in sickness or old age, or during periods of study. In the latter case the husband had the duty to give her all the assistance he could, and could not force his wife to take up unskilled work if she preferred to undergo professional training. On the other hand, the Law made it more difficult to be a ' mere housewife ' without family responsibilities.

East German women, as a group, had to face greater difficulties than their sisters in the Federal Republic. A far higher proportion of them were engaged in the economy and yet they had endured greater difficulties shopping, greater difficulties in finding dry-cleaners, hairdressers and launderettes, and greater difficulties in getting repairs done. This situation had been changing for the better. And it must not be forgotten that East German mothers did at least find it much easier to get their children into nurseries than did mothers in Western countries.

It was impossible to say just how East German women viewed their government, how they reacted to the advantages and disadvantages of living in the DDR. As in other countries few women took part in politics. Only about 26 per cent of the SED members were women, and in 1970 only one woman, Margarete Müller, had reached candidate membership of the Politburo. Another woman, Dr Grete Wittkowski, was President of the State Bank, and there were women members of the Council of State and Council of Ministers. With official encouragement women had been gradually taking on jobs and entering professions formerly monopolised by men.

## THE SOCIALIST CONSTITUTION OF 1968

At the seventh congress of the S E D in 1967 Walter Ulbricht called for a new constitution for the D D R. Within a year a new constitution had replaced that of 1949. Why this change? The official explanation was that the D D R had become a socialist state and needed a socialist constitution. This might have been part of the truth. But more important was the leaders' determination to emphasise the sovereignty of the D D R, its difference from West Germany, and to underline to the world, and the people of East Germany, that there was no going back on their version of socialism. The new constitution was also in line with changes in some of the other East European states. Perhaps too, it was designed to offer hope to the East German people, that the dictatorial methods which had made the old constitution a dead letter would soon be a thing of the past.

Article 1 of the new constitution made clear the intended change. The DDR was described as ' a socialist state of the German nation ', instead of merely a ' democratic Republic '. Unlike the old constitution, the new one recognised the leading role of the ' Marxist-Leninist party ' and the ' socialist ownership of the means of production '. A number of rights of the individual were deleted—the right to strike and the right to emigrate, for instance. As for the formal institutions of the state, the Volkskammer lost some of its power to the Staatsrat (Council of State), which was set up after the death of President Pieck in 1960. In the Staatsrat its Chairman directed its work. Thus Herr Ulbricht's *de facto* power in this body was formally recognised. The government or Council of Ministers (Ministerrat) lost some of its power to the Council of State and was entrusted mainly with economic affairs. In turn the Council of Ministers was given more independence vis-à-vis the Volkskammer.

All in all, the constitution of 1968 was a little more realistic than that of 1949, and somewhat more authoritarian. Whether the provisions of the constitution would be observed was widely doubted.

## INTO CZECHOSLOVAKIA

Apart from giving unswerving support to the Soviet Union and the Warsaw Pact, the DDR's main preoccupation in foreign affairs was the battle for recognition. It found no difficulty in gaining recognition from the other Communist states including China. And after the rapprochement between Moscow and Belgrade, Tito and Ulbricht exchanged ambassadors in 1957. After Fidel Castro won power in Cuba that state forfeited its relations with Bonn by recognising the D D R. But until 1969 the D D R failed to win recognition from either the Western states or from any of the countries of the Third World. Only in 1969 was the D D R able to improve its official representation abroad. More will be said about this in the next chapter.

With its Warsaw Pact allies the D D R enjoyed, at the official level at any rate, good relations in the 1950s. They were united by ideology (except for Poland and Hungary in 1956), had common economic interests—and common fears about their own survival. In the case of the U S S R, Poland and Czechoslovakia, there was the additional fear of West German ' revanchism '. The greater flexibility shown by Bonn in the 1960s and its trade offensive in Eastern Europe caused Ulbricht some worries. He feared his allies would be prepared to exchange ambassadors with Bonn without getting assurances on frontiers and recognition of the D D R. Only in the case of Romania were these fears realised. The same might have happened in the case of Czechoslovakia but for the intervention of the Warsaw Pact forces in August 1968. Whether or not Herr Ulbricht played any significant role in persuading the Russians that something had to be done about the situation in Czechoslovakia, it is safe to assume he was worried about it. The liberals associated with the name of Alexander Dubcek, who took over the Czechoslovak C P in January 1968, were engaged in experiments which Ulbricht must have feared would catch on in the D D R. The East German frontier with Czechoslovakia was open, and thousands of East German tourists visited the country in 1968. A S E D Politburo resolution of 25 July 1968 regretted that the Czechs underestimated ' the anti-socialist forces at work in their country and the dangers of interference from Bonn '. Subsequent meetings between delegations of the other Warsaw Pact parties with the Czechs, including an encounter by Ulbricht and Dubcek at Karlovy Vary on 12 August, apparently did nothing to still the fears of the Soviet, D D R, and other East European leaderships. The result was that their tanks and troops poured into Czechoslovakia on 21 August.

The D D R officially regained its sovereignty in 1955 but in its relations with the U S S R it has remained less than an equal. These relations are governed by the stationing of large concentrations of Soviet forces on East German soil and by the fact that roughly three-quarters of the D D R's trade is done with the Soviet Union. Nevertheless Western observers noticed a somewhat more independent attitude on the part of East German leaders during the 1960s. This was believed to be due to the D D R's growing economic strength, its apparent stability, the great need for the Soviet Union to find allies in the Communist camp against China, and, perhaps, Herr Ulbricht's personal conviction that he was far more experienced at the top than any of the Soviet leaders. The relations between the two states were formally governed by treaties signed in 1955 and 1964.

M

# 10  West Germany in The Sixties

The time between Dr Erhard assuming office in 1963 and his next appointment with the electorate, in September 1965, was not an easy period for him. It would have been difficult for any man to fill Adenauer's shoes, and the ex-Chancellor, despite his advanced age, still wanted to play a role in German politics. He remained a member of the Bundestag and as Chairman of the CDU criticised his successor. In effect he claimed Erhard was becoming soft on the 'Reds' and was endangering West Germany's good relations with France. This naturally encouraged his rivals to remain active. But he had troubles in other directions. There was a growing crisis in the Ruhr, a continuing crisis in agriculture and a new crop of scandals connected with Germany's dark past.

The crisis in the Ruhr mining industry did not suddenly arise in 1963. It had been going on since about 1958 and was similar to that facing the coalmining industries in other countries: oil was replacing coal as a means of cheap, economical fuel and therefore only the most efficient mines would survive in the shrinking market. In 1958 West Germany used 125.2 million tons of hard coal. The amount in 1963 actually rose to 127 million tons, but fell in 1965 to 114.4. In 1967 it was down to 97.1 million tons. The amount of mineral oil rose year by year over this period from 27.3 million tons in 1958 to 124.8 million tons in 1967. The amount of natural gas, though still small, rose greatly over the same period. In about the same years some 250,000 miners lost their jobs. Subsidies, tax on oil and protection against foreign coal were the main weapons used to fight the crisis. Nevertheless, in the sixties it appeared to be a losing battle. Critics have claimed more could have been done to attract outside industry to the area.

The crisis of West German agriculture is illustrated by two figures. Firstly, between 1949 and 1965 the number of farms declined by 488,000. Secondly, between 1950 and 1965 the number of those working in agriculture fell from over five million to just under three million. As was only to be expected the farmers were increasingly angry and demanded a ban on imports.

## TROUBLE IN THE BUNDESWEHR

Another headache for Dr Erhard was the controversy which surrounded the retirement, in 1964, of Vice-Admiral Hellmuth Heye, the Parliamentary Commissioner for the Armed Forces. Due in large measure to the efforts of the Social Democrats, the West German soldier has far more rights than either earlier German soldiers or the soldiers of most other countries. He is supposed to be a 'citizen in uniform': as such he can take part in political activities, join a trade union, though not strike. If he commits a serious offence, he will be tried by a civilian court for there are no military courts in the Federal Republic. On the Swedish pattern a Parliamentary Commissioner (*Wehrbeauftragter*) will work to protect the rights of individual soldiers and take up their grievances. Because of opposition from the right it took over a year and a half's discussion before the first Commissioner was appointed. He was an ex-general and was subsequently dismissed for alleged homosexual offences. His successor was ex-Admiral Heye who came from an old military family and had been a C D U member of the Bundestag. In three articles published in 1964 in the weekly magazine *Quick*, and in an interview in *Der Spiegel*, the Admiral claimed that there was a danger that the Bundeswehr was developing into a 'state within a state'. When told by his critics that such allegations belonged in his annual report to parliament rather than in a popular magazine, Heye retorted that after two and a half years in the post he felt more drastic action was required to make parliament and public take note. The Admiral was subsequently forced out of office. Heye's view that all was not well in the Bundeswehr seemed to be vindicated by a number of cases of brutality, involving deaths of servicemen, which came to light in 1963-64.

Differences over the running of the armed forces, the rights of servicemen and so on led, during the Chancellorship of Dr Erhard, to the resignations or dismissals of three top officers including General Trettner, Inspector General of the Bundeswehr.

That the struggle between the traditionalists and the democrats in the Bundeswehr still was not solved as West Germany entered the seventies was indicated during the 'Grashey Affair' at the time of the Grand Coalition. General-major Helmut Grashey, deputy commander of the West Germany Army, delivered a lecture, early in 1969, at the staff academy of the Bundeswehr in Hamburg. In his lecture he said it was time to throw out the ideas of the 'citizen-in-uniform' which, he claimed, had been merely a concession to the S P D. He attacked the Commissioner and the civil administrators of the armed forces. Grashey's superior, General Albert Schnez, commander of the Federal Republic's land forces, shielded Grashey from attack. He himself had failed to get a top N A T O post because of Dutch objections based on his wartime record. After the setting up of the S P D-F D P coalition in 1969, Helmut Schmidt, Social Democratic Minister of Defence, ordered the removal of Grashey, from the Defence Ministry to another command. Grashey, however, decided to retire. In a semi-secret report to his staff officers, which became public in January 1970, Schnez fully endorsed the views of his subordinate.

Over the years the Bundeswehr has also been plagued by rumours of corruption, allegations of military inefficiency, and accidents often caused by faulty equipment. Just one example, up to May 1970, 120 Starfighters had crashed with the loss of 56 pilots.

ELECTION 1965

The differences in the Christian Democratic camp remained bitter and deep before, during, and after the election of 1965. Remarkably perhaps in these circumstances, the C D U/C S U emerged once again as the strongest party with 47.6 per cent of the vote and 245 seats. But the Social Democrats also improved their position winning 39.3 per cent and 202 seats. The Free Democratic vote slumped to 9.5 per cent and this gave them 49 seats. The F D P was less credible than it had been in 1961 as a party of new initiatives in both foreign and internal policy, for of course it had once again been enjoying office with the Christian Democrats. The S P D, which in 1961 had campaigned for television sets for old-age pensioners, clean air and ' modern weapons ' for the Bundeswehr, became even vaguer in 1965. This might have cost it votes. Most of its hard policy campaigning was done for it by its intellectual fringe headed by the famous author Günter Grass. He saw his task as winning over floating middle-class voters who might otherwise vote F D P or for the neutralist splinter group the German Peace Union (D F U). He spotlighted the ' forgotten ' issues such as the recognition of the Oder-Neisse Line and legalised abortion because ' 10,000 women die every year in West Germany from the consequences of illegal ones '. Another famous and controversial intellectual, Rolf Hochhuth, author of *The Representative* wrote a pro- S P D paperback. It is doubtful whether the intellectuals made much impact. And they were in serious danger of being disowned by the party leaders who were playing it safe. One serious election analyst, Prof. Erwin K. Scheuch of Cologne, wrote after the election that the S P D had undoubtedly gained from its attempt to woo the Catholics but, he continued, ' it

was badly advised when it believed it had to do away with policy '.
It had underestimated the electors. Willy Brandt was later to admit
that he too thought the party had concentrated too much on its
' image ' and not enough on policy. One ugly aspect of the campaign,
and it was not the first time it had happened, were the continuous
attacks on Herr Brandt because he was born illegitimate and because
he had been an emigrant. What should have been a mark in his
favour, his wartime journalistic activities in Sweden against Nazism,
was used to discredit him. So dispirited was Herr Brandt after the
election that he announced his intention of retiring as Chancellor
Candidate of the S P D.

It took Prof. Erhard a good deal of hard bargaining to resurrect
his coalition with the Free Democrats. And as the leading Hamburg
weekly *Die Zeit* commented, ' Erhard is building a coalition in which
all the participants are dissatisfied '. Another leading paper, *Die
Frankfurter Allgemeine Zeitung*, thought the coalition was in danger
of developing the ' neurotic turbulence of a Strindberg marriage '.

Apart from the growing crisis in the Ruhr coal-field and
arguments about Länder finance, two of the major problems which
faced the Erhard government were what to do about the new
nationalists and the student revolt.

## THE NEW NATIONALISTS

Numerous attempts had been made in West Germany over the
postwar period to found a successful far-Right party. Up to the 1960s
the most successful had been the Socialist Reich Party led by Col.
Otto Ernst Remer and Fritz Dorls (among others). Set up in October
1949 and openly Nazi, the party achieved notable successes in the
Land elections in 1951 in Lower Saxony (11 per cent of the vote)
and Bremen (7.7 per cent). It elected 16 members in Lower Saxony
and 8 in Bremen. In October 1952 the party was banned as unconstitutional. This ban did not stop the setting up of new Right-wing
parties every year since 1952. These were all without success. One
party did manage to stand out among the many Right-wing groups.
This was the German Reichs Party (D R P) established in 1950. Two
of the more significant leaders were Adolf von Thadden and Wilhelm
Meinberg, holder of the Nazi party's gold medal, former S S officer
and Nazi member of the Reichstag. Perhaps more important than
the D R P in these years as a means of carrying out Nazi ideas were
the products of many far-Right publishing houses. The most important of these was that belonging to Dr Gerhard Frey publisher of
*Die Deutsche National-Zeitung und Soldaten-Zeitung* and other
journals. Dr Frey boosted circulation by attacks on S P D politicians

as traitors, attacks on Israel and with articles designed to show stories about Nazi crimes were myths and that in reality the Allies were the war criminals.

After the setting up of the National Democratic Party (N P D) in November 1964 the fortunes of the far Right appeared to be improving. The hard core of the new party were former members of the D R P. They joined together with remnants of the Refugee Party, and other Right-wing groups. Fritz Thielen of the D P was elected Chairman. His Vice-Chairmen were Wilhelm Gutmann (Refugee Party), Adolf von Thadden and Heinrich Fassbender (a veteran of several far-Right failures).

Despite the limited time available to it, the new party gained about 600,000 votes or 2 per cent of the valid votes in the Federal election of 1965. It was in 1966 that the world started to take notice of the N P D. At the Land election in Hamburg held in March of that year it managed 3.9 per cent of the poll. This rose to 7.4 per cent in Bavaria and 7.9 per cent in Hesse in November. The party gained representation in both regional parliaments. Its success was a factor in the fall of Dr Erhard. The F D P, on the other hand, failed to return any of its members to the Bavarian parliament. The formation of the Grand Coalition of the Christian Democrats and the S P D at the end of the year helped the N P D to further successes. Between April 1967 and April 1968 it gained seats in Schleswig-Holstein, Rhineland-Pfalz, Lower Saxony, Bremen and Baden-Wüttemberg. The ' rise ' of the National Democrats caused a healthy reaction among German trade unionists, students and many other West Germans. However, it should be pointed out that the party had gained ' only ' 60 seats out of a total 849 in these Länder parliaments.

Who were the nearly two million West Germans who had given their votes to this party of revenge and resentment? They were more likely to be Protestant than Catholic, especially Protestants in Catholic areas. They were more likely to be inhabitants of villages, small and middle-sized towns than large towns. Those in small businesses, officials and the middle classes were over-represented among N P D voters but N P D supporters came from every occupation and social group. Trade unionists were under-represented among N P D supporters; refugees over-represented, though not remarkably so. Men tended to vote N P D more frequently than women. The party attracted all age groups but the Nazi generation (30 to 59) was strongly represented and it did best in what were the hard-core Nazi areas in the 1920s and early 1930s. It also did well in areas where there had been a relatively high proportion of non-

voters. It made gains from the F D P, to a lesser extent from the
s P D, and from the c D U/c s U.

The members of the N P D were similar to its voters. Their political
backgrounds were, as one would expect, more markedly far right.
In 1966 twenty per cent of the members were former Nazi party
members. As the party expanded its membership this sank to 9 per
cent by the end of 1967. Of 18 members of the party's first Federal
Executive Committee 12 were former active Nazis. At the Land
level, 300 of the party's 446 officials in 1968 had earlier far Right
connections. But only 14 of its 60 members of Länder parliaments
were former Nazi party members.

In their programme and political utterances, although they stressed
that they stood by the constitution of the Federal Republic, the N P D
leaders advocated measures which bore a striking resemblance to
those advocated by Nazi and nationalists before and after 1933.
Xenophobia is one of the key elements of the N P D programme as
published in 1967. The very first words are ' foreign power ', which
' oppresses divided Germany in a divided Europe . . . The Germans
still bend to the will of the victors who have divided Germany and
Europe among themselves '. The N P D is presented as an organised
protest against materialism which can only be overcome by recognising past ideals that are now despised. The older generation
wrongly sits in the dock while the young are seduced to turn away
from German history. In this way Germany is capitulating spiritually
as well as it did militarily, with the result that foreign rule will
become permanent. As far as the state is concerned, the N P D wants
strong government, with a strong President directly elected by the
people. All laws introduced under the influence of the victors are
to be removed from the statute book. In education the N P D calls
for a national, centralised educational system, based on proven
German methods. Experimentation is to end. Education must be
based on the natural connection between People and Fatherland,
Family and Homeland (*Heimat*). The economy is to based on
entrepreneurial initiative and state planning. Government expenditure must be curbed. But German agriculture must be protected
and encouraged, the workers must be guaranteed their jobs against
foreigners. Codetermination should not mean outside trade union
officials in the factories. In its defence policy the N P D demands a
policy aimed at European defence: ' We need a military force strong
enough to deter every possible enemy '. Foreign troops should be
withdrawn from Germany. The Bundeswehr needs a soldierly spirit,
must be free of trade-union or any other political influence, and
must be free of civilian administrators. Former Waffen-s s men

should be given the same treatment as other former members of the
German armed forces, and former P O Ws must receive compensation
which is at least equal to that of former political prisoners. The
N P D rejects the view that Germany alone was guilty for the last
war and demands the return of 'East Germany', meaning the
territories beyond the Oder-Neisse, and the Sudetenland. The
Federal Republic has the responsibility for 'Middle Germany'
(D D R).

What were the causes of the National Democratic Party's relative
success in the second half of the 1960s? With the magnetic and
authoritarian personality of Dr Adenauer out of the way Right-wing
voters, not very committed to Christian Democracy as such, possibly
felt the new C D U/C S U leadership no longer represented their
aspirations. Secondly, the Free Democratic Party's Left-wing was
becoming more vocal and was attracting to the party other Left
liberals. Prof. Ralf Dahrendorf, the noted liberal sociologist, son of a
S P D politician and critic of German traditionalism, joined the F D P
in this period. Thirdly, the spread of 'Gaullist" ideas and the
failure of the Western Allies to achieve German reunification helped
to create the new nationalism. In 1965, according to a poll carried
out by the Emnid Institute, 69 per cent of West Germans put the
reunification of Germany before European unity. In 1951 only
55 per cent had done so. (In the period 1955-56 over 75 per cent had
done so.) Perhaps too, the fact that the N P D leaders tried hard to
appear, by far-right standards, sensible, respectable, middle-class
spokesmen, operating within the constitution, helped it to gain old-
fashioned nationalists and former Nazis grown 'soft' in the
affluent society. The economic recession of 1966-67 certainly
provided the party with coal-miners and farmers who felt they had
been forgotten by the orthodox politicians. The setting up of the
grand coalition of Christian and Social Democrats in December 1966
strengthened this feeling. The machine politicians, *die Bonzen*,
appeared to be ganging up against *der kleine Mann*, the 'little man'
or the man in the street. Resentment against foreign workers was
also a likely cause. According to figures published by the Ministry
for Economic Affairs in Bonn, there were 329,000 foreign workers
in West Germany in 1960 (1.5 per cent of the labour force). The
number rose year by year until it reached 1,313,000 or 6.1 per cent
of the labour force, in September 1966. It then started to fall. Finally,
the N P D appealed to Refugee party and D P members who had not
managed to find a home in one of the other three parties.

With growing concern abroad and demonstrations, sometimes,
ending in violence, every time the N P D held a major meeting, the

Federal Republic's major politicians were under increasing pressure
to find a solution to the N P D. There were those who argued that the
mere existence of such a party was an insult to Hitler's victims and
that therefore the party should be banned. Others believed that any
attempt to drive the N P D underground would make matters worse,
especially as it appeared to be keeping within the letter of the law.
Some worried about the Republic's image abroad, others about the
bait it offered to Left-wing student militants. Some of the more Right-
wing Christian Democratic and Free Democratic politicians feared
that any action to ban the National Democrats would cost them the
support of their own more extreme followers, who sympathised with
many of the things said by N P D politicians. The most embarrassing
aspect of the N P D's success was that it would qualify for public
funds. Under the Party Law (*Parteiengesetz*) of July 1967 West
German political parties have the right to financial assistance from
public revenue. It was later laid down that parties gaining 0.5 per
cent of the vote would qualify. By the start of the 1970s the Federal
Republic had not decided what to do about the N P D.

## THE GRAND COALITION

As mentioned above, Prof. Erhard was under fire from his own
colleagues, as well as the opposition, and was faced with the rise of
the N P D, with the student revolt and with an economic recession.
The number of unemployed, though small, started to rise. Another
blow fell in July 1966. At elections in North Rhine-Westphalia the
Social Democrats made considerable gains coming within two seats
of winning an absolute majority. Erhard's critics in his own party
were emboldened by this result. In August Herr Eugen Gerstenmaier,
C D U President of the Bundestag, told the world that it was time
Erhard went and that he himself was prepared to take his place. The
Chancellor's fate was virtually sealed on 27 October when the F D P
announced its intention to withdraw from the government. Erhard
countered by reallocating F D P posts to his Christian Democratic
Ministers. But the following day he had yet another problem. The
Bundesrat decided to reject the budget proposals. The Land elections
in Hesse a matter of days later finished off 'rubber lion' Erhard.
Though the S P D only achieved a slight increase in its already
absolute majority, the 2.4 per cent decline in the C D U vote was
seen as a defeat for Erhard. The following day the Social Democrats,
with F D P assistance, got a motion through the Bundestag asking
Erhard to give parliament a chance to vote on a motion of confidence. By 10 November the Christian Democrats had agreed on a
new Chancellor candidate, Dr Kurt Georg Kiesinger, Prime Minister

of Baden-Württemberg, and nominee of Franz-Josef Strauss. Who
would the Doctor seek as his coalition partners? The Free Democrats were not enthusiastic about renewing their
partnership with the C D U/C S U. The Christians were not very
attracted to them. There was bad feeling because of the break-up of
the government, and they still opposed Strauss, and, in any case,
were not strong in numbers. The Social Democrats had the numbers,
and in recent years had come to favour a 'Grand Coalition' with
the Christian Democrats. They had the backing of (C D U) Federal
President, Heinrich Lübke. Would the Social Democrats accept
Franz-Josef Strauss? They had strongly attacked him in the past
but the chance of office helped them to modify their opposition to
him. For them it was a very difficult position. Herr Erich Mende,
F D P leader, could not guarantee that all his group would support a
mini coalition of S P D and F D P. Even had such a government been
formed with the full backing of all the F D P group it would have
rested on a small majority. It would have inherited an economic
crisis which, had it got worse, could have seriously dented the image
of the S P D. Such a government would have favoured a more flexible
Eastern policy, but, it was argued, it would be under sharp attack
from the Christian Democrats for being soft on the Reds, or as a
government of ' renunciation politicians ', that is, those prepared
to renounce Germany's interests. Further S P D leaders, notably
Herbert Wehner, argued that if they could enter a strong government, they could prove to the electorate that they were competent
ministers and this would improve their chances at the next
election.

Dr Kiesinger's government included the following prominent
politicians: Herr Brandt, as Vice-Chancellor and Foreign Minister,
Prof. Karl Schiller (S P D), Minister of Economics, Herr Strauss,
Finance Minister, Dr Gerhard Schröder (C D U), Defence Minister,
Herbert Wehner (S P D), Minister for All-German Affairs, Dr Gustav
Heinemann (S P D), Minister of Justice, and Paul Lücke (Interior),
Kai-Uwe von Hassel (Refugees) and Hermann Höcherl (Agricul-
ture) of the C D U/C S U, and Georg Leber (Transport) and Carlo
Schmid (Bundesrat affairs) of the S P D. In all there were eleven,
including the Chancellor, C D U/C S U Ministers, and nine Social
Democrats.

The new government gave the S P D their first taste of office since
before 1933 but rank-and-file members, including parliamentarians,
were far from happy about it. They found a spokesman in Günter
Grass. In open letters to both Kiesinger and Brandt he attacked the
Chancellor. ' Is there not in the S P D/C S U/C D U a man with a clean

enough record to take over the office of Chancellor?', he asked. He was of course referring to the fact that Dr Kiesinger had been a member of the Nazi party and had held a highly responsible post in the Foreign Office under the Nazis. Grass argued that Kiesinger's appointment helped to make the N P D's ex-Nazis respectable, an argument the National Democrats were later to use themselves. They also pointed out that Prof. Schiller had been a Nazi party member. To make matters worse, in the first year of the Grand Coalition the recession deepened and the S P D's electoral stock fell. In three regional elections in that year it lost ground.

When Herr Brandt took over as Foreign Minister it was expected that Bonn would make at least a partial reappraisal of its policy towards the D D R and East Europe. Brandt's policy was that of 'small steps' towards minor improvements in relations between East and West. The Foreign Minister also felt that the Hallstein Doctrine had outlived its usefulness. During Dr Erhard's term of office Bonn's relations with the Third World had worsened. Its close relations with Israel had led to a deterioration of its relations with the Arab states. In October 1964 Herr Ulbricht had paid a state visit to Cairo and Bonn had sought revenge against President Nasser by recognising Israel. Ten Arab states then broke off diplomatic relations with the Federal Republic. Under Adenauer, Bonn had broken off relations with Yugoslavia and Cuba when they recognised East Germany. The Arab states did not give full and formal recognition to the D D R but the danger was that they would do so making it so much more difficult to resume relations with Bonn in the future. The Social Democrats could not persuade their colleagues to abandon the Doctrine mainly because of the attitude of the C S U. In 1969 Egypt, Iraq, Sudan, Syria, South Yemen and Cambodia recognised the D D R. Bonn no longer had relations with the five Arab states but complications arose with Cambodia. Bonn did not break off relations as such but recalled its Ambassador declaring he 'is and will remain recalled'. This provoked Cambodia to break off relations. In Eastern Europe the Federal Republic had achieved success by establishing diplomatic relations with Romania in January 1967. This had represented a dent in the Hallstein Doctrine for Romania retained its ties with East Berlin. Bonn claimed that it was prepared to make exceptions in the case of the Soviet Bloc states because they were not free to decide between the two Germanies. Because it would not recognise the Oder-Neisse frontier or the D D R, or sign the Non-Proliferation Treaty, or clearly renounce a nuclear role, the Federal Republic was unable to establish formal relations with any of the other Warsaw Pact countries though in 1968 it once again exchanged ambassadors with Belgrade. Yugoslavia retained its relations with the D D R.

## THE S D S AND THE STUDENT REVOLT

Certainly up to the mid-1950s German students tended to be conformist in their political views. Towards the end of the 1950s some change was noticeable. This was provoked by rearmament including the reintroduction of conscription which directly affected students, the campaign against nuclear arms, the changes for the better in Eastern Europe, the failure of Adenauer's policy to achieve reunification, the struggles of countries like Algeria for independence, the emergence of new social models in China and Cuba, the ' Leftward ' trend in the Vatican and the other churches, and the poor conditions which the students had to put up with. The scandals concerning ex-Nazis and the *Spiegel* Affair (see p. 155) in the early 1960s further contributed to make students more critical of their society.

The changing pattern was seen in the development of the S D S, *Der Sozialistische Deutsche Studentenbund*, the Socialist German Students' League. This body had been set up after 1945 as the official Social Democratic student body and for years had been regarded as one of the most moderate of the European socialist student organisations. However, at a congress held at Frankfurt in the summer of 1959, the S D S turned sharply Left just at a time when the parent body was turning Right. In the following year the S P D dissociated itself from the S D S. Deprived of the main sources of its funds, the S D S might have failed but for the assistance it received from certain Left-wing academics—Professors Wolfgang Abendroth of Marburg and Ossip K. Flechtheim of the Free University of West Berlin were the most prominent—who formed a sponsoring society, *Der Sozialistische Bund*. The S D S was able to hold its own against the new Social Democratic University League (S H B).

The Free University of West Berlin had by this time gained a special position in higher education in West Germany. Modelled on American lines, its structure had encouraged its students to take a greater part in running things than was traditionally the case at German universities. In this way its students gained in self-confidence. It had built up a high reputation for its political science teaching, thus attracting to it some of the more critical students attracted to that discipline. Both parts of Berlin became competing markets of world culture and ideas which the students savoured drawing from both. The Free University admitted a fair number of refugee students from the D D R some of whom claimed to be Marxist and socialist, but against the S E D. Large numbers of students came from West Germany proper, some of whom sought to avoid military service by studying in West Berlin (where the conscription law is not in force). Given this special position of the Free University it is not surprising that the increasing critical awareness of West German students should manifest itself there.

In the 1960s the S D S was able to organise a number of headline-making demonstrations in West Berlin. The first of these was in December 1964, when several hundred students demonstrated against the then Congolese Premier, Moise Tshombe. In February 1966, 1,500 students took to the streets against American policy in Vietnam in a march authorised by the authorities. In December of the same year 1,000 students defied the police to make a similar protest. In April 1967 2,000 turned out against American Vice-President Hubert Humphrey. In between there were several demos, including a sit-in involving 3,000 against the university authorities for preventing the use of official buildings for political meetings. More dramatic was the reception given the Shah of Iran who had abuse and tomatoes hurled at him. On that occasion, 2 June 1967, a 26-year-old student Benno Ohnesorg was shot in the back by a plain-clothes policeman. A demonstration of 4,000 followed to protest against the shooting, and silent marches were held throughout West Germany on the day of his funeral, involving 100,000 students.

1968 and 1969 saw more student demonstrations and more violence in many parts of West Germany. The approaching federal elections raised the temperature and made students more political. So did the student revolt in Paris in May 1968, the N P D, the assassination attempt against S D S leader Rudi Dutschke in April, the continuing Vietnam War and the passage of the emergency powers' laws (*Notstandsgesetze*) by the Federal Parliament. The fact that the bulk of the members of the Bundestag belonged to the government parties seemed additional proof that West German democracy was a sham. During this period the S D S moved further and further away from the traditional Marxist, state-socialist ideology, in favour of a mixture of the teachings of the Russian anarchist Bakunin, the American ' New Leftist ' Herbert Marcuse, Mao Tse-tung, and the South American revolutionist Che Guevara. Trotsky and Lenin also gained, or retained, a few admirers.

Despite the successes of the S D S it remained a small body amongst the total student population. In the autumn term of 1966 the Christian Democratic student organisation (R C D S) with 2,200 members was the largest student political sociey. It was followed by the S H B with 1,500 members. The S D S came third with 1,200 and the League of Liberal Students (L S D) fourth with 900. A year later the S D S had 2,500 members, the S H B, which was moving in the direction of the S D S, 2,000, and the L S D 1,100. The R C D S was in a state of complete stagnation. Nevertheless, all these student bodies put together represented only a small proportion of the student body of nearly 300,000 students in the mid-1960s. The traditionalist fencing fraternities (*Verbindungen*) had more members. And a survey published in *Der Spiegel* (19 June 1967) showed that the great majority of students had no clear, and certainly no Leftist, political orientation. However, many students could be won for occasional S D S activities because of a vague concern for some of the issues mentioned above, and a feeling of dissatisfaction about conditions at the universities and in the schools.

German schools are overcrowded and especially in the agricultural areas conditions are bad. In the 1950s the number of single-class schools with one teacher for all grades was actually increasing. The war had caused great destruction of school buildings. Even so, in 1961, 50 per cent of them dated from before 1905. Traditional regional differences had been accentuated by the federal system. In Hesse, with a population of about five million in 1965, 11.6 per cent of the appropriate age group were able to pass the *Abitur*, the university matriculation exam in 1964. In the Rhineland, with a population of about three and a half million, only 5.1 per cent got their *Abitur* in 1964. As Prof. Dahrendorf, for one, has often pointed out, it is still very difficult for working-class children to get an education commensurate with their abilities. Children from agricultural areas, Catholics and girls are others who could be described as the educationally underprivileged. This lack of opportunity is indicated by the fact that only about four or five per cent of university students in West Germany are from working-class homes, although the majority of people are working class. In Britain and the D D R the proportions are much higher. In the early 1960s about one third of the West German population lived in towns of over 100,000. At the same time 53 per cent of students at West German universities came from these towns. Unlike those of Britain or East Germany most students in the Federal Republic in the 1960s had to finance their studies themselves. This obviously made it more difficult for the less well off. It meant too that the majority of better-off students were dependent on their parents. Many students have to take jobs. In 1965 Prof. Dahrendorf, in *Die Zeit* (23 April), summed up the situation of the German universities as follows: the

German university admits too few students; of those who are admitted too many leave without qualifying; those who do complete their studies study too long; what they learn is too little in terms of quality and quantity.

## BRANDT BECOMES CHANCELLOR

As we have seen, after the S P D joined the Grand Coalition it suffered a number of electoral reverses. In 1969 the climate of opinion started to move more in its favour. The economy took a turn for the better and this became associated in the public mind with Prof. Karl Schiller, the Social Democratic Minister of Economics. Only Chancellor Kiesinger was regarded as more popular among the government politicians. In March the S P D got another boost by the election of Dr Gustav Heinemann to the Federal Presidency. The election took place earlier than expected because of the unscheduled retirement of Heinrich Lübke. For some years the East Germans had attacked Herr Lübke claiming that he had designed and built concentration camps during the war. This he had always denied. In January 1968 the weekly *Der Stern* broke the news that J. Howard Haring, an American handwriting expert who had worked for General Motors, I B M and Shell, as well as for the District Attorney of New York, had stated his view that signatures on wartime blueprints of concentration camps were undoubtedly Lübke's. Pressure on Herr Lübke grew until he was finally forced to go.

Dr Heinemann was opposed by Dr Schöder in the Federal Meeting. About 90 per cent of the Free Democratic delegates voted for the Social Democrats indicating to the S P D as *Die Frankfurter Allegmeine Zeitung* saw it, that they could be reliable coalition partners. Dr Heinemann was the first Social Democrat to be President in Germany since the death of Friedrich Ebert in 1925.

The federal elections of 1969 were hard fought considering the two main contenders had been, and were still during the election, in a coalition government together. The changes were not dramatic. With 15.2 million votes (46.1 per cent) the Christian Democrats received only 300,000 fewer than in 1965. The S P D gained over 14 million votes, an increase of roughly 1.2 million, which represented 42.7 per cent of the poll. The Social Democrats increased their parliamentary strength by 22 giving them 224 seats as against 242 for the Christians. The F D P slumped from over 3 million votes to 1.9 million (5.8 per cent) emerging with 30 seats, a loss of 19. The dreaded N P D attracted 1.4 million votes (4.3 per cent) which did not qualify them for representation in the Bundestag. The Left-wing A D F gained only 197,570 (0.6 per cent).

The Social Democratic gains were made predominently in white-collar, dormitory areas, for instance, around Cologne and Bonn, in Hamburg and the nearby districts in Schleswig-Holstein. The S P D failed to attract more working-class support but it got itself across to the younger white-collar and professional people. This could be a long-term danger to the Christian Democrats for as the economy changes there are more of these voters. They tend to be either indifferent to or, at least, less bound to the churches, a fact which has led a minority in the C D U/C S U to ask whether they ought not to drop the ' C ' from the title of their party. West Germany is becoming more urbanised and since 1961 it has gained less support than the S P D in these areas. In the towns of over 100,000 inhabitants it gained 62 seats in 1957 as against 27 for the S P D. In 1961 the figures were 41 and 49, in 1965 30 and 60, and in 1969 14 and 76 respectively. In 1965 33.2 per cent lived in such towns. These people were more convinced by the S P D's 'We'll create the modern Germany' than the C D U/C S U's 'It depends on the Chancellor '. The Christian Democrats argued: We built the affluent society without the S P D; look at the state of ' Socialist Britain '; the S P D's ' soft ' line on Eastern policy had been exploded by the Soviet invasion of Czechoslovakia; and the student agitators were close intellectually and even personally to the S P D. These arguments did not have the desired impact.

The Free Democrats of Walter Scheel lost ground as a result of their recent swing to the Left. The results indicated that the C D U and the N P D had gained from F D P losses. That a great many of those who gave their second vote to the F D P wanted a coalition with the S P D was indicated by the fact that they gave their first votes to the candidates of Brandt.

The Left-wing A D F or Action for Democratic Progress undoubt-edly suffered from its association with Soviet Communism. It was an alliance of the neutralist D F U, the recently formed German Communist Party (D K P, not to be confused with the K P D which still claims to exist underground) and other tiny groups. The D K P failed to condemn the Soviet action in Czechoslovakia. Most S D S students and supporters would not consider voting for these orthodox Communists and those associated with them. The A D F was hit as well by the argument that a vote for it was a wasted vote.

Herr von Thadden's candidates lost some of their protest support when the economic situation improved. There is no doubt that the long-sustained campaign against the N P D frightened off some people who thought it was not respectable.

The Christian Democrats fumed against the possibility of the S P D/F D P coalition and offered talks to the leaders of both parties. After the success of the coalition negotiations between the Social and Free Democrats, Herr Brandt was elected Chancellor on 21 October by 251 votes to 235 with 5 abstentions and 4 invalid. As a successful candidate for Chancellor must receive more than half the votes of the Bundestag's total membership he needed 249 votes. Thus he was elected by a margin of only two votes. All S P D and F D P members were present and it can therefore be assumed that three of the F D P had either abstained or spoilt their papers.

The main appointments in the new coalition were: Willy Brandt, Chancellor; Walter Scheel, F D P Leader and former Minister for Economic Aid, Foreign Minister; Prof. Karl Schiller, former Rector of Hamburg University, Minister of Economics; Helmut Schmidt, former wartime Lieutenant and veteran S P D defence spokesman, Minister of Defence; Hans-Dietrich Genscher (F D P), Minister of Interior; Georg Leber (S P D), the leader of the Building Trade Union, Minister of Traffic, Posts and Telecommunications; Josef Ertl, the right-wing Bavarian Free Democrat, Minister of Agriculture. A non-party appointment, that of Prof. Hans Leussink as Minister of Education and Science, caused some surprise. Herr Leussink is a professional engineer and former Rector of the Karlsruhe Technical University. In all the Cabinet comprised 12 S P D members, 3 F D P and Herr Leussink. One important S P D member not in the government was Herr Herbert Wehner, Minister for All-German Affairs in the Grand Coalition. Herr Wehner took on the important job of leading his party's group in the Bundestag.

The most pressing problem calling for immediate action was a revaluation of the currency. From 1952 onwards West Germany had a surplus on its foreign trade and many economists believed the Mark was undervalued. A huge surplus in 1967, partly the result a drop in imports brought on by the recession, and the international monetary crisis of November 1968 brought renewed demands from West Germany's allies to revalue the mark. As the Christian Democrats opposed this nothing was done. The controversy became dramatic during the election with Kiesinger and Strauss opposing, and Schiller favouring, revaluation. In two days the equivalent of $540 m. flowed in. The foreign exchange markets were closed temporarily. The old government allowed the mark to ' float '. The new Cabinet at its first meeting revalued the currency by 9.28 per cent which made West German exports dearer abroad and foreign imports cheaper. This decision, like that to float the mark, hit Federal Germany's agriculture. Measures to protect it brought the

N

old government into conflict with the other members of the Six. After hard bargaining the new mini-coalition was permitted by the other Common Market states to grant subsidies of various kinds to West German agriculture.

The new coalition faced some tough problems, the principal one of which was how to stay in existence, and attacks on government policy by former F D P leader Erich Mende did not augur well for its future.

# 11   The Social Democratic Decade

BRANDT AND OSTPOLITIK

The 11 years 1969–80 were a period in which West Germany seemed to gain a greater importance, a new stature, in the international community. This was made possible by the Federal Republic's continued economic expansion, and by its active diplomacy. The *Ostpolitik* of the early years of the S P D-F D P coalition laid the foundations of this new influence.

Willy Brandt outlined his policy towards Poland in a press conference after his election as Chancellor on 21 October 1969. He welcomed the idea of opening diplomatic relations in the near future. A week later he indicated his view of relations with the German Democratic Republic. He reiterated the traditional West German position on the unity of the German people, commenting, 'Even if there exist two states in Germany, they are not foreign countries to each other; their relations with each other can only be of a special nature'. He then went on to offer the East Germans negotiations at government level without discrimination on either side, which should lead to contractually agreed co-operation. For the first time a West German Chancellor had recognised the existence of the German Democratic Republic. Willi Stoph, Chairman of the Council of Ministers of the D D R, found Brandt's statement full of contradictions but 'there was a hint in it of a more realistic assessment of the situation created in Europe as a result of the Second World War'. On this basis, Walter Ulbricht presented a draft treaty on relations between the two German states to President Heinemann After more statements, some delays, correspondence and backstairs diplomacy, Brandt and Stoph met at Erfurt (D D R) on 19 March 1970. The people of that ancient town gave Brandt an enthusiastic welcome which seems to have taken the politicians of both states somewhat by surprise. The two heads of government conferred again in the West German town of Kassel on 21 May. In the meantime the two states had signed a postal agreement and Bonn announced measures aimed at helping the other Germany to export more to the Federal Republic and thus reduce its trade deficit. As a further gesture to the S E D, the Bundestag repealed the so-called 'safe conduct' law. Highly offensive to the East German leadership, this had granted certain S E D politicians immunity from prosecution on visits to West Germany. It had been originally introduced at the time of the abortive S P D–S E D talks of 1966. Negotiations also followed with the U S S R, Brandt fully understanding that on their success depended the future of relations with East Germany. A treaty on the renunciation of force was signed in Moscow on 12 August 1970 by the two states. Thus 31 years after the signing of the notorious Hitler-Stalin Non-Aggression Pact the Federal Republic and the Soviet Union had agreed on a treaty which made a genuine contribution to peace and understanding. Article 3 bound the two nations to respect the territorial integrity of all states in Europe within their existing frontiers, including the Oder-Neisse line and the frontiers between the D D R and the Federal Republic. The treaty opened the way for the other agreements which followed. In December the Federal Republic and Poland signed a treaty Article 1 of which stated that the signatories agreed that the Oder-Neisse line 'shall constitute the Western state frontier of the People's Republic of Poland'. With the initialling of the treaty the Polish government announced its intention to allow those ethnic Germans who wished to leave for the Federal Republic to go. The position of West Berlin was regulated by the Four Power agreement of 3 September 1971. The West gained Soviet recognition of the close ties between West Berlin and the Federal Republic and its guarantee of the unimpeded movement of people and goods between the Western Sectors and West Germany. West Berliners were, in future, to have normal opportunities to visit East Berlin and the DDR for tourist, cultural and business reasons. In return the Western Powers recognised, once again, that the Western sectors are not part of the Federal Republic or governed by it. The treaty put paid to the West German practice of holding important state occasions in West Berlin, such as the election of the Federal President or plenary sessions of the Bundestag. The West Germans were, however, authorised to maintain a permanent liaison agency in West Berlin. In return the Soviet Union gained the right to install a consulate-general there. The three Western Powers, by signing the treaty, did not give up their view that the whole of Berlin remains under Four Power control. Even after they later recognised the DDR they still continued to exercise their right to send patrols, unhindered by the East Germans, through East Berlin. As for the West Germans, the three Western Powers had pointed out in 1949, 1954 and 1967 that West Berlin was not a *Land* of the Federal Republic. For them West

German laws had not applied in West Berlin, only identical laws agreed by the parliament of West Berlin. The military service laws and the emergency powers laws of the Federal Republic, for instance, do not apply in West Berlin. From the standpoint of the Four Powers, therefore, West Germany was losing nothing by the 1971 treaty.

The most fundamental of the treaties which arose from the *Ostpolitik* was the so-called Basic Treaty (*Grundvertrag*) between the Federal Republic and the Democratic Republic. Signed on 21 December 1972, it obligated both states to develop good neighbourly relations on the basis of the aims and principles of the United Nations' Charter. The two states further agreed to respect the sovereignty of each other, to renounce force, to work for disarmament and to solve the practical and humanitarian problems which stood between them. In 1974 the Federal Republic and the DDR agreed to exchange special representatives, not ambassadors, having diplomatic status. In a letter to the East German government Herr Brandt reaffirmed that the Basic Treaty did not contradict West Germany's aim to work for the right of self-determination of the German people and for German reunification. In 1973 there were other great strides forward in *Ostpolitik* with the establishment of full diplomatic relations between West Germany and Finland, Czechoslovakia, Hungary and Bulgaria, the admission of the two German states into the United Nations and the opening of the Helsinki Conference by 32 states of Eastern and Western Europe, Canada and the United States.

Herr Brandt had no easy time in trying to get the *Ostpolitik* accepted in Bonn. Many Christian Democrats claimed that he was giving much away and getting very little in return. With his slender majority he was abandoning some of the most cherished principles of all previous administrations—the position of West Berlin as a *Land* of the Republic according to Article 23 of the Basic Law, the right of the Federal Republic to speak for all Germans, the non-recognition of the DDR, the rejection of the Oder-Neisse frontier and the right to their *Heimat* of those expelled from beyond it, and the Hallstein doctrine. The reality of the situation was, however, that West Germany's ability to enforce its claims weakened with every year which passed. The world felt West Germany had re-emerged in a way which no one had dreamt of in 1945 or even 1949, and should be content to acquiesce in these losses. By clinging to its old claims West Germany was inviting suspicion and hostility in Eastern Europe, and growing impatience in the West. Though there were critics of Brandt's *Ostpolitik* in the United

States, Bonn's most powerful ally was seeking détente with the Soviet Union and therefore welcomed Brandt's basic approach. As for the Soviet Union, this period was a good time to negotiate with the Kremlin leadership. They feared that the growing Sino-American friendship could be at their expense. By landing a man successfully on the moon in 1969 the Americans had shown that the Russians had no advantage over them in this area. For these, and other, reasons the Soviets were prepared to come to the conference table. The initiatives of the S P D-F D P government greatly increased the prestige and moral stature of the Federal Republic in all those states which had been belligerents in the Second World War. Nor did the Basic Treaty do anything to lessen the feeling of kinship between the citizens of the two Germanies. As former Governing Mayor of West Berlin Brandt knew better than most Bonn politicians the realities, in human terms, of the division of Germany. This was also true of some of his colleagues. Herr Genscher, F D P Minister of Interior, was born and brought up in Halle (D D R) and still had relations there. Professor Schiller was born in Breslau, now in Poland, and Annemarie Renger, S P D Bundestag President was born in Leipzig. Egon Bahr, who did so much of the negotiating with the East Germans on Brandt's behalf was born in Treffurt (DDR). His aim, like Brandt's was, in no small degree, to improve the situation for those millions of Germans suffering through the partition. This they certainly did. The two million West Berliners could now visit the D D R without much difficulty. Once again they could phone their relations in the other half of the city. Between June 1972 and May 1978 19.58 million visits by West Berliners were recorded in East Berlin or East Germany proper. In 1977 alone there were 3.4 million visits by West Berliners in the D D R including East Berlin. The three million or so Germans who had left the DDR between 1949–71 could once again visit their relatives without the danger of being arrested as deserters. In 1976 3.1 million West Germans visited the D D R, in 1977 2.9 million did so. Because of the Basic Treaty roughly 6.5 million West Germans living in the frontier areas became eligible to visit the frontier region of the D D R. In 1977 around 443,000 such daily visits were made. In the other direction it proved easier for old age pensioners from the D D R to visit West Germany. In addition, up to the end of 1977 an estimated 215,000 East Germans under retirement age had been able to visit the Federal Republic on 'compelling family business'. This included attending weddings, funerals, etc. The *Ostpolitik* also resulted in many thousands of ethnic Germans from Eastern Europe being permitted to emigrate to West Germany. In both political and human terms Brandt's policy was a success. His personal achievement was recognised in 1971 when he was awarded the Nobel Prize for peace, the first German to be so honoured since Carl von Ossietzky, the pacifist, in 1935.

## DOMESTIC REFORMS

Brandt was anxious that his government should be a reforming administration and a number of reforms were embarked upon. More money was spent on education at all levels and the school leaving age was raised to 16. Retirement pensioners got more as did other welfare claimants. Tenants were given more rights. A law was passed to encourage wider share ownership by workers and other rank-and-file employees. Efforts were made to improve the motorways and railways. The Brandt government was also far sighted enough to decide to establish an oil reserve *before* the oil crisis of 1973. It came too late, however, to make any difference when the oil embargo was imposed. The age of majority was reduced to 18 giving the vote to an additional 2.5 million young people. Believing the Federal Republic should be able to compete more effectively with the DDR in sport, the government gave more federal aid to sports' organisations. This did not halt the tide of DDR successes. At the Mexico Olympics (1968) West Germany had gained only five gold medals against the DDR'S nine. Subsequently, at Munich (1972) and Montreal (1976) the DDR increased its lead. At Montreal it was second with 40 gold compared with the USSR (47), USA (34) and West Germany (10). Nevertheless, West Germany's olympic achievements compared well with those of Britain, France and Italy. All these improvements were fairly non-controversial, all were well within the Federal Republic's financial means.

Much more controversial was legislation connected with codetermination. This met with opposition from the Right-wing of the FDP and the majority of the Christian Democrats. One argument used was that such legislation would frighten off foreign investors, especially American investors. In November 1971 the *Betriebsverfassungsgesetz* (Factory Constitution Law) was passed with the votes of the SPD, FDP and 21 Christian Democrats. This strengthened the right of individual employees to be informed and to be heard on matters concerning their place of work. The Works' Council (*Betriebsrat*) was given more authority and trade unions were given the right of entry into the factory provided they informed the employer of their intention to do so. It is convenient to mention here that after years of argument a new Codetermination Law came into effect on 1 July 1976. This improved employee representation on the supervisory boards of companies outside the coal and steel industries. The main provision was that in the 650 major companies accounting for 70 per cent of West German output, the employee representatives on the boards were increased from one third to one half. Though this represented a big improvement from the employees' point of view, it did not give them the kind of parity representation enjoyed by their colleagues in coal and steel. First of all, the chairman is agreed by both sides. But if share-holders and employees cannot agree on a chairman the shareholders' nominee becomes chairman. Secondly, out of the ten employee representatives, one must be a senior executive. Of the rest, three are trade union nominees, usually leading trade union officials from outside the firm, and the other six are various categories of employees from within the firm.

YOUTH AND TERRORISM

The Bundeswehr continued to grow under the Social Democrats as under the Christian Democrats, so did the number of conscientious objectors to military service. In 1968 11,952 had applied to be recognised (5,588 were so recognised). In 1970 19,363 applied for recognition (9,351). By 1977 the number of applicants had risen to over 70,000. With over 495,000 men under arms in 1979, the West German armed forces were second only to the French in numbers in Western Europe. The West Germans spent more per capita on arms than Britain or France, but less per capita as a percentage of gross national product. The SPD-FDP regime continued to expand provision for alternative service for objectors, usually in hospitals or agriculture, and cut conscription from 18 to 15 months in June 1972. Brandt's Chancellorship seemed to augur well for the reintegration of the minority of potentially Left-wing students into more conventional political movements. Despite the increasing numbers of conscientious objectors, to a considerable extent this did in fact happen. But a small minority of the minority remained so alienated from society that they were prepared to use violence to change it. Led by Andreas Baader, a drifter and adventurer, Ulrike Meinhof, journalist and daughter of a curator, and Gudrun Ensslin, a philosophy student and pastor's daughter, the so-called Baader-Meinhof gang pulled off a jail break, held up banks, bombed police stations, and attacked American Army camps and the Right-wing Axel Springer press building in Hamburg. The violence was frightening, especially for the great majority of West Germans for whom the greatest political catch-phrase was *Sicherheit*—security. The reaction of the SPD-FDP government was to rush through a whole series of measures, in June 1972, tightening up the firearms regulations, extending the power of judges to hold suspects in custody, extending the range of activities of the paramilitary *Bundesgrenz-schutz* (Federal Frontier Defence Force) and of the *Verfassungs-schutz* (the West German equivalent of the American FBI). Baader, Meinhof and some others were arrested in June 1972. Some of their confederates continued with their acts of violence. In February 1975 the chairman of the West Berlin C D U, Peter Lorenz, was kidnapped and ransomed. In April the West German Embassy in Stockholm was seized and blown up. The terrorists concerned were apprehended but not before two diplomats had been killed. The wave of violence reached its climax in 1977. In April of that year Baader, Ensslin and Jan-Carl Raspe were sentenced to life imprisonment, Meinhof had committed suicide in prison. In revenge Baader's comrades murdered Siegfried Buback, Chief Federal Prosecutor, and his driver. On 30 July Jürgen Ponto, Dresdner Bank chairman, was killed resisting a kidnap attempt. Hans-Martin Schleyer, President of the Federation of German Industry, a leading employers' organisation, was kid-napped after a battle in which his driver and three bodyguards were killed. Among the demands of the kidnappers was the release of 11 convicted terrorists including Baader, Ensslin and Raspe. To reinforce their demands the urban guerrillas joined forces with the Palestinian Liberation Organisation (P L O) to hijack a Lufthansa airliner with 86 passengers and crew on board. Eventually the plane was allowed to land at Mogadishu in Somalia. A brilliant rescue operation by the *Bundesgrenzschutz* was mounted. The three leaders, held in Stamnheim prison near Stuttgart then killed themselves in a last act of defiance. Herr Schleyer was murdered. Terrorism had been defeated—at a price. More legislation, giving the police wider powers of search and arrest, and making it possible to bar defence lawyers from trials of suspected terrorists, was introduced. All that the Baader-Meinhof group had achieved was a slightly more authori-tarian Federal Republic with Bonn's government quarter looking like an armed camp. Not too much significance should be attached to the terrorists, they had less of a cause than almost any other group operating in Europe, the Middle East or South America.

If the West German reaction to terrorism was understandable, it was more difficult to understand the so-called *Berufsverbot*. On 28 January 1972 the heads of the governments of the *Länder* chaired by Willy Brandt, had agreed principles for dealing with public employees (*Beamte*) who were members of political extremist organisations. Basically, they decided, public employees would have to undertake to uphold the Basic Law. Membership of organisations which fought against the constitutional order would usually result in a conflict of loyalties, in these cases the employer would have to decide what to do. This agreement of principles led to a good deal of controversy. The practice of vetting public officials was not new, new was the restatement of the principles and the publicity given to a number of individual cases. Usually, the teachers, postmen, engine drivers and minor officials excluded from the public service were leftists and many were members of the German Communist Party (DKP). The problem was that the DKP, since 1968, was a legal organisation. Totally committed to Moscow it remained among the least attractive of Western Europe's Communist parties. However, was there any danger in allowing its members, and there were very few of them, going about their lowly tasks in the public service? Was not their exclusion from the public service another step along the road to fear, suspicion and conformity? Such actions provided no protection against the thousands of Soviet bloc spies in the Federal Republic. That there was a danger of undue conformity was revealed by the *Wehrbeauftragter*. The first SPD member to hold this position, Karl Wilhelm Berkhan, found that conscripts were reluctant to stand up for their rights. He believed this was in part the result of increased unemployment which made young men fear taking risks.

ELECTION 1972

Willy Brandt as Chancellor lived, in political terms, if not recklessly, then at least dangerously. He had a small majority and a coalition partner with a record of previous splits and defections. At a stroke his majority was halved when three FDP Bundestag deputies, including former leader Erich Mende, joined the CDU in October 1970. Worse was to come. In October 1971 came the first anti-*Ostpolitik* defection from the SPD, followed by two others in February 1972. When the Budget was rejected on 28 April 1972 by 247 votes to 247 with one abstention, it was clear an election could not be far away. On 16 May Dr Günther Müller, former Chairman of the Young Socialists, was expelled from the SPD for (right-wing) anti-party activities. This reduced the coalition deputies to just half (248) of the Bundestag deputies with full voting rights (that is, all the deputies except those from West Berlin). The treaties with the Soviet Union and Poland were ratified because most of the Christian Democrats simply abstained (after American representations) rather than voting against them. Another blow was struck against the Brandt administration when Karl Schiller resigned on 7 July over differences on economic policy. In this situation of Parliamentary stalemate Brandt deliberately got himself defeated on a confidence motion by getting his cabinet to abstain. On 22 September President Heinemann could announce fresh elections.

Brandt's victory was by no means certain. His government came under attack from right-wing defectors, including Schiller, who left the s p d altogether before the elections, and the left-wing Young Socialists. The Christian Democrats, led by the moderate Rainer Barzel, attacked the government for selling out the national interests and for damaging the market economy. There were also doubts about the administration's ability to deal with the terrorists. During the Olympic Games held in Munich in September, Palestinian terrorists killed 11 Israelis and one police officer during a police battle to free Israelis held hostage. The results of the elections held on 19 November came as a shock to the cdu/csu. Only once before in its history had the s p d done better. In terms of seats the s p d won 230 (224 in 1969), the cdu 176 (193), csu 48 (49) and fdp 42 (30). With 45.9 per cent of the popular vote the s p d had, for the first time, outdistanced the cdu/csu (44.8). The Free Democrats had improved their position from 5.8 per cent to 8.4 per cent. The npd vote had slumped to a mere 0.6 per cent and the dkp got only 0.3 per cent. The s p d owed their success to the increased support they had received from youth, women and the working class. There can be no doubt that Brandt's personal popularity had been a crucial factor in the victory.

Willy Brandt's personal triumph was short-lived. In April 1974 Günter Guillaume, a personal assistant to the Chancellor was arrested as an East German spy. Brandt resigned on 6 May taking upon himself the political responsibility for what he called his carelessness in the affair. It was widely believed he could have continued and resigned for personal reasons. He had been Chancellor for nearly five years, which was longer than Kiesinger or Erhard, and was in the Adenauer class in terms of his significance. Aged 60, he remained in the Bundestag and was active as s p d chairman.

The Bundestag elected Helmut Schmidt Chancellor by 267 votes to 225, including three coalition deputies, on 16 May. Schmidt (born 1918), the son of Hamburg school teachers, had studied economics at Hamburg University before taking up politics. He had been the Interior Minister in the Hamburg *Land* administration (1961–5), chaired the s p d Bundestag caucus (1967–9), served as Defence Minister (1969–72), Minister of Economics and Finance (July-December '72) and Finance until May 1974. The new Foreign Minister was Hans-Dietrich Genscher (f d p). Other important appointments included: George Leber (s p d) Defence, Egon Franke

(S P D) Inter-German Relations, Hans Apel (S P D) Finance, Professor Werner Maihofer (F D P) Interior. The only woman member of the government was Dr Katharina Focke (S P D) Minister for Youth, Family and Health. This ministry was, up to 1980, almost the only one held by women.* In 1961 Elizabeth Schwartzhaupt (C D U), the first woman minister in the history of the Federal Republic, was appointed to it by Dr Adenauer. Schmidt's administration comprised 11 S P D members and four F D P.

### HONECKER TAKES OVER THE D D R

Brandt's *Ostpolitik* represented both an opportunity and a challenge to the S E D. On the one hand, the East German leaders welcomed relations with Bonn and the non-Communist world with all the advantages international recognition would bring. On the other, they feared their fragile stability could be shattered by Bonn's embrace. As we saw above (p 187) several Arab states and Cambodia started off a wave of recognitions of the D D R in 1969. By the end of the year 11 states of the Third World had recognised East Berlin. The breakthrough with the Western industrial states came after the signing of the Basic Treaty with the Federal Republic. Switzerland was the first such state to recognise the D D R in December 1972. Belgium was the first N A T O state to accord recognition to East Germany (27 December). Britain and France waited until 9 February 1973. The United States and Canada were among the last states to agree recognition in September 1974 and August 1975 respectively. That the D D R was not going to let past political quarrels and propaganda stand in the way of diplomatic relations was shown when it took up full relations with Iran in December 1972 and Franco Spain in January 1973. Both regimes had provided the East German media with many anger-filled hours in the past. In the case of Iran, oil was a consideration. It is not clear what the D D R was to get out of rushing into relations with Spain. When Erich Honecker was photographed with President Ford of the United States, and then Chancellor Schmidt at the Helsinki Conference on Security and Co-operation it was for the S E D a dream come true. The party felt it had stormed the final summit, taken the last stronghold, in the long war for recognition. The East German leaders believed such symbolic pictures must surely give them the seal of approval in the eyes of their own people. The photographs emphasised, they believed, the point once again that even the West had recognised that there was no alternative to the S E D in the D D R.

The man who had fought so hard for this dream to come true, Walter Ulbricht, died on 1 August 1973. Ulbricht had been deprived

* Marie Schlei was Minister for Economic co-operation, 1976–78

of much of the glory and credit for what was happening by being forced to resign as First Secretary of the S E D in May 1971 just before the VIII Congress of the party. As expected, Honecker took his place. Ulbricht was given the purely honorary title of 'Chairman of the S E D' and was allowed to remain head of state. But his true position was indicated by the speed with which speech writers forgot he had ever had anything to say, his portraits disappeared, institutions named after him were renamed, and he was downgraded in the history books. In October 1972 the Council of State was deprived of most of its power. By the time Ulbricht died physically, he had long been dead politically. His modest funeral was the outward recognition of this. He had to pay the price for being, in his final years as S E D boss, just a little independent of Moscow, for wanting to drive a harder bargain with West Germany than the Soviet leaders needed, and perhaps not least, for keeping Erich Honecker waiting too long.

## NEW CONSTITUTION

Herr Honecker immediately re-emphasised the Soviet connection. This was given formal expression in the new constitution of October 1974. Article 6 declared that the D D R 'is for ever and irrevocably allied' with the U S S R. Gone was Article 8, paragraph 2 of the 1968 constitution which pledged the D D R to work to overcome the division of Germany. (In most other respects the basic elements of the 1968 constitution remained.) The Friendship Treaty between the D D R and the U S S R of 7 October 1975 bound East Germany even more closely to the Soviet Union. Eternal friendship between the two was the promise contained in Article 1. Economic co-operation and integration became obligatory under Article 2, and Articles 4 and 8 bound the two states to give military assistance to each other in case of attack. Article 9 seemed to deny the possibility of any separate East German foreign policy, for it stated that both would consult each other, in the interests of both states, on all international questions and would act from a common position. The East Germans proved to be good allies for the Soviet Union, backing its line in the international Communist movement, at the U N, and giving economic and military aid to the Soviet Union's clients in the Third World especially Vietnam, South Yemen, Ethiopia, Mozambique, Angola and the African National Congress guerrillas in Rhodesia.

In his domestic policies Erich Honecker attempted to secure his own position by getting his own men promoted, swung for a time to the 'left' in his economic ideological policies, tried to placate his people with the limited means available, and confronted the

domestic challenge caused by better relations with West Germany.
In his personnel policy Honecker pushed those who had been
associated with him in his long years as head of the Free German
Youth (F D J). One of his associates, Horst Sindermann, became
Chairman of the Council of Ministers (Prime Minister) in October
1973. Honecker's rival, Stoph, was kicked upstairs to the powerless
Council of State. Though the old men of the Politburo seemed to
take a long time to fade away, Honecker contented himself with
having others promoted. Following the pattern of the Soviet
Politburo, the Minister of Defence (1973) and the Minister for State
Security (1976) became full members of the Politburo. Honecker revealed his own appetite for power by taking over as Chairman of
the National Defence Council in 1971. This body would run the D D R
in time of war. He also was formally elected Chairman of the Council
of State in October 1976. In this he could claim he was only following
the good example of the Soviet leader Leonid Brezhnev. In general
Honecker tended to down grade economic experts in the first years
of his stewardship, preferring instead political/ideological specialists
like himself. Later he was forced to some extent to reverse this
because of the D D R's economic difficulties. Thus Willi Stoph was
reinstated as Chairman of the Council of Ministers in 1976, and the
economic expert Günter Mittag reverted to his previous role as
Central Committee secretary for the economy. He had lost this in
1973.

In economic/ideological questions Honecker swung 'left' in his
first years as S E D Secretary. This could have been merely part of a
campaign to show his allies that the D D R was a truly orthodox
Soviet bloc state and to let his own people know that better relations
with the Federal Republic did not mean there would be any con-
vergence of the two German systems. One such measure was the
nationalisation of the remaining mixed and private firms, in order, as
the S E D put it, to further the development of Socialist production
relations, and remove 'certain symptoms of recapitalisation in the
D D R'. This happened in April 1972. At that time these enterprises
were responsible for over 14 per cent of national income. They
employed nearly two million adults as against nearly 6.7 million
employed by the socialist sector. They were mainly in food and
textiles. This measure was possibly a sop to still the anger of some
because of the relatively high standard of living of those in the
semi-private and private sectors. Later this policy was partially
reversed. Starting in July 1974 Honecker used the term 'Communist'
in reference to the members of the S E D. In contrast to previous
policy he put much more emphasis on the K P D of Thälmann at

the expense of the old s P D. Again, this could have been part of the policy of *Abgrenzung* (delimitation) between the ideology of the West German s P D and the s E D. Later on this emphasis was toned down, probably because of the negative reception it got from the D D R population and even the ordinary members of the s E D. At the IX Congress of the s E D in May 1976 there were 1,914,382 members and 129,315 candidate members of the s E D out of a total population of only 16.89 millions. In the writer's experience many of them were merely fellow travellers. In such a situation and with an acute shortage of labour the s E D leaders remained limited in what they could do both politically and economically. It is significant that between the VIII and IX congresses the proportion of party members from the intelligentsia had risen while the proportion from the manual working-class had fallen. There is a clue here to the failure of the 'left' line. The s E D programme adopted in 1976 in the end represented a compromise between the old 'independent' Ulbricht emphasis on the uniqueness of the D D R's Socialism and Honecker's emphasis on the Soviet orthodoxy of the D D R. The new s E D statute agreed at the IX Congress in May 1976 also represented a compromise. However, Herr Honecker followed the Soviet example of changing his title from First Secretary to General-Secretary—a title last used at the height of Stalinism, 1950–53. Finally, the new *History of the SED* published in 1978 marked some retreat from the ' left ' line of the early Honecker period with Ulbricht reappearing, but some rewriting of history to give Honecker a more prominent role!

RAISING LIVING STANDARDS

The s E D leaders continued to attempt to raise the standard of living in the 1970s. No doubt there was a sincere desire to see their people enjoying a better life, but, in addition, they realised that improved contacts with West Germany made this of paramount political importance. In 1980 the citizens of the D D R still measured their own success by comparing their life to that of their relatives in the West. The possession of consumer durables continued to rise in the D D R. In December 1973 a new currency law permitted D D R citizens to accept foreign currency gifts of up to 500 Marks (then £125). They could continue to receive gifts in kind as well. This law was designed to encourage West Germans to give their relatives West Marks (badly needed by the D D R), encourage East Germans hoarding them to spend them, raise living standards of significant numbers of East Germans and end a potentially dangerous situation which put many East Germans outside the Law (by illegally holding foreign currency). The new ruling did all of these things. It led to a boom in the

Intershops which sold Western goods against Western currency only. It also created antagonisms between those who possessed Western currency and those who did not. It exposed once again the weakness of the DDR Mark. It led to those with badly needed skills—plumbers, painters, carpenters, bricklayers—who were self-employed or who did private work in their own time, to demand payment in West Marks. In 1979 a weak attempt was made to rectify this situation.

In 1971, 1972 and again in 1976 old age pensions were increased by higher percentages than ever before. The lowest paid workers were also given some improvement in their pay. To halt the decline in the birth rate generous allowances were granted to mothers with longer paid leave as well. Interest free loans were available to young couples to buy furniture and other fittings. If they got on with having a family they could, depending on how many children they had, avoid repaying the loan altogether. There was indeed some improvement in the birth rate but experts did not think this would be a long term trend. The high divorce rate, the large number of women employed and the changing attitudes of women would seem to confirm this view.

At the end of the 1970s the economic situation of the DDR appeared gloomy. The Republic had been hit by the world energy crisis with the Soviet Union, the main oil supplier, increasing its prices in accordance with world trends. The DDR increased its indebtedness to the USSR and Western states to maintain living standards. The world slump and the DDR's shortage of labour restricted its economic activities further.

ABGRENZUNG

As we have seen, in the Constitution of 1974, and in many other ways, the SED attempted to deny that Germany existed. It is interesting that the 1974 Constitution was not, unlike that of 1968, put to a referendum. There was fear it would provoke too much discussion. The introduction of compulsory military training in schools in 1978 was more political than military in its intention acting as a kind of ideological rearmament. There was much discussion too about 'real existing Socialism' meaning the DDR's version not that of the SPD, Eurocommunists—like the Spanish and Italian Communists—or Czech reform Communists. That the SED leaders did not welcome any reform ideas imported from the West was made clear to its intellectuals. Those who did not understand the message were fined (author Stefan Heym), put under house arrest (Robert Havemann), jailed (SED author Rudolf Bahro), forcibly ejected from the DDR (folk singer Wolf Biermann and author Reiner Kunze) or allowed to leave (jazz singer Christiane Wunder and others).

By 1980 the SED had largely failed in its *Abgrenzung* policy. Although the majority of the DDR's citizens had not experienced any other political system, they still seemed to regard West Germany as their closest neighbour. They continued to watch West German television and found it difficult to accept the official view that the Federal Republic headed by the SPD and the FDP represented a threat to anyone.

## ELECTION 1976

When Helmut Schmidt took over as Chancellor in 1974 he faced the problems associated with the world energy crisis. The Federal Republic too, like other industrial states was facing inflation and unemployment. In the regional elections the SPD lost ground. By the time the Federal elections came round in 1976, politically, the situation did not look all that rosy for the coalition. Yet the Federal Republic had weathered the international economic crisis better than almost any other industrial state. Indeed, the independent Hamburg weekly, *Die Zeit* (11 June 1976) showed that between February 1973 (Schmidt had been Chancellor since May 1974) and March 1976 West German prices had increased by 20.5 per cent. This compared with an increase in Switzerland of 22.6 per cent, USA 30.2, Holland 32.5 and much higher increases in Britain, France, Italy and Japan. In the election campaign it was easy for the SPD–FDP to win the battle of statistics whether the figures related to employees' incomes, public sector debts, strikes, growth or unemployment. No wonder the SPD quoted the London *Financial Times* and the American *Newsweek* referring to the Federal Republic as a model. If unemployment, low compared to many other industrial states, was up, so was unemployment pay at 68 per cent of the previous wage. Retirement pensions had been doubled since 1969 and there were many other social improvements. The Christian Democrats claimed they wanted freedom instead of socialism, less bureaucracy, and a tougher line with the East. This time the Christian Democrats presented Dr Helmut Kohl as their Chancellor candidate. Herr Kohl, a tall, friendly, 46-year-old Catholic, who had been the Prime Minister of the Rhineland-Palatinate from 1969, lacked the Bonn and international experience of Chancellor Schmidt. In his own party Kohl was a moderate. Once again the SPD faced the anger of Franz Josef Strauss, the fury of the Axel Springer press, the money of big business and the restrained but clear opposition from the Catholic

Church. Despite all this, the Social Democrats must have been disappointed with the results.

The S P D vote fell to 42.6 per cent, roughly their 1969 position. The F D P proportion went down to 7.9 per cent, only twice had they been lower—1957 and 1969. The Christian Democrats could be well pleased with their 48.6 per cent share. Only in 1957 had they gained a higher proportion of the vote. The losses of the S P D were right across the country and were not confined to any one group, though they lost in middle class Catholic areas more than in any others. They had lost the advantage among the first-time voters. As usual the Christian Democrats had done well among the old. The real winner of the election was Herr Strauss whose C S U had done better than ever in Bavaria. In near civil war conditions in the Christian Democratic camp Herr Strauss was chosen to lead the C D U/C S U in the 1980 election. Worries about the economy and about easier divorce and abortion (in Catholic areas) probably go a long way to explaining the S P D's difficulties. Many S P D members felt the party should have offered the voters, especially the young, a little bit of idealism, even utopianism.

With a majority of ten the S P D-F D P coalition managed to retain office up to 1980. It pursued a policy of cautious reform at home and cautiously flexed its muscles abroad. Save only perhaps in its industrial democracy and certain aspects of its welfare system, it would be going too far to describe West Germany as a model. It still had the problems which faced the other industrial states—inflation, unemployment, the dangers as well as the opportunities produced by the micro-chip, pollution, the maldistribution of wealth, the integration of a considerable alien workforce, the dangers inherent in the growth of police power to deal with modern crime, the risks involved in maintaining a large military establishment. Yet the Federal Republic seemed to be able to cope better than most of its friends, neighbours and rivals.

# Further Reading

CHAPTERS 1—3

W. T. Angress, *Stillborn Revolution*, London, 1963

A. J. Berlau, *The German Social Democratic Party 1914-21*, Columbia, 1949

E. H. Carr, *German-Soviet Relations 1919-39*, Baltimore, 1951

F. Carsten, *The Reichswehr and Politics, 1919-33*, Oxford, 1966

R. T. Clarke, *The Fall of the German Republic*, London, 1935

R. Coper, *Failure of a Revolution*, Cambridge, 1955

H. L. Dyck, *Weimar Germany and Soviet Russia 1926-33*, London, 1966

E. Eyck, *History of the German Republic* (2 vols), Oxford, 1962

H. Gatzke, *Stresemann and the Rearmament of Germany*, Baltimore, 1954

D. J. Goodspeed, *Ludendorff*, London, 1966

H. Gordon, *The Reichswehr and the German Republic 1919-26*, Princeton, 1957

R. Grunberger, *Germany 1918-45*, London, 1964

S. W. Halperin, *Germany Tried Democracy 1919-33*, London, 1963

R. N. Hunt, *German Social Democracy 1918-33*, London, 1964

L. Kochan, *The Struggle for Germany 1914-45*, Edinburgh, 1963

P. J. Pulzer, *The Rise of Anti-Semitism in Germany and Austria*, New York, 1964

J. P. Nettl, *Rosa Luxemburg* (2 vols), London, 1966

A. Nicholls, *Weimar and the Rise of Hitler*, London, 1968

A. Rosenberg, *The History of the German Republic*, London, 1936

A. J. Ryder, *The German Revolution of 1919*, Cambridge, 1967

C. Schorske, *German Social Democracy 1905-17*, Harvard, 1955

G. Stolper, *The German Economy, 1870 to the Present*, New York, 1967

H. A. Turner, *Stresemann and the Politics of the German Republic*, Princeton, 1963

P. Viereck, *Metapolitics, The Roots of the Nazi Mind*

J. W. Wheeler-Bennett, *The Nemesis of Power, The German Army in Politics 1918-1945*, London, 1953
*Hindenburg, the Wooden Titan*, London, 1936

CHAPTERS 4 AND 5

W. S. Allen, *The Nazi Seizure of Power*, Chicago, 1965
E. K. Bramsted, *Goebbels and National Socialist Propaganda*, London, 1965
A. Bullock, *Hitler, A Study in Tyranny*, London, 1952
H. T. Burden, *The Nuremberg Rallies, 1923-39*, London, 1969
J. S. Conway, *The Nazis Persecution of the Churches, 1933-39*
A. Dallin, *German Rule In Russia, 1941-44*, London, 1957
L. Fermi, *Illustrious Immigrants*, Chicago, 1968
S. Friedlander, *Pius XII and the Third Reich*
W. Frischauer, *Himmler, The Evil Genius of the Third Reich*, London
A. Frye, *Nazi Germany and the American Hemisphere, 1933-41*
C. FitzGibbon, *20 July*, New York, 1956
P. Fleming, *Invasion 1940*, London, 1957
J. F. L. Fuller, *The Second World War*, London, 1948
R. Goldston, *The Life And Death Of Nazi Germany*, London, 1967
G. P. Gooch, *German Mind And Outlook*, London, 1945
C. W. Guillebaud, *The Economic Recovery of Germany 1933-39*, London, 1939
B. H. Liddell Hart, *The Other Side of the Hill*, London, 1948
K. Heiden, *Hitler*, London, 1936
H. A. Jacobson, *Decisive Battles of World War II*
T. L. Jarman, *The Rise and Fall of Nazi Germany*, London, 1955
L. de Jong, *The German 5th Column in the Second World War*, London, 1956
E. Kogon, *The Theory and Practice of Hell*, London, 1950
F. Kracauer, *From Caligari to Hitler*, Princeton, 1947
H. Krausnick, *Anatomy of the s s State*, London, 1968
W. C. Langsam, *Historic Documents of World War II*, London, 1959
D. Lerner, *The Nazi Elite*, Stanford, 1951
G. Lewy, *The Catholic Church and Nazi Germany*, London, 1964
R. Manvell and H. Fraenkel, *Doctor Goebbels*, London, 1960
    *Hermann Goering*, London, 1962
    *The July Plot*, London, 1964
    *Heinrich Himmler*, London, 1965
    *The Canaris Conspiracy*, London, 1969
H. Mau and H. Krausnick, *German History 1933-45*, London, 1959
A. Milward, *The German Economy At War*, New York, 1964
G. L. Mosse, *Nazi Culture*

P. Phillips, *The Tragedy of Nazi Germany*, London, 1969
T. Prittie, *Germans Against Hitler*, London, 1964
G. Reitlinger, *The Final Solution*, London, 1953
   *The s s, Alibi of a Nation*, London, 1956
G. Ritter, *The German Resistance*, London, 1958
H. Rothfels, *The German Opposition to Hitler*, London, 1961
H. Schacht, *Account Settled*, London, 1949
F. v. Schlabrendorff, *The Secret War Against Hitler*
D. Schoenbaum, *Hitler's Social Revolution*, London, 1967
A. Schweitzer, *Big Business in the Third Reich*, London, 1964
W. Shirer, *Berlin Diary*, London, 1941
   *The Rise and Fall of the Third Reich*, London, 1960
H. Speidel, *Invasion 1944*, Chicago, 1950
G. H. Stein, *The Waffen s s*, London, 1966
R. H. Stevens (trs.), *The Testament of Adolf Hitler*, London, 1961
Thyssen F., *I Paid Hitler*, New York, 1941
H. Trevor-Roper, *The Last Days of Hitler*, London, 1947
   *Hitler's Table Talk*, London, 1953
   *Hitler's War Directives 1939-45*, London, 1964
U N E S C O, *The Third Reich*, London, 1955
E. Wiskemann, *The Rome-Berlin Axis*, London, 1966
Sir C. Webster and N. Frankland, *The Strategic Air Offensive Against Germany 1939-1945*, H M S O, 1961
A. Werth, *Russia at War*, London, 1964
Z. A. B. Zeman, *Nazi Propaganda*, London, 1964
J. P. Stern, *Hitler, the Führer and the People*, London, 1975

CHAPTER 6

N. Balabkins, *Germany Under Direct Controls*, New Brunswick, 1964
M. Balfour, *Four Power Control In Germany and Austria 1945-46*, London, 1956
L. D. Clay, *Decision in Germany*, New York, 1950
H. Feis, *Churchill, Roosevelt, Stalin*, Princeton, 1957
C. FitzGibbon, *Denazification*, London, 1969
W. Friedmann, *The Allied Military Government Of Germany*, London, 1947
Gimbel, *The American Occupation of Germany*
A. Grosser, *West Germany From Defeat to Rearmament*, London, 1956
J. Joesten, *Germany What Now?*, Chicago, 1948
W. Leonhard, *Child of the Revolution*, London, 1957

J. S. Martin, *All Honourable Men*, Boston, 1950

D. Middleton, *The Struggle for Germany*, New York, 1950

J. P. Nettl, *The Eastern Zone and Soviet Policy in Germany*, London, 1951

B. Ruhm von Oppen, *Documents on Germany 1945-55*, London, 1955

J. L. Snell, *The Origins of the East-West Dilemma Over Germany*, New Orleans, 1959

E. Wiskemann, *Germany's Eastern Neighbours*, London, 1956

H. Zink, *The United States in Germany*, Princeton, 1957

H. Krisch, *German Politics under Soviet Occupation*, New York, 1974

CHAPTERS 7 AND 10

K. Adenauer, *Memoirs*, London, 1966-68

R. Augstein, *Konrad Adenauer*, London, 1964

K. Bölling, *Republic In Suspense*, London, 1964

M. Balfour, *West Germany*, London, 1968

G. Braunthal, *The Federation of German Industry in Politics*, Ithaca, 1965

R. Chaput de Saintonge, *Public Administration in Germany*, London, 1961

D. A. Chalmers, *The Social Democratic Party of Germany* 1968

D. Childs, *From Schumacher to Brandt*, London, 1966

R. Dahrendorf, *Society and Democracy In Germany*, London

K. W. Deutsch and L. Edinger, *Germany Rejoins the Powers*, London, 1949

L. Edinger, *Kurt Schumacher*, Oxford, 1965

L. Edinger, *Politics in Germany*, Boston, 1969

A. Elon, *Journey Through a Haunted Land*, London, 1967

F. Erler, *Democracy in Germany*, Harvard, 1965

F. Golay, *The Founding of the Federal Republic of Germany*, Chicago, 1958

W. F. Hanrieder, *West German Foreign Policy 1949-63*, Stanford, 1967

A. Hartley, *Germany East/West*, London, 1968

A. Heidenheimer, *Adenauer and the* C D U, The Hague, 1960
*The Governments of Germany*, London, 1966

R. Hiscocks, *Democracy in Western Germany*, London, 1957
*Germany Revived*, London, 1966

K. Jaspers, *The Future of Germany*, Chicago, 1967

S. King-Hall, R. K. Ullmann, *German Parliaments*, London, 1954

U. Kitzinger, *German Electoral Politics*, Oxford, 1960

J. L. Knusel, *West German Aid to Developing Nations*, London, 1968

G. Loewenberg, *Parliament in the German Political System*, Ithaca, 1966

R. G. Neumann, *The Government of the Federal German Republic*

P. H. Merkl, *The Origin of the West German Republic*, New York, 1963
*Germany, Yesterday and Tomorrow*, New York, 1965

R. G. Opie, 'Western Germany's Economic Miracle', *Three Banks Review*, March 1962

E. L. Pinney, *Federalism, Bureaucracy and Party Politics in Western Germany*

E. Plischke, *Contemporary Government of Germany*, London, 1964

R. J. C. Preece, *Land Elections in the German Federal Republic*, London, 1968

T. Prittie, *Divided Germany*, London, 1961

I. Montague, *Germany's New Nazis*, London, 1967

J. Richardson, *Germany and the Atlantic Alliance*, London, 1966

Lord Russell, *The Return of the Swastika?*, London

J. E. Smith, *The Defence of Berlin*, London, 1963

H. Speier, *German Rearmament and Atomic War*, Evanston, 1957
*West German Leadership and Foreign Policy*, Evanston, 1957

H. J. Spiro, *The Politics of German Codetermination*, Harvard, 1958

W. Stahl, *The Politics of Post-war Germany*, New York, 1963

F. J. Strauss, *The Grand Design*, London, 1965
*Survey, Germany Today and Tomorrow*, London, October, 1966

K. P. Tauber, *Beyond Eagle and Swastika*

R. Tilford and R. J. C. Preece, *Federal Germany: The Political and Social Order*, London, 1969

H. C. Wallich, *Mainsprings of the German Economic Revival*, New Haven, 1955

P. Windsor, *German Reunification*, London, 1969

F. A. Váli, *The Quest for a United Germany*, Oxford, 1968

P. Weymar, *Konrad Adenauer*, London, 1957

P. Windsor, *City on Leave*, London, 1963

W. D. Graf, *The German Left Since 1945*, Cambridge, 1976

CHAPTERS 8 AND 9

D. Childs, *East Germany*, London, 1969
'East Germany: Towards the 20th Anniversary', *World Today*, October 1969

J. Dornberg, *The Other Germany*

T. M. Forster, *The East German Army*, London, 1967

W. Hangen, *The Muted Revolution*, London, 1968

A. M. Hanhardt, *The German Democratic Republic*, John Hopkins, 1968

L. Hornsby, *Profile of East Germany*, London, 1966

F. v. Nesselrode, *Germany's Other Half*, London, 1963

J. E. Smith, *Germany Beyond the Wall*, Boston, 1968

H. Köhler, *Economic Integration in the Soviet Bloc*, New York, 1965

R. Solberg, *God and Caesar in East Germany*, New York, 1961

CHAPTER 11

J. Becker, *Hitler's Children*, London, 1977

W. Brandt, *People and Politics*, London, 1978

D. P. Conradt, *The German Polity*, New York, 1978

K. H. F. Dyson, *Party, State and Bureaucracy in Western Germany*, Beverly Hills, 1977

A. Hearnden, *Education in the Two Germanies*, Westview, 1976

H. Lippmann, *Honecker and the New Politics of Europe*, London, 1973

P. C. Ludz, *The Changing Party Elite in East Germany*, Cambridge Mass, 1972

M. McCauley, *Marxism-Leninism in the German Democratic Republic*, London, 1979

E. Moreton, *East Germany and the Warsaw Alliance: the Politics of Detente*, Boulder, 1978

G. Pridham, *Christian Democracy in Western Germany*, London, 1977

T. Prittie, *The Velvet Chancellors*, London, 1979

J. Sandford, *The Mass Media Of The German-Speaking Countries*, London, 1976

K. Sontheimer and W. Bleek, *The Government and Politics of East Germany*, London, 1975

J. Steele, *Socialism With A German Face*, London, 1977

R. Tilford, *The Ostpolitik and political change in Germany*, Farnborough, 1975

W. Gerhard, *Community and Conflict in the Socialist Camp*, London, 1975

P. Windsor, *Germany and the Management of Detente*, London, 1971

J. M. Starrels and A. M. Mallinckrodt, *Politics in the German Democratic Republic*, New York, 1975

The writer has used many German sources in preparing this book. The bibliography is meant merely as a guide for the English-speaking reader.

# General Index

# Index of Persons